NEW YORK REVIEW BOOKS
CLASSICS

POETS IN A LANDSCAPE

GILBERT HIGHET (1906–1978) was born in Glasgow, Scotland, to a middle-class family. He showed an early facility with Latin and Greek, reading Homer, Virgil, and Aeschylus for pleasure by the time he was sixteen. He attended Glasgow University, and later Oxford's Balliol College, sweeping up most of the available prizes and scholarships along the way. In 1937 Highet joined the faculty of Columbia University, becoming a full professor at thirty-one. He taught at Columbia until 1972 (with the exception of a period during WWII, when he was stationed as an officer in Washington, D.C. and later assisted in the return of looted goods in Europe), becoming a legend for his animated and inspiring lectures. A very public intellectual, Highet served on the boards of *Horizon* magazine (1958–77) and the Book-of-the-Month Club (1954–78), was chief literary critic for *Harper's* (1952–54), and hosted a cultural affairs radio program, *People, Places, and Books* (1952–59), that was broadcast on more than three hundred stations in the U.S., Canada, and the U.K. Highet wrote, translated, or edited some twenty books, of which *The Classical Tradition* (1949) and *The Art of Teaching* (1950) remain the best known. He was married to Helen MacInnes, a successful writer of espionage novels, from 1932 until his death from cancer in 1978.

MICHAEL C. J. PUTNAM is MacMillan professor emeritus of classics and comparative literature, Brown University. Among his recent books are *Poetic Interplay: Catullus and Horace* and *Jacopo Sannazaro: The Latin Poetry*. In May 2009 he was awarded the Centennial Medal by the American Academy in Rome. He is a member of the American Academy of Arts and Sciences and of the American Philosophical Society.

POETS IN A LANDSCAPE

GILBERT HIGHET

Preface by
MICHAEL C.J. PUTNAM

NEW YORK REVIEW BOOKS

New York

THIS IS A NEW YORK REVIEW BOOK
PUBLISHED BY THE NEW YORK REVIEW OF BOOKS
435 Hudson Street, New York, NY 10014
www.nyrb.com

Library of Congress Cataloging-in-Publication Data

Highet, Gilbert, 1906–1978.
  Poets in a landscape / by Gilbert Highet ; introduction by Michael Putnam.
     p. cm. — (New York Review Books classics)
  Originally published: London : Hamish Hamilton, 1957.
  ISBN 978-1-59017-338-1 (alk. paper)
  1. Poets, Latin—Homes and haunts. 2. Latin poetry—History and criti-
cism. 3. Rome—Intellectual life. 4. Rome—In literature. 5. Landscape in
literature. 6. Literary landmarks—Italy. 7. Italy—Description and travel. I.
Title.
  PA6047.H5 2010
  871.092'2—dc22
  [B]
                                        2009036325

ISBN 978-1-59017-338-1

Printed in the United States of America on acid-free paper.
10 9 8 7 6 5 4 3 2 1

CONTENTS

	Page
PREFACE	vii
INTRODUCTION	
Italy	11
Translations	12
Thanks	15
I: CATULLUS	
Life and love	17
Sirmio	40
Clodia	46
In fair Verona	52
II: VERGIL	
Landscape	56
The village and the farm	64
The cities	72
The place of the tomb	78
III: PROPERTIUS	
Umbria	83
Enigmatic melancholy	86
Cynthia	91
The springs of Clitumnus	95
Death and transfiguration	102
IV: HORACE	
A career open to the talents	114
Tivoli	121
The Odes	126
The Sabine farm	137
The Letters	153

CONTENTS

V: TIBULLUS

    Style   161
    Consolation   164
    Rite of spring   167
    The dark woods   174

VI: OVID

    Contrasts   177
    Success and disaster   184
    Sulmo   191

VII: JUVENAL

    The making of a satirist   198
    Aquinum   203
    The lost inscription   210

VIII: ROME

    The gate   214
    The boiling streets   219
    City of the soul   225
    The hill of palaces   229
    The heart of the city   240

NOTES   249

INDEX   267

PREFACE

Though a distinguished scholar of the Classics with more than a dozen books to his credit, Gilbert Highet (1906–78) is remembered, first and foremost, as a teacher, from his many years as professor at Columbia, from his varied roles as radio commentator and editor, and from his writings on pedagogy. A dapper and courtly Scotsman firmly established in New York, he was known for his politeness and charm. An editor who worked with him said that he never seemed condescending or tried to pull scholarly rank. Though respected, especially in his later years, as a mentor of graduate students, his true audience was not his colleagues, however much they benefited from books like *The Classical Tradition* (1949) or *Juvenal the Satirist* (1954). It was the educated public at large, cultivated laymen who were drawn to his work by the wide range of his learning, by his great gift of making analogies between different cultures and aesthetic environments, by his fluency of style.

Poets in a Landscape shows off these virtues at their finest, evoking the beauty of the different parts of Italy from which seven of Rome's greatest poets emanated. Through Highet's sensitive eyes we come to know one poet after another, starting with Catullus, born around 85 BCE, and ending with Juvenal, whose uncertain birth date can be placed sometime after the middle of the first century CE. We plot a geographical course from the north of Italy, starting in the Po valley at Verona, birthplace of Catullus, and Mantua (modern Mantova), near which Vergil was born. We then move south to Asisium (modern Assisi), the home city of Sextus Propertius, near the border between the provinces of Etruria and Umbria.

With the chapter on Horace we journey farther south across the

vii

Apennines to reach the province of Apulia and one of its central towns, Venusia (modern Venosa). The account of the elegist Tibullus draws us back to the outskirts of Rome and to Pedum, in the Alban Hills east of the city. With Ovid, youngest of the Augustan poets, we move due east, to Sulmo (modern Sulmona) in the high hills of Samnium. Juvenal, writing a century later, takes us in turn directly south to Aquinum, on the Via Latina between Rome and Capua. A final chapter returns us to the metropolis itself.

The native landscapes of these poets are as diverse as the poets themselves, whether we are contemplating the olive groves at Sirmio (modern Sirmione), Catullus's peninsular home jutting from its southern shore into the Lago di Garda, or the lakes around Mantua, home to Vergil's beloved swans, or the hill towns of Umbria onto one of which Propertius projects his own biography as complement and counterpart to the many deaths that the civil war, fought between Antony and the future Augustus, brought to nearby Perusia (modern Perugia) in 40 BCE.

Their later careers, too, transported all seven poets into different settings, equally distinctive and fascinating. Highet takes us to Horace's Sabine farm, in the hilly terrain east of Rome, where he wrote his masterpiece, the first three books of *Odes*; to Naples, Vergil's fostering home for the core of his career; and to the Latian countryside southeast of Rome, where we join Tibullus in celebrating the Roman festival of the Ambarvalia, a fertility rite held in honor of the goddess Ceres. We travel the length of the peninsula in the poets' imaginations, going with Horace to Tarentum on the picturesque coast of the Ionian Sea, and with Vergil, especially through his splendid catalogues, to a variety of peoples and places embracing virtually the whole of the Italian peninsula. About the Mantuan poet's love of his homeland, for example, Highet writes:

Poets have been the most successful in conveying the love of country, even if they were temporarily embittered or pessimistic. Among them, Vergil is one of the most eloquent. The emotions which other writers put into describing the torments and ecstasies of sexual love, the doubts and raptures of man's approach to God, the intricate fascinations of explaining one's own personality, Vergil devotes to the land of Italy and the men who work it.

But the city of Rome is the center, and Highet tellingly gives it his last chapter, one of his longest (only Horace is allotted more pages). It is a commonplace of Latin literary history that none of Rome's finest poets was born in the city that was the empire's heart. Lucretius alone, who receives but passing mentions in *Poets*, might claim that honor, but in fact we remain in ignorance of his origins. Nevertheless Rome was the city that chiefly claimed their attention, whether literally, because in several cases they lived there, or figuratively, because it served as touchstone for many of their most telling ideas and attitudes, sometimes uttered in allegiance, sometimes in negative reaction to its political ideals.

Though Catullus makes passing references to his native Verona, he was irresistibly attracted to Rome. The most urbane of poets is also one of the most urban. When he describes his estate as lying east of the city, he suggests that it might be called either Sabine or Tiburtine (near Tibur, modern Tivoli). Those who wish Catullus harm, he pronounces, would call it Sabine, which is to say crude or rustic after an Italian tribe dwelling nearby. Those who cherish him choose Tiburtine, which allows him to style his property as "suburban" (*suburbana*), allied with the sophisticated city rather than the boorish countryside.

Horace would make the opposite point, inviting his patron Maecenas to leave the city, with its "smoke and commercialism and hubbub" (*fumum et opes strepitumque*), and to dine with him, that is to say, to share his life of the mind and its subtlety. In his first eclogue, Vergil imagines one of his bucolic characters visiting Rome and salvaging his lost land through the good offices of a "young god," while his other protagonist is departing into exile after losing his property—in Vergil's words—to an "impious, barbarous soldier." Already at the start of his career Vergil sees Rome and its power as dichotomous—benign and supportive, or self-serving and destructive.

One of Ovid's most moving poems is the third in his first book of "Sadnesses" (*Tristia*), penned during the initial years of his exile. It tells of the night of his departure from Rome, and we gaze with him on the moonlit urban world. Juvenal's third satire, by contrast, finds a man named Umbricius leaving behind, with relief, the jarring, corrupt realm of the city for the "sweet retreat" of Baiae on the Bay of Naples, the landscape that Vergil cherished. He urges his satirist friend (equated by Highet with Juvenal the poet) to visit his own native Aquinum, whenever he needs "to be restored." The poem ends with a moving echo of Vergil's initial eclogue, a further reminder of the creative, multileveled tension between Rome and its poets, between city and country, between martial energy and imagination, that is a steady, stimulating theme for its greatest minds.

If landscape is the topic that holds *Poets* together, it is also an excuse for a series of rich, evocative meditations on the originality of each of these seven masters. Some of Highet's critical judgments are now dated. We would no longer speak of Vergil's first masterpiece, his *Eclogues*, as consisting of "little bucolic poems" or even make reference to his "two great poems" by contrast with the collection that preceded them. No reader would now judge that Ovid "had no eye for landscape" or that his poems' "chief subject, almost their sole subject, is heterosexual gratification." And Highet's staunch adherence to the "biographical fallacy," as well as the high moral tone that permeates the volume as a whole, lead him to remark, for instance, on Tibullus's "grave psychical trouble."

Nevertheless many of the book's evaluations remain as relevant today as they were half a century ago. Highet is illuminating about Propertius's "art of omission" and his gradual transition from *amor* to *Roma*, as we follow a spiritual odyssey from his mistress Cynthia, in his initial elegy, to the materfamilias Cornelia, in his last. Highet rightly criticizes scholars who apply strict logic to the interpretation of this challenging poet instead of the imagination that he demands. And he writes eloquently of Horace's "civilized wisdom," of his unusual move from satire to lyric, of the contradictions and conflicts that abound in his poetry.

The same holds true for the digressions throughout the text that enhance rather than frustrate the reader's perceptions. From a discussion of Vergil, we also ponder the importance of Greek civilization for Rome. In his exploration of Tibullus's artistry, Highet educates us on the importance of style in poetry. Horace receives the most accolades, for subtlety of thought, exactness of phrasing, the music of his rhythms, and sheer abundance of insights brilliantly expressed.

What remains as strong as ever is the clarity, precision, and elegance of Highet's writing, the work of someone who patently delights in teaching and has the knack of enlivening his subject by telling references throughout these pages. Immense learning enhances, but never overwhelms, his judgments. Highet is as much at home in modern as in ancient literature. A reference to Tennyson, for example, helps us merge Catullus's poems 31 and 101, as studies in happiness and loss. And the abrupt transitions he finds in the poems of Eliot and Pound allow us to see with a more practiced appreciation what makes the different elements in the poetry of Propertius coalesce. Likewise we find ourselves visualizing the words of poets by means of examples from medieval or Renaissance art, or hearing them through a range of musical analogies from Bach to Hugo Wolf and Gabriel Fauré. It is not coincidental that, during his discussion of Horace, Highet turns to Bach on three occasions to point up the exactitude, rhythmic intensity, and cumulative force of Rome's greatest lyricist. The same virtues that permeate the book are also present in the limpid translations that, with their assured virtuosity, complement the varied authors under scrutiny and bring them vividly before the Latin-less reader.

This is a very personal volume in ways that take us beyond the teaching of a great educator. The journey through the countryside of Italy, and through the minds of its superb poets, is a shared one. The "we" that is a constant presence throughout the book includes both Highet himself and the anonymous "travelling companion" of the dedication, his wife, the novelist Helen MacInnes. During his time of writing she was at work on *North from Rome* (1958), published the year after *Poets in a Landscape.* I am also happy to think that, with the book's reprinting, under the auspices of *The New York Review of Books* and of the American Academy in Rome where some of the research for it was conducted, this collaboration can now expand to embrace new generations and to introduce them, with undiminished vitality, to the beauties of the Italian *paesaggio* and to the ever valuable poets that it inspired two millennia ago.

—MICHAEL C. J. PUTNAM

POETS IN A LANDSCAPE

To my Travelling Companion

INTRODUCTION

ITALY

ITALY is a land full of presences. It has produced many great statesmen, brilliant artists, admirable musicians, superb poets. Each of these has left something of his spirit in Italy. Scarcely any other country has preserved so much of a richly varied past. If it were not for the courage and vitality of the Italians, they would be dwarfed by their own history.

Every visitor feels the grandeur and beauty of the Italies of the past. For one, the most impressive thing is the revelation of Renaissance art in its full magnificence: the paintings of Botticelli, the sculptures of Michelangelo, the architecture of Palladio. Another will plunge with delight into the world of the Middle Ages: its violence and its saintliness are still preserved in the fortress-towers of San Gimignano, in the tombs and castles of the proud Scaligers, in the rock-hewn hermitage of Saint Francis. Another will prefer Italy of the seventeenth and eighteenth centuries, dominated by that strange combination of strength and delicacy, austerity and pomp, which is called baroque: when he thinks of Italy, he will remember Bernini's Roman fountains, the church of the Salute on the Grand Canal of Venice, the palace of Caserta, the paintings of Tiepolo, and the most amazing building in Europe, the basilica of St. Peter in Rome.

Most of my life has been spent on the study and interpretation of Roman and Greek history, philosophy, literature, and art. Now, although I knew that much of the Greco-Roman world survived in Italy, still it was a tremendous surprise for me to discover the nature of that survival, and to experience its intensity. All the other Italies presented themselves, each with its own peculiar style and energy. But the Italy which was moulded by Rome and educated by Greece, the Italy which was for many centuries the focus of a magnificent civilization covering the whole of the known world, the Italy of Cicero and Vergil, Scipio and Hadrian, Romulus and Constantine—that Italy became real to me as it had never been before.

In this book I have tried to set down something of that realization of Roman Italy; and in particular, of Italy as the home and inspiration of seven of the greatest Roman poets.

In the months I spent there, I saw and experienced much else, which I have excluded—although it would have been profoundly moving for me to recall such things as the noble temples of Sicily, whose sunlit isolation has something of the deep power of Greek tragedy; the tomb of the empress Galla Placidia in Ravenna, with its frail otherworldly mosaics; the silent streets of Herculaneum, surrounded by cliffs of the volcanic mud which overwhelmed the town, and now lying far beneath its noisy, chattering, modern successor; the amazing vividness and variety of the Greek and Roman sculptures of the Vatican Museum, which fill gallery after gallery with a pagan immortality; the translucent fresh waters of the fountain of Arethusa bubbling up on the margin of the salt sea; Mount Etna, that restless giant, towering grim against the sunset; the Christian Romans sleeping underground in the catacombs; and the pagan Etruscans still feasting in their tombs, gazing at the visitor with an enigmatic smile. There are too many memories to make a single picture.

Instead, I have endeavoured to recall some of the greatest Roman poets, by describing the places where they lived, recreating their characters, and evoking the essence of their work. This book is meant for those who love Italy, and for those who love poetry.

TRANSLATIONS

The translations are my own. They are all, as nearly as possible, in the exact metre of the original.

Latin hexameters are rendered, not by the English five-foot iambic line, which is always too short to give the full sweep of the original, but by a six-foot iambic. This resembles the metre used by Robert Bridges in *The Testament of Beauty*, and (more distantly) that employed by Richmond Lattimore in his translation of the *Iliad*.

The Latin elegiac couplet cannot be properly translated by the English 'heroic' couplet. The shape and emphasis of the two metres are quite different. In the Latin elegiac, the first line, six feet in length, is the more important. The second line, one foot shorter, with a marked pause in the middle, moves more slowly; its poetic content is smaller and its energy is less than that of the first line. The effect is beautifully reproduced in the elegiac couplet composed by Schiller and translated into English by Coleridge:

> In the hexameter rises the fountain's silvery column;
> In the pentameter aye falling in melody back.

But in the English 'heroic' couplet the second line is the same length as the first, and is in fact a little stronger than its predecessor, because of the rhyme. As we hear the rhyming word at the end of the first line, a certain expectation builds up in us, which is only satisfied by the little climax created through the appearance of the rhyme at the close of the second: thus—

> In vain the sage, with retrospective eye,
> Would from the apparent What conclude the Why.

I have therefore translated Latin elegiac couplets by a combination of English six-foot iambics and five-foot iambics (without rhyme): like this—

> Through many nations, over many seas, I travelled
>   to pay this service, brother, with my tears:
> to lay these final offerings upon your grave,
>   and, to your voiceless ashes, speak in vain.

Other metres used by the Roman poets in lyrics and epigrams
I have copied as exactly as I could—allowing for the change from
a quantitative system to an accentual system. There is good pre-
cedent for this. The witty little metre used by Catullus for some
of his merriest poems, the eleven-syllable, was perfectly adapted
to English by Tennyson:

> O you chorus of indolent reviewers,
> Irresponsible, indolent reviewers,
> Look, I come to the test, a tiny poem
> All composed in a metre of Catullus . . .

Tennyson and other poets (for instance, Carducci in Italian) have
also converted the more difficult Alcaic and Sapphic metres into
the accents of their own languages. The slight strangeness of effect
which such adaptations produce is to my mind more valuable to
those who wish to appreciate the inwardness of Latin poetry than
the familiar ring of a rendering into some native metrical pattern.

In addition, I have tried to match the original poems line for
line. If a translator takes a poem ten lines long and turns it into a
version containing sixteen lines, he has altered its proportions and
sacrificed an important element of its art. Even the punctuation of
the original, its enjambements and its pauses, ought in an accurate
translation to be reproduced as far as possible; and this I have
attempted to do.

One last point. Some Roman poetry is austere and dignified;
some is light and gay; some is chatty and irreverent. Not all the
'classical' poets wrote loftily 'classical' poetry. The language of
Roman elegy, for instance, is far closer to everyday conversation
than the language of epic and didactic poetry; and in epigrams we
find words and turns of phrase which are frankly prosaic and col-
loquial. It is the duty of the translator to choose words and phrases
from his own language and his own time which reflect the varying
tones of the original poems on which he is working; and not to

turn a cheerful, down-to-earth epigram which sounded very contemporary to its contemporaries into an antique and remote lyric filled with thee and thou, hasteth and hearkeneth. The occasional colloquialisms in these translations therefore all correspond to something equally colloquial in the originals; and those versions which seem to pass abruptly from grave to gay represent similarly abrupt transitions in the Latin poems themselves.

THANKS

I owe much gratitude to many friends who have helped me by suggestions and criticisms. In particular, my thanks go to that excellent scholar and lively writer, Gilbert Bagnani, who has been kind enough to read the entire book through in manuscript and to send me his comments. For any mistakes and omissions which remain, he is not responsible. Then, for bibliographical assistance, let me express gratitude to the library staff of the American Academy in Rome, to the reference department of Columbia University Library, and to that expert bibliographer Dr. Mark Jupiter of Columbia. Professor Lily Ross Taylor of Bryn Mawr gave me much valuable advice while I was working at the Academy, and Dr. Bertha Tilly (herself the author of an admirable scholarly work on Vergil's Latium) provided some excellent information from her long experience in the recreation of Roman Italy. Acknowledgment is made to Mrs. W. B. Yeats and to Messrs. Macmillan & Co. for permission to quote 'The Scholars' from Collected Poems of W. B. Yeats.

Throughout the country my wife and I were welcomed with warm-hearted hospitality both by Italians and by foreigners living in Italy. Among the latter let me mention with special gratitude the young English couple who, although it was their private home and we were interrupting what should have been a peaceful morning of sunshine and leisure, were good enough to admit us to S. Antonio in Tivoli, and to show us the remains of the villa where the poet Horace may have lived, in the stimulating though sometimes difficult company of his patron Maecenas.

The Italians who treated us kindly are too numerous to mention. Still, I think with particular pleasure of a visit to what may have been the house of the poet Juvenal, on a hillside some miles above Aquino. When the guide and I arrived, panting and sweating, nothing was visible, except a roofless old church, a few farm buildings, and the remains of a Roman terrace. A few children appeared. We spoke to them. They looked terrified, and remained silent. Their mother emerged, warily. After listening to our questions, she said, 'The old man would know.' Now the old man hobbled round the corner of the house; and indeed he did know. He pointed out the remaining fragments of Roman habitation, and showed us round the church. He remembered the visit of another scholar, who 'measured everything and took pictures everywhere'. (It was probably Count Michelangelo Cagiano de Azevedo, who wrote a careful little book on Aquinum.) Alas, he could tell us nothing about the Juvenal inscription. Still, as he talked, the group gradually enlarged itself. More children appeared. Several pretty girls with cheerful smiles came out, followed by tough hearty red-faced men; and soon there were twenty or thirty people all chatting with us and laughing. Although we had two or three miles to walk back downhill in the hot sun, we had to have several glasses of white wine, and then take a picture of the entire settlement. What they thought I was, I shall never know; but they made me kindly welcome. For me, they were the descendants of Juvenal's own tenants and countrymen; and they made me realize how Juvenal projected himself into his friend Umbricius, the man who, tired of the noise and corruption of the big city, retired to a small town where it was possible to live with spade in hand tending the young plants, and

even in a lonely corner,
to make himself the landlord of a single lizard.

I

CATULLUS

LIFE AND LOVE

HE came from the north. He lived a brief, passionate, unhappy life. He wrote magnificent poetry. And he introduced a new word for 'kiss' into the European languages. Although he was a superb poet, only one solitary copy of his poems survived the Dark Ages—a single battered manuscript, preserved in his home, Verona. Yet, even if that lonely copy had perished and all his poems had been lost, one of his creations would have remained. Whenever a Frenchman says *baiser*, whenever an Italian speaks of *un bacio*, when a Spaniard says *besar* or a Portuguese *beijar*, they are using the word which this poet picked up and made into Latin to amuse his sweetheart. The woman was unworthy. The poet died. The word lives.

His name was Catullus. Apart from his poignant and violent poems, we know very little about him. Even in ancient times, he was not universally studied and revered as a 'classic'. Other poets admired him and learned from him; but he was not exactly suitable to be taught in schools and colleges. He is still unsuitable. It is extraordinarily difficult to read and discuss one of Catullus's poems of passionate love in any classroom; and still more difficult if, two or three pages away, the readers can see another poem which begins and ends with a revolting obscenity. It is more difficult again to explain, even to oneself, why one of the very few passionately sincere love-poets in western literature should have degraded his own work and offended his own admirers by crude jokes and deliberate filth. Other poets have been daring. Few have said what they felt with such trenchant clarity. Few have suffered such bold, arrogant emotions. Few have written so little—sixty or

17

seventy pages—and still covered such a vast range of feeling. Few have been so outrageously direct and so maddeningly inconsistent.

Catullus's sixteenth poem is a comic reproach to his two friends, Furius and Aurelius. They had scolded him because the love-poems he wrote to his new mistress were too frank, too gushing: so many thousands of kisses. . . . They said 'All that is immoral, oversexed, weak.' Catullus replied that his poetry was truly masculine. And he shouted that he would prove it on their bodies. 'You, both of you, I shall * you and ** you, just to show that I am not a weakling.' This was at the beginning of his love affair, when he had written only a few of his most famous love poems. At the end of the same affair, when he hated and despised his mistress so much that he would not address a poem to her directly, he composed a bitter and poignant farewell message to her, the last sigh of his love. And he dedicated it to the same two friends, Furius and Aurelius, who had once reproached and tried to restrain him. It begins with a long eulogy of their selfless loyalty. Once, not so long ago, they were brutes and perverts, because they disapproved of Catullus's poems. Now they are faithful comrades. By addressing them in this poem, he admits he was wrong. The final renunciation of his love he entrusts to the men who did not desert him either in his happiness or in his misery.

The violence of the farewell letter to his girl is hard to endure, but it is explicable. It is harder to understand how the same young man can have brutally insulted his friends, and then, not too long afterwards, called on them to support him in his worst trial. There is nothing like Catullus's combination of rude violence and heart-warming affection in the work of most lyric poets: in Shelley, in Keats, in Rilke, in Baudelaire, in Chénier, in Goethe or Hugo. The nearest parallel to him is Rimbaud. All lyric poets are hard to understand, but Catullus is almost impossible. There is no single good book on him and his work, in any language. Yeats was right, when he said that Catullus himself would terrify the scholars who try to understand him.

Bald heads forgetful of their sins,
Old, learned, respectable bald heads
Edit and annotate the lines
That young men, tossing on their beds,
Rhymed out in love's despair
To flatter beauty's ignorant ear.

All shuffle there; all cough in ink;
All wear the carpet with their shoes;
All think what other people think;
All know the man their neighbour knows.
Lord, what would they say
Did their Catullus walk that way?[1]

His full name was Gaius Valerius Catullus. He was born in
87 B.C., in the northern city of Verona. Nowadays we are apt to
think that all the peninsula of Italy must be inhabited by Italians.
But in his time it was not. Sicily and the south were largely Greek.
The northern part was heavily settled by Celts. Only the centre
was held by Italian peoples, and even they were intermingled with
Etruscans and other strange races. Before conquering the western
world, Rome had to begin by conquering Italy. Verona was a
Celtic settlement, which was taken over by the Romans and con-
verted into a 'colony' only a year or two before Catullus was
born. Well before his time, the Celts of northern Italy had given
up their distinctive dress and customs. In appearance at least they
were assimilated to the Romans. But traces of their original lan-
guage and of their peculiar character are likely to have lingered on
for many generations.

Of course no one can tell whether Catullus was of Celtic stock
or not. He never speaks of himself as anything but a Roman
citizen. Still, he did bring into the Latin language two or three
strange words, which may conceivably be Celtic in origin; and his
name has been thought by one expert to be Celtic. Also, we see in

[1] Yeats, 'The Scholars', from *Collected Poems* (Macmillan, London, 1950),
p. 158.

his nature a desperate passion, an unreasonable, almost suicidal fervour very unlike the emotions of all other Roman poets. We know this was not merely a fashionable pose, since no other Roman author manifested these ardent and dangerous excitements; and, since Celtic myth and Celtic poetry are full of similar ardours and frenzies, we may well imagine that Catullus either was a Romanized Celt, or else—like Yeats—without being truly Celtic lived among Celts and learned from them their superb, devoted, all-or-nothing attitude to the world. The greatest of all Celtic heroes was Cuchulain, who (in one legend) died fighting the waves of the sea, slashing their crowns off with his sword.

If the idea were not a little pedantic, we could arrange all Catullus's poems, one hundred and sixteen of them, in such a way as to produce an outline biography of the poet. As we have them, they are set out, not by date or by content but more or less by shape: all the short elegies and elegiac epigrams together, all the long elaborate poems together, and the light colloquial and lyrical poems together at the beginning. This gives us a fine impression of Catullus's lively mind, excitable temperament, and spiritual versatility. It is far more variegated and confused than Shakespeare's sonnets. But when read as a book is meant to be read, straight through from beginning to end, it is virtually unintelligible. Obviously it was not published in this shape by Catullus, but was put together out of several diverse collections after his early death.

Still, these poems contain almost everything we know of him. Only a few facts are given by any other source. Long afterwards, St. Jerome mentioned him, copying from an earlier biography the bare facts that he was born in 87 B.C. and died in 57 when he was thirty. We know, from allusions in his poems, that he lived until 54 B.C. at least; but he did die young, perhaps aged thirty-three. We hear also that he attacked Julius Cæsar in his poems, but later apologized. Virtually all the rest is inference from his poetry.

There were three important events in his life. The first was the death of his elder brother. The second was his tour of duty as a government official in Asia Minor. The third was his love affair with a beautiful and conscienceless woman called Clodia. All three meant failure and heartbreak for him. He was a man doomed to suffer.

The elder brother died while Catullus himself was young, gay, and thoughtless. So he himself says.

As soon as I became a youth, verging on manhood,
    during the flowery springtime of my life,
love was my constant sport. How well I know the goddess
    who mingles passion with sweet bitterness!
But all concern for love affairs was lost in mourning
    for my brother. Lost, for ever lost to me,
dying, my brother, you broke all my happiness,
    my home was buried for ever in your grave.
Dead together with you are all my favourite pleasures—
    pleasures your love had nourished while you lived.[1]

For the grave of his brother, who died and was buried near the ruins of Troy, Catullus created one of the most poignant little elegies ever written—saying, as he was bound to say (and as the tombstone itself said), the ritual words of greeting and farewell, but blending them into an utterance of sincere and passionate grief.

Through many nations, over many seas, I travelled
    to pay this service, brother, with my tears:
to lay these final offerings upon your grave,
    and, to your voiceless ashes, speak in vain.
Since fate has taken you from me, brother, for ever,
    poor brother, carried off before your time,

[1] Catullus 68.15–24.

now let me satisfy the ancient sad tradition
   and do this sacrifice upon your tomb.
Receive it, and receive my tears of love and mourning:
   and so for ever, brother, hail and farewell.[1]

The death of his brother aged Catullus suddenly. Their father
was alive, and was an important figure in Verona; but Catullus
writes as though he had never existed. It had been to his elder
brother that Catullus turned for sympathy, and even for indulg-
ence. It was his elder brother who, as Catullus gratefully acknow-
ledges, 'let him play' even after he was grown up. At his death, the
weight of responsibility and the gloom of maturity fell upon
Catullus—and by then he was scarcely able to endure them.

He was recalled from Rome to Verona. Apparently he was told
that his duty was to take life seriously, to give up his 'constant
sport', and to embark on the same administrative and political
career which his older brother had entered. He spent some miser-
ably lonely months in the northern city. He threw off a number of
pieces on local scandals (scarcely intelligible today); and he com-
posed some highly-wrought modernistic poems, inspired by
certain masterpieces of Callimachus, Sappho, and other Greek
writers, but filled with poignant personal touches of remorse and
aspiration. At last, when he was about thirty, he left Italy for Asia
Minor as an aide to the governor.

Catullus's journey to Asia was an attempt to make something
of his life. He had done little except make love and write poetry.
He was spending too much money. He had no career. He had no
clear future. All around him, less intelligent and less sensitive men
were rising high in politics, becoming distinguished lawyers and
orators, carving out their futures with the sword, enriching them-
selves with the plunder of the western world. Julius Cæsar and his
gang were preparing to share the loot of Gaul: they were to
become millionaires on the proceeds, and some of them, even the
least worthy, to emerge as powerful statesmen.

[1] Catullus 101.

Quick, quick, Catullus, turn your face to the wall, and die.
That tumour Nonius is a Roman magistrate;
Vatinius swears (and lies) by his hopes of the consulate.
Quick, quick, Catullus, turn your face to the wall, and die.[1]

Julius himself was already planning to overthrow the republic
which he had fatally weakened, to make himself its saviour, and
at last to become the monarch of his enslaved fellow-citizens.
Towards the very end of his life, Catullus produced several out-
rageous and unprintable poems about Cæsar and his chief engin-
eer, Mamurra, calling them crooks and wastrels, womanizers,
perverts, accomplices in mutual vice. Cæsar felt the wound, and
knew that the scar would be indelible; but he recognized talent
when he saw it. He made a gesture of friendship towards Catullus,
which evoked a contemptuous epigram:

I am not really anxious for your approval, Cæsar.
Whether you're white or black, I do not care.[2]

Yet, after a while, Catullus seems to have been won over by the
almost irresistible charm of Cæsar's intelligence and personality;
perhaps also by the fact that Cæsar was a friend of his family, so
that it had been base disloyalty to attack him. He apologized, and
dined with Cæsar: the two were reconciled, the wily manipulator
and the passionate poet. In one of his finest poems, Catullus spoke
quite sincerely of 'the achievements of great Cæsar' in the
northern campaigns against the Celts in Gaul, Britain, and
Germany. He may have been a vile crook, Julius Cæsar, but he
was also a great man, and Catullus was forced to recognize his
greatness. It would be touching to imagine that, as Thornton
Wilder suggests in his *Ides of March*, he sat beside Catullus on his
deathbed, talking with him and comforting him; but it is scarcely
credible. When the young poet died, Cæsar was engaged in
crushing the Gauls during their struggle for freedom.

[1] Catullus 52.
[2] Catullus 93.

It was in the spring of the year 57 B.C., when Catullus was about thirty, that he joined the staff of the governor of Bithynia, a province in northern Asia Minor. Like a young Briton going to India in the nineteenth century, he was expected both to learn the principles of government and to make some money. Every intelligent and properly educated young Roman with reasonable means could, if he used his will-power and his brains, become a powerful administrator and help to govern the world. It seems likely that his brother had been on a similar mission when he died. Catullus may have hoped to pursue the same kind of career and succeed in it, but he was soon disillusioned.

Memmius, his chief, was a cool and self-centred man, who might by now have been quite forgotten had he not been associated with two great poets. It was to Memmius that the eloquent apostle of Epicureanism, Lucretius, addressed his poem *On the Nature of the Universe*—hoping to convert him, and through him other Roman noblemen, to the creed of Epicurus. But he was so far from being converted to the tranquillity, economy, and reverence which are part of Epicureanism that he bought the little house and garden in Athens where the master Epicurus used to teach, and then planned to destroy them in order to put up a new building. Cicero (who had little sympathy for Epicureans but much for history) had to write and ask him not to commit such an act of vandalism.

What duties he gave Catullus to do in Asia, we cannot tell. Catullus learned nothing, and often complains (in untranslatable language) that Memmius got the best of all his staff. If there was any cash going, it went directly and irrevocably to Memmius. But at least Catullus had an opportunity to visit the beautiful and historic Greek cities of Asia Minor; he saw the lonely mountains and savage forests of the desolate country where Troy had once reigned, long ago. Still, he returned to Italy almost as poor as when he left. One of his drollest poems tells how, after he came back, his friend Varus introduced him to a girl. The girl asked him how well he had done in Asia. Badly, badly, said Catullus, the governor was a real shark. But at least (she went on) you brought home the usual palanquin with eight slaves to carry it? Catullus could not resist showing off before a pretty girl. 'Oh yes, certainly,' he said, 'I managed that.' 'Splendid,' she replied, 'be a dear boy and lend me the palanquin and slaves tomorrow: I have to go to an important religious ceremony.' He got out of that only by a bald lie:

> Oh now, that was an error: dear old Cinna,
> my friend, *he* is the man who owns the litter—
> though, quite frankly, it really doesn't matter:
> I keep using it, just as though I'd bought it.[1]

Poor, ridiculous young man. He had imagined himself returning from Bithynia with statues and rare books, gold and jewels, enough to enjoy all his pleasures and dazzle all his rivals: he would hold the gorgeous East in fee. But he came home lonely, penniless and discouraged.

The greatest experience of his life began long before his journey to the East. This was his love for Clodia.

She was a really formidable woman. Even her enemies admitted that she was beautiful. She had huge burning eyes (so they nicknamed her 'the ox-eyed', after the goddess Hera). She was talented, she danced exquisitely, she loved poetry. She came from one of the most famous and most arrogant and violent families in Rome, the Claudian house. She and her brother had changed their names from Claudius and Claudia to Clodius and Clodia, so that they might sound proletarian—as though a socialist nobleman in England were to change from Lord William Hendricks to Bill Enry. Both she and her brother were absolutely devoid of moral standards. It was he who, disguised as a flute-girl, smuggled himself into the secret festival of the Good Goddess in order to seduce Cæsar's wife. He and his sister, it was credibly believed, indulged in a little incest from time to time. Clodia was married to a rich and worthy statesman, Metellus. But Metellus died with suspicious abruptness. After that she was rich and free. She could do virtually anything she wanted; and she did.

[1] Catullus 10.29-32.

Catullus met her before her husband's death. He was young.
He had come to Rome in order to complete his education and
(his father hoped) to enter political life. He had letters of intro-
duction to several distinguished men who could encourage and
guide him—including Hortensius, the second greatest orator in
Rome, and probably Clodia's husband Metellus, who had been
governor of the province in which Verona lay. Clodia was a
Roman lady, rich and well-connected: he a youngster from a new
colonial city. Like Oscar Wilde entering the United States, he had
'nothing to declare except his genius'. At first, he was so over-
whelmed by her beauty, her charm, and her powerful personality
that he could scarcely speak. But with remarkable tact and
delicacy, he sent her a poem explaining his silence. Only twelve
lines long, it was a bouquet of exquisite compliments. Since it
would have been gross to use her own name, he gave her a new
poetic name, so shaped that the two were interchangeable in
poetry. Whenever he read his poem to her, he could insert her
real name. In published copies, she was discreetly concealed.
Because she had literary taste, was sensitive, and was by nature
passionate, he compared her to the lyric poetess Sappho of Lesbos,
and named her 'Lesbia'. To express his immediate, overwhelming
love of her, and the awe she inspired in him, he turned into Latin
verse (in the original metre) a poem by Sappho on the over-
powering physical ecstasy of love and the pain of deprivation. By
voicing his frank envy of her husband (or perhaps one of her
established lovers), he made—although with graceful indirectness
—a declaration of his own love for her.

Surely that man equals the gods in heaven—
if it be not blasphemy, he excels them—
he who sits and, constantly, in your presence,
    watches and hears you
laugh with sweetness such that my shaken senses
leave me helpless. Lesbia, at the moment
when I first caught sight of you, then my voice was
    struck into silence,
tongue benumbed, light delicate flame pervaded

every limb, loud inward alarms were ringing
through my ears, while suddenly both my eyes were
covered with darkness.[1]

Clodia coquetted with him. She did not reproach him or send
him away.

A little later she gave him some encouragement. He was now
able to sit with her, and to watch her without the fearful tension
of those first meetings. He ventured to call her his 'girl': the word
is less absolute than 'mistress', and may imply only a playful
devotion. In the same poem he described her as his 'radiant long-
ing'—'radiant' because of her great glittering eyes, 'longing'
because he had not possessed her. Once again in this poem, instead
of speaking to her outright, he made an indirect declaration of
love; but this time the poem was a subtle mixture of passion and
humour. He addressed it, not to her, but to her pet sparrow. He
chose a light metre, something far less fervent and serious than the
lyric stanza of Sappho. He used colloquial language here and
there, the beginnings of intimate love-talk. The rhythm and the
words are light and gay, like the hopping twittering bird. Most
readers have always been amused by the little piece, and some
have introduced naughty double meanings into it. Yet it is basic-
ally a sad poem, in which only a tiny thoughtless prisoned
creature is happy, and two human beings are thwarted and
miserable.

Tell me, sparrow, you darling of my darling,
whom she plays with and fondles in her bosom,
you who peck when she offers you a finger
(beak outthrust in a counterfeit of biting),
when that radiant star of my aspiring
turns towards you, as a pleasant little playmate,
one small bird, to console her when she suffers,
by your love to relieve her burning passion—
could I possibly play with you as she does,
could I lighten the pain that still torments me?[2]

[1] Catullus 51.
[2] Catullus 2.

The 'burning passion' which needed comfort from the mock kisses of a little bird is hinted at, but not explained. Clodia was like Anna Karenina, beautiful and ardent, married to a sober, much-occupied politician. She needed love (she could tell the hot-headed young poet), her heart was full of love, and she had no one, nothing to give it to except her pet bird.

A little later, the bird died. Juliet of Verona once spoke to Romeo of such a bird, saying:

> 'Tis almost morning; I would have thee gone;
> And yet no further than a wanton's bird,
> Who lets it hop a little from her hand,
> Like a poor prisoner in his twisted gyves,
> And with a silk thread plucks it back again,
> So loving-jealous of his liberty.

Romeo, like Catullus, answered:

> I would I were thy bird.

And Juliet replied:

> Sweet, so would I;
> Yet I should kill thee with much cherishing.[1]

Clodia's bird was killed with much cherishing. But at the moment, Catullus could feel no real sorrow. Instead, he wrote a light and cheerful lament for the dead bird, full of slang, and pet-diminutives, and jokes concealed by mock grief. Yet this poem also was filled with tactful approaches to Clodia: beginning with a gay invocation to Venus (she thought Venus was her patron goddess,

---

[1] Shakespeare, *Romeo and Juliet*, 2.2.176–183.

and had a special statuette of the divinity, on which she hung her lovers' spoils) and ending with a reference to her beautiful eyes—a reference which, nevertheless, she cannot altogether have enjoyed.

> Weep, weep bitterly, Venuses and Cupids,
> weep too, weep, every sympathetic spirit.
> My girl's sparrow has left this life for ever,
> that poor sparrow, the darling of my darling,
> whom she loved like the apple of her dear eyes.
> He was really a sweet: he knew his mistress
> just as well as a daughter knows her mother.
> All day long he would hardly leave her lonely,
> hop hop cheerily everywhere around her,
> greeting her with a sweet and special chirrup.
> Now he travels the solitary darkness
> towards that region from which there's no returning.
> Well, confound you, you barbarous and cruel
> Death! you swallow up everything that's pretty:
> now you've massacred a pretty little sparrow.
> Shame, oh shame! And alas, you naughty sparrow,
> you, yes, you are to blame: my darling's lovely
> eyes are swollen and red with weeping for you.[1]

This is one of the gayest and most informal short laments ever written, full of words and phrases which never occur in serious poetry. There is even something comical about the idea of the little sparrow hopping away down the long dark avenue of death. Throughout the poem we can feel a bubbling excitement and gaiety, only half-suppressed. Obviously Catullus has come much closer to his love.

Still, there is something ominous about the two poems. They are both about a living thing that Clodia loved. The first, light though it is, is full of passion, excessive passion which can scarcely find an outlet. The second, light though it is and playful though it is, concerns death. Catullus understood intuitively that Clodia

[1] Catullus 3.

killed the thing she loved; and the death of the devoted bird is a
foreshadowing of his own death.

At least he was happy for a time. Long afterwards, when he
had grown older and Clodia had been, not once but again and
again, unfaithful to him, he still remembered the rapture of their
early love. He blessed his friend Allius who had lent the two a
house to meet in: it was (he said) like a fresh draught of water to a
thirsty man. Other poets, after their first success in love, recall the
woman's body or her voice or her passionate acts or their own
prowess. Crude though his words often may be, Catullus is excep-
tionally sensitive in this. He scarcely describes the meeting, but
sums up his long expectation and the glory of his possession in a
single picture—the picture of a beautiful woman coming in from
the sunlight to a darkened house, and pausing for a moment with
one foot on the threshold. It might be a painting by Vermeer,
except for the difference of emotional tension. Vermeer is calm,
his sunlight is tinged with autumn and afternoon, time moves
slowly in his pictures. Catullus is hopeful, tense, brilliant: he lives
an eternity of passion and bittersweet suffering in a single heart-
beat.

A brook glittering clear on the airy mountain-top
   leaps from the source deep among mossy rocks,
to roll with headlong speed down through a sloping valley
   and cross the highroad through the jostling crowds,
bringing sweet freshness to relieve the weary traveller . . .
   Such was the help that Allius gave me.
He opened up a broad path through a closed domain—
   giving my lady and myself a home
where we might meet and satisfy the love we shared.
   There, with soft footsteps, my white goddess entered,
and, as she crossed the well-worn threshold, stopped, with shining
   foot poised upon the slender sandal-tip.[1]

[1] Catullus 68.57–61, 66–72.

That was a serious and ambitious poem—an elegy, decorated with elaborate images and mythical parallels, and tinged with the melancholy of disillusionment, the death of hope. But we also have the poem he wrote much earlier, in the first exultation of triumphant love. It is in the same light metre as his sparrow poems. Like them, it contains some slang; it adds a little note of popular superstition (the idea that it is dangerous to count anything valuable—the same notion which makes primitive people hate census-takers); but it also has a foreboding of death below its glittering surface.

> Life, my Lesbia, life and love for ever!
> All that gossip of grave and reverend elders—
> close your ears to it! it's not worth a penny.
> Suns can sink and return again next morning:
> our brief day, when it once has been extinguished,
> must pass into a sleep that has no waking.
> Give me kisses—a thousand, then a hundred,
> one more thousand and then another hundred,
> then one thousand again, and still a hundred.
> After that, when we've run up many thousands,
> let's destroy the accounting and forget it,
> so no envious character can hurt us
> when he hears we have had so many kisses.[1]

This is the poem in which Catullus used his own word for 'kiss': *basium*. There had been plenty of kissing in Latin before him. The comic playwright Plautus has some inventive variations on the theme. The love poets of the generation after Catullus were experts in kissing. But Catullus was the first, and for some time the only, writer to use *basium*. (The regular word is *osculum*.) It is not easy to tell its origin; but it seems likely that it was a Celtic word which Catullus brought down to Rome. Perhaps, when he first used it, Clodia laughed; then he taught her to like it, wrote poems which contained it, and made it at home in Latin.

[1] Catullus 5.

There is a second kiss poem, less successful and less famous than the first. It appears to echo the same idea, thousands of kisses and thousands more. 'How many kisses are enough?' asks Lesbia, and Catullus answers, 'As many as the sands of north Africa, or the stars in the sky—the stars which watch the secret love-adventures of men and women.'[1] Yes, but here we can feel the first cold breeze blowing upon his passion. In the former poem, the couple were together, wholly together with the world locked out. In this, they are no longer 'we', but 'you' and 'I'. In love there is always one who kisses, and one who offers the cheek. The former poem showed Lesbia kissing Catullus; in this poem Catullus is giving the kisses to Lesbia; and she is asking him how many kisses will satisfy him—which implies that she herself is approaching satiation.

Later she was unfaithful to him: openly; deliberately; defiantly. At first, he tried to reconcile himself to her infidelities. In the elegy where he recalled their earliest love-meeting, he wrote:

> Although she cannot be content with me alone,
>   I'll bear my lady's rare, discreet adventures
> rather than seem to be a nagging busybody.
>   Often the queen of heaven, mighty Juno,
> mastered her blazing wrath when her husband was at fault,
>   and yet she knew the escapades of Jove.[2]

There is also a bitter epigram in which he actually speaks of marriage to Clodia, and at the same time admits it is hopeless. She loved her freedom too much to be faithful to any man.

> My woman says that she'd prefer to marry no one
>   but me, even if Jupiter asked for her love.
> Ah yes: but what a woman says to an eager lover,
>   write it on running water, write it on air.[3]

[1] Catullus 7.
[2] Catullus 68.135–140.
[3] Catullus 70.

The language of Roman love poetry is extremely subtle. There are many different words and phrases to describe different aspects of a love affair; and they must all be taken into account when one tries to translate such poems. For instance, Catullus usually calls Clodia his 'girl', *puella*. Once he calls her his 'lady', *era*—a rather formal word used by servants to describe the lady of the house; and twice his 'mistress', *domina*—that also began by being a word of respect, became part of the common language of lovers, and grew into the regular term for 'lady' in the Romance languages, *dame, donna, dona*. Only here does Catullus speak of Clodia as his 'woman', *mea mulier*. So used, it is not a regular lover's word at all. It must be intimate and colloquial: the ordinary Italian now uses it, when he calls his wife *mia moglie*. It must mean that Catullus thought of Clodia, not as a casual flame, but as the woman he wanted to marry.

Although he had had his share of love affairs, he himself was apparently meant for marriage and for the happiness of a home. He wrote three of his longest and most elaborate poems about marriage. Each is in a different style. One is a long magnificent mythological piece about the wedding of Peleus and Thetis, who were to become the parents of Achilles. One, apparently an adaptation from Sappho, is an exquisite double chorus to be sung in antiphon by the bridesmaids and groomsmen as they await the bridal procession. And one is a bright lyric in the Italian style, combining naughty jokes with tenderness in a way that few other poets could achieve. They are all too long to translate here, but the most touching stanza of all must be quoted: an anticipation of the baby which is to be born to the young Italian couple:

> Soon let a little Torquatus
> stretch his soft hands
> from his mother's lap,
> smiling sweetly to his father
> with baby lips half open.[1]

[1] Catullus 61.209–213.

The man who could write that, and other delightful passages in the wedding poems, was intended to be happy with a woman who loved him faithfully. But he knew that he could never marry Clodia. She became bolder and crueller in her infidelities, in her open debaucheries. He suffered the most agonizing of all tortures possible for a lover, the torture which is like being strained and twisted on a rack until the body loses its natural shape and all the limbs become monstrosities—the combination of love and hate, adoration and loathing. Other lovers have had to endure this. It is the theme of some of Shakespeare's sonnets, it was one of the secrets of Baudelaire's wasted life. But no poet has ever felt it more bitterly nor expressed it more vividly than Catullus.

> My mind has been so broken by your guilt, my Lesbia,
>   and so destroyed itself by faith in you,
> that now it cannot wish you well if you turn to virtue
>   nor cease from loving you in all your vice.[1]

The most famous of all his poems on this theme is simply a couplet containing the impossible, unendurable antithesis:

> I hate and love. You ask, perhaps, how that can be?
> I know not, but I feel the agony.[2]

And there is one remarkable monologue, written while he was making a desperate effort to leave the woman for ever. It is in a harsh and rather unusual metre, called *scazon*, 'the limper', in which each line ends with three heavy syllables: usually it images clumsiness or fatigue, and here it reflects painful effort. The language is deliberately unpoetic, often slangy. It shows us Catullus, still in love and yet knowing the woman is hopelessly unworthy of his love, looking back in sombre regret to the happiness

[1] Catullus 75.
[2] Catullus 85.

which he will never know again, struggling desperately to be
liberated from his obsession, and yet, whenever he thinks of
Clodia, visualizing her in the arms of her future lovers.

You poor Catullus, don't be such a crass-brained fool!
All that is obviously lost, you must write off.
The sun shone brightly on you once, in days gone by,
when you would follow everywhere the girl led on—
the girl I loved as no girl ever will be loved.
Yes, then we had a thousand thousand pleasant games,
and you enjoyed them, and the girl did not hold back.
It's true: you lived in sunshine then, in times long gone.
Now she refuses. You then must refuse, you too:
don't follow when she runs, don't live a poor fool's life;
control your heart, endure it all, and be steel-hard.
Good-bye now, girl. Catullus has become steel-hard.
He will not chase you, beg for you against your will;
but you will surely suffer when you're asked no more.
You devil, you. What kind of life will you lead now?
Who will come courting you, and who will call you sweet?
Whom will you love, and whose girl will they say you are?
Whose lips will you be kissing now, with love-sharp bites?
No, no, Catullus, be determined: be steel-hard![1]

This remarkable poem is a dramatic monologue in which
Catullus both records his suffering and endeavours to master it.
It is more like certain works of Browning (for instance, the
Soliloquy of the Spanish Cloister) than anything else in our lan-
guage. Catullus begins abruptly with violent self-reproach, com-
manding himself to forget the woman for ever. Then, inevitably,
he recalls the past, when he was happy with her, even although he
kissed and she merely offered her cheek. But this takes him to the
present, and to some repulse which he has just received—crueller
and more unforgettable than any other: he realizes that the past is
irrecoverable, and tells himself that it *must* be forgotten. There-

[1] Catullus 8.

after, to strengthen his resolution, he speaks roughly to the absent Clodia, asserting that he is determined to free himself from her power. This turns his mind to the future. Thinking of the unknown but certain lover who will supplant him in Clodia's arms, he imagines her kisses (using his own word, *basia*) and her lustful bites; and at that, in agony, he breaks off with one more assertion of his will-power, which sounds almost too emphatic to be trustworthy. We feel that in a few days he will give way once more, and once again beg Clodia for an hour alone with her. In spite of its awkward metre and its prosaic, deliberately slangy wording, this is one of the most poignant love-poems ever written. It sounds agonizingly real.

While he brooded on his misery, Clodia went from one lover to another. One of them was Catullus's friend, the brilliant young politician Caelius Rufus—so that a new torment, the torment of friendship violated, was added to Catullus's agonies. But Caelius left her. She had many other lovers, and finally became an amateur prostitute. Like a street-walker, she would pick up anyone, and make love to any man in any filthy back alley. Other rich and noble ladies were to do the same later in the history of Rome: an emperor's daughter, Julia; an emperor's wife, Messalina. Roman women had been held strictly in check for so many centuries that, when they broke the chain, some of them lost all their self-respect and self-control, and would do disgraceful things in public merely to demonstrate their independence.

The last of Catullus's poems in which he mentions Clodia was written after he had convinced himself that she was utterly worthless, and after he began to feel able to live without her. Once he had been too shy to speak directly to her, and had addressed his early love-poems to her pet bird. Now he was too full of bitterness and loathing to speak directly to her, and asked two trusted friends to give her his message. But he chose for it exactly the same Sapphic metre in which he had composed the earliest of all his lyrics to her; he repeated one word in exactly the same place in the stanza (the word *identidem*, 'constantly'); and, as in several of his poems to her, he ended with an image of death.

You, my two old friends, who remain my comrades
whether I may journey to furthest India,
where the sea-beach booms to the pounding monsoon's
    thunderous combers,
or among Hyrcanians, supple Arabs,
fierce Sacae, or dangerous Parthian bowmen,
or to where seven mouths of the Nile, debouching,
    darken the azure,
or perhaps may travel the Alpine passes
towards the new-won triumphs of mighty Cæsar,
Rhine, the Gauls' frontier, and the terrifying
    outermost British,
you whom I know willing, wherever heaven
sends me forth, to share my adventures with me,
take for me these words to my girl, a message
    short and unpleasant.
Give her my good-bye, her and all her lovers,
whom she hugs so close to her in their hundreds,
loving not one, yet with her constant lusting
    leaving their loins limp.
Gone is all my love, which she once respected—
murdered through her guilt, as a flower blooming
out upon the edge of the meadow, falls when
    touched by the ploughshare.[1]

This beautiful and horrible poem is a masterpiece of technique, as well as an utterance of unforgettable sincerity. The entire lyric contains only three sentences—just as the first Lesbia poem (translated on pp. 26–7) contains only two. The four opening stanzas, highly elaborated, contain several different themes: a wonderful description of all the extremes of the known world, a contrast between tried friendship and faithless love, and a gloomy resolution to go anywhere, anywhere to escape from the woman's influence. The sound effects are exceptionally subtle. It might seem to be impossible to convey the roar of the Indian Ocean in only five words, but Catullus does it. In three vowels he evokes

[1] Catullus 11.

the long loud-mouthed bellowing of the wind, and in the repetition of one booming syllable, the repeated thunder of the breakers: *longe resonante E O A tunditur unda.* The metre is the metre of the poetess of Lesbos, the passionate Sappho, so that it links this poem with Catullus's earliest poem to his 'Lesbia'. The word *identidem* strengthens the link; for in the first poem it was applied to the happiness of a lover who could sit 'constantly' with her and hear her talk; and in this, it describes the 'constant' demands of her insatiable lust. In addition, Catullus slurs its last syllable into the following word and then slurs the last syllable of that word too, so that the whole phrase sounds like a savage sneer: *identidem omniumilia rumpens.* The final words of the stanza are a loathsome expression, very close to downright obscenity. They mean that Clodia exhausts her men sexually. She uses them up, and, instead of invigorating them as a truly loving woman would do, destroys their manhood in satisfying herself.

This last theme also comes out in the strangest of all Catullus's poems. It is a work too long and too special to translate here, but it can be summarized. It is a dramatic treatment of a very curious and ancient myth, apparently older than the religion of the Olympian gods: the myth of the devoted youth and the cruel goddess who is both his lover and his mother. She is Cybele, who lives in the wild jungles and has fierce lions as her attendants. He is Attis or Atys. Either because he had sworn to be faithful to her and then broken his oath with a human girl, or because she dominated him and demanded a blood-sacrifice, or because he wished to keep himself her pure servant for ever (different reasons are given in different versions of the myth), he castrated himself, fled from his home, and lived for ever as her votary, far from civilization, in a group of eunuchs like himself, making wild music and dancing furious dervish dances. That this is a very ancient myth is shown by the fact that both Attis himself and the later worshippers of Cybele who imitated him used a *stone* knife. Catullus's poem on this myth is a technical and psychological masterpiece. It is written in a fantastically difficult metre, the rhythm of the eunuchs' savage dance, on which he plays many subtle variations. Most of it is a monologue, uttered, not by the original Phrygian dervish, but by a Greek youth of Catullus's own time, who has been seized with the frenzy of the goddess, has joined her cult, has sailed to the wild regions where she reigns, and there has dedicated himself to her by castrating himself. After recovering from the wild exultation in which he mutilated his body, he looks back with bitter remorse on his life as a normal young man among friends and lovers. But the goddess hears his lament, and sends her lions to drive him, raving with terror and subjection, into the forests which are her domain. This is a portrait of a manic-depressive during the phase of depression, at the end of which mania grips him once more.

But it has another hidden significance, which has not been noticed. This is that it is a translation into mythical terms of Catullus's relation to Clodia. It is the desperate complaint of a young man who was once happy and normal, but who has been seized and dominated by a female demon. The demon does not stand for comfort and satisfaction, not even for the ecstasies of sexual fulfilment. She is a primitive spirit, living in dark jungles and served by fierce animals. The man can have no peaceful and balanced relationship with her. Although she is feminine and he is (or was) masculine, he must be utterly subservient to her. Her aim is to take away his manhood, to destroy him and yet to keep him alive as a slave and a symbol of her power. (In his farewell poem to Clodia, written much later, Catullus said she treated all her lovers in the same way, 'leaving their loins limp', almost unmanning them.) His early normal life is now cut off from him by a gulf as wide as the sea. He can hope for nothing in the future except a succession of orgies, joyless fits of insane excitement and unsatisfied desire, separated by periods of deathlike unconsciousness and hopeless remorse.

Catullus probably wrote this terrible poem before he ever saw the wild mountains and forests where the goddess Cybele had her home. It is not a piece of landscape-painting. It may, however, have been written in anticipation of his visit to Asia Minor, the country full of dark cults and ancient myths. It is really a psychological revelation, and its true theme is the fascination and terror which can be inspired in a sensitive soul by the subliminal powers of orgiastic religion and the dominating character of an evil woman. If we ask why the ancient and hideous myth of Cybele and her servant Attis should have suggested itself to Catullus as a symbol of his relationship to Clodia, we need only remember that it was a collateral ancestor of hers, the vestal virgin Claudia, who escorted Cybele into Rome on her first arrival; and that the temple of Cybele stood on the Palatine hill, not far from the house of Clodia. Often in that house, during his ecstasies and agonies, Catullus must have heard the clash of cymbals, the wild cries, and the weird rhythms of the drums echoing from the temple, and must have compared the destiny of those fanatics, devotees of a powerful goddess at once lovable and hateful, to his own life as the slave of a cruel but irresistible mistress.

SIRMIO

We know little of what Catullus did during his year in Bithynia. (Imagine Lord Byron as assistant principal of the Highways and Rivers Bureau of a small province in India.) But at least he managed to buy a little yacht, in which (like Byron) he visited the cities of Asia and the isles of Greece. He loved the little craft so much that he sailed at least part of the way home to Italy in it, and finally had it taken overland to the one place in the world where he could be truly happy.

This was Sirmio. It is still a delightful spot.

Sirmio (now called Sirmione) is a slender tongue of rock, covered with trees and gardens, which juts out from the mainland for two or three miles into Lake Garda, near Verona. The lake itself, the largest in Italy, is nobly beautiful. Not that it is calm and gentle. It is a powerful body of water, surrounded by steep hills on almost every side, with mountains rising in the background. Sheets of rain can sweep over it, cold Alpine winds can whip up its waters until

it rises into billows that boom like the sea.[1]

[1] Vergil, *Georgics*, 2.160.

Yet in rough weather, when the lake and the sky and the mountains are all a mass of changing grey, the whole region is thoroughly invigorating: sombre, yet manly. And when the sun strikes the waters and scatters a million broken rays upon them, the whole surface seems to be dancing and laughing for mile upon mile. To stand far out on the peninsula, to see the vistas of blue and pale gold receding among the cloud-shadowed hills, and to hear the water, clean and brisk, lapping almost all around, is a rare delight. Sirmio then seems like a stout little boat sailing forward through the welcoming waves.

Here, on Sirmio, Catullus had a country place. Here, after his trip to Asia, he returned, and dedicated his yacht to the Heavenly Twins, Castor and Pollux, who sent him good weather throughout his voyage. And here he wrote a poem of deep relief on his homecoming. It is in the 'limping' metre, to image his exhaustion: the last three syllables of each line throb heavily like a tired heart; but after a short rather formal beginning, it ends with cheerful colloquialisms, as though sunlight were breaking through mist.

> Of all the islands and of all the almost-isles
> which Neptune, god of water, set among clear lakes
> and in vast seas, you, Sirmio, are sole bright gem.
> With what relief and gladness now I see your face,
> scarcely believing I have left the far-off lands
> of Asia, and can gaze upon you safe and sound!
> Ah, what is nearer heaven than relief long-sought,
> when the mind drops its burdens, when we, still worn out
> with travel and exhaustion, reach at last our home
> and lay our bodies down to rest in the longed-for bed?
> For all our labours this is surely rich reward.
> Now greetings, lovely Sirmio, and share my bliss!
> Enjoy it too, you waters of the Lydian lake:
> and all the jollity of home, come on, laugh! laugh![1]

[1] Catullus 31. He calls the lake Lydian because the Etruscans, who came from Lydia in Asia Minor, settled its shores. Its Roman name was Benacus.

To visit Sirmio today is to do as one often does in Italy: to walk back through the Middle Ages into ancient Rome. The peninsula lies a few miles away from the main road passing south of Lake Garda from Milan to Verona. We leave the highway at the village of Desenzano, and drive north to Sirmio. Leaving the mainland, the car runs out along a thin tongue of land between shallow coastal waters; just at the narrowest point, it passes a tiny harbour, and then makes its way slowly through a stone gate pierced in a powerful medieval wall. The wall cuts off the broadest and most fertile part of the peninsula, defends the fishing village that lies behind it, and in the Middle Ages must have made the place a splendid stronghold. It is commanded by a massive castle standing within a moat of its own, which scowls down upon the village like an armoured knight with his visor closed. This was a castle of the powerful Scala family, rulers of Verona. It must have been impregnable to anything except an artillery bombardment. Now it is empty, except for a caretaker and for tourists climbing its steep stairs and strolling along its ramparts. There are some Roman remains inside—among which it is a shock to see a large inscription bearing the name of CLODIVS.

Leaving the castle behind and walking out through the village, we find the peninsula growing more hilly and more thickly wooded. There are a few spacious country houses standing in their own grounds; some new villas being built rather hurriedly, as in every once secluded spot in the world; a hotel or two; an old deserted country church high on a hill; gardens and olive groves.

At last, at the broad tip of the Sirmio peninsula, we reach a strange place. It looks like a huge collection of sumptuous cave-dwellings. As we walk among the olive-trees towards the water, suddenly we find that the ground has been opened up beneath our feet. Below many cubic yards of earth, below the roots of the olive-trees, lie rooms of brick and stone, arches, corridors, vaults, now ruined and uninhabitable, but built with that accuracy, solidity, and massive grace which are the marks of the best Roman architecture. At the extreme northern end, where the peninsula drops down to the lake shore, rows of rooms gaze through broken walls like the eyes in a skull. They look like caves. So, long ago, the natives of the place, remembering the poet who loved Sirmio, named them 'The Grottoes of Catullus'.

They are not grottoes, and they did not belong to Catullus. They and the other rooms and corridors which have been excavated in Sirmio are the remains of a huge and sumptuous palace built some time after Catullus died. We do not know who built it and lived in it. But its rooms are so many, its structure so complex, and its situation, gazing out over the lake, so magnificent, that we can be sure it was one of the many superb country-houses built for rich and noble Romans in the peaceful first century of the Empire. The emperor Tiberius constructed several such houses in splendid situations on the high slopes of Capri, almost midway between blue sea and blue sky; there are remains of many more around the bay of Naples; but this is the largest such mansion yet discovered in northern Italy.

Thus Sirmio sums up one of the differences between Roman Italy and medieval Italy. It has the remains of two ancient and mighty buildings upon it. One is a luxurious country-house, looking benignly towards the lake and the mountains, undefended and indefensible, peaceful, built wholly for relaxation and happiness. The other is a grim medieval fortress, mistrusting even its closest neighbours and servants, looking away from the lake, and watching the narrow causeway of land from which an attack might come.

As for the name 'grottoes', that is the familiar misnomer. Many Roman buildings, abandoned in the Dark Ages, were silted up, buried, and forgotten. Trees grew in their earth-filled rooms, and then—as the ground-level gradually rose—above their roofs. Their arches, filled in with soil and débris, supported fertile hills. When they were rediscovered, so far below the new surface of the earth, the Italians could not believe they had once been above ground; thought they were subterranean resorts devoted to coolness, quietness, and privacy; and so called them 'grottoes'.

In 1880 Tennyson visited Sirmio. He was over seventy, and his health was failing. But he was delighted by seeing the home of Catullus, spent the entire day there, and wrote a pleasant little poem about it—inspired by the rhythm of the dancing waves over which he was rowed to reach the peninsula.

Row us out from Desenzano, to your Sirmione row!
So they row'd, and there we landed—'O venusta Sirmio!'
There to me thro' all the groves of olive in the summer glow,
There beneath the Roman ruin where the purple flowers grow,
Came that 'Ave atque Vale' of the Poet's hopeless woe,
Tenderest of Roman poets nineteen-hundred years ago,
'Frater Ave atque Vale'—as we wander'd to and fro
Gazing at the Lydian laughter of the Garda lake below
Sweet Catullus's all-but-island, olive-silvery Sirmio![1]

After the old poet returned to his home in England, he recalled his visit to Sirmio with delight, described it to his friends, and spent the evening reading one of them the poems of Catullus, while he explained their various beauties of form, expression, and sound. Still, with characteristic sensibility, he did not speak of the imposing ruins at the end of the peninsula as being the home of Catullus. He could see that it was a palace.

The palace is still being excavated. Some day an inscription or a statue may be dug up, which will give us the name of its owner. Dr. Degrassi, who is superintending the dig, believes that such a sumptuous house can only have belonged to a member of the imperial family. Yet in northern Italy there were many rich men (such as the younger Pliny) who had the wealth to build such a place, and the romantic reminiscent nature to place it where a great poet of the past had once lived.

But this was not Catullus's country home. He never had enough money to build or maintain such a château. Once, inviting his friend Fabullus to dine, he had to warn him that the guest would have to provide everything usually provided by the host—the food, the wine, and the spices, and a girl . . .

for your Catullus
now has nothing but cobwebs in his pocket.[2]

[1] 'Frater Ave atque Vale', Tennyson, *Poetical Works* (Oxford, 1953), 533.
[2] Catullus 13.7–8.

And once he wrote a little poem on his farm. Furius (one of the two faithful friends) had asked him whether it faced north, south, or what? Catullus replied:

> My farm, Furius, doesn't face the south wind,
> no, nor yet the refreshing western zephyrs,
> nor harsh Boreas, nor the eastern breezes.
> But it faces a most appalling mortgage:
> there's a draft that is absolutely lethal![1]

He tells us how much the mortgage was, too: it came to about £1500 of our money. His farm would be no more than a little house built in the country style, without marbles or statues or mosaics or luxury; but set in a garden, among a few olive-trees, on the windswept cape of Sirmio. It is there, walking on the sweet grass, and not among the massive arches of the later palace, that we can best imagine Catullus.

The air is clear and cool there. It moves constantly; the lake water is seldom still; marching clouds move over the distant mountains; contours and lights change and develop. This is not a soft and sleepy landscape. Wherever the eye falls, there are strong-boned hills, and ridges climbing higher and higher to the Alps. On one side of the peninsula there is a gentle slope towards the water, but on the north and east there are steep cliffs about a hundred and fifty feet high, with the waves breaking far below.

Above the still unexcavated areas of the palace, the ground is ridged and hummocked. It is covered with tall grass, bushes, thistles, and wild parsley. This is too chill and windy to shelter many colonies of birds, but a few hardy little creatures hop and flutter among the stones. They are sparrows—the seven-hundredth descendants of Lesbia's doomed pet. Among them, one single black butterfly wavers and careens in the wind. The olive-trees, descendants of those which Catullus owned, are planted in regular rows; but they hate regimentation. Each of them has grown into a

[1] Catullus 26.

different shape, knotted and bitter, strengthened but tortured by its constant battle against the wind from the mountains.

When Dante passed through hell with his master Vergil, he saw that, among the damned souls, the suicides were tormented by being enclosed within the shapes of bleak and haggard trees, while the lustful, who had been driven by storms of passion during their lives, were condemned to fly eternally like leaves or spume before an irresistible gale ceaselessly sweeping through the darkness.

It is good for us to think of Catullus returning to his northland from enervating Asia or corrupt Rome, and, for a time, being happy in 'relief long-sought, when the mind drops its burdens'. Yet he was a man doomed to misery. We come closer to his soul when, with his single small volume of poems (a promise of far richer possibilities unfulfilled) in our hand, we stand above the endlessly rolling waves that beat on Sirmio, and watch the olive-trees, twisted into shapes like those of tormented prisoners, tossing their arms wildly in the air, and feel upon our faces the tearful violence of the restless and passionate wind.

CLODIA

And Clodia?

Ah, Clodia.

Her life ended not in despair, but in derision. She did not mind degrading herself to any depth in order to get attention and excitement. From her garden, she could watch the young men swimming in the Tiber, and signal to them. She would sleep with a grinning Spaniard—who, says Catullus, kept his teeth brilliant by polishing them with his own urine. She would pick up strangers in vile taverns and in filthy back streets. But she could not bear to be neglected. When Caelius Rufus left her, she prosecuted him for attempting to poison her.

The charge was ridiculous. (She added others, equally ridiculous.) The evidence was flimsy. Clodia did not know what moderation was. She attempted to strengthen her case by asserting that Caelius had defrauded her of some money she had lent him, that he had attempted to murder an Egyptian diplomat, had tried to raise a riot in Naples, and so on. She hoped that, even if he were acquitted on some charges, he might be found guilty on others; and that, even if he were cleared of them all, his character would be blackened and his career as a rising statesman ruined.

But Caelius was not a sensitive and soft-hearted poet. He was a brilliant, sensual, ruthless young politico—less like De Musset than D'Annunzio. He did not intend to be sacrificed to a revengeful woman. He determined to rebut all the charges and burn up all the slanders against him by showing Clodia herself to be an irresponsible, vicious, and utterly selfish woman. As his two defenders, he was lucky enough and shrewd enough to get old Crassus, the deaf, sober, politically blameless millionaire, the Herbert Hoover of his age; and the man who spent his life and met his death in resisting the extremes of oligarchy and democracy, the greatest speaker of his time or any other time, Marcus Tullius Cicero. (Cicero enjoyed his duties. Not only was Clodia the sister of the man who had helped to drive him into exile and caused his private house in Rome to be utterly destroyed, but she was the widow of one of his old acquaintances, whom she had possibly assisted in dying, and whose memory she was constantly dishonouring. His wife even thought Clodia had been trying to oust her, and to marry Cicero, since he was both distinguished and rich.)

The speech Caelius made in his own defence has disappeared. We know only that it was bitingly effective. He coined many epigrams about his ex-mistress. He said she was 'willing in the dining-room, chilling in the bedroom'. He called her a 'twopenny Clytemnestra'; 'Clytemnestra' because she looked bold and domineering like a tragedy queen, and because that particular queen had murdered her husband; 'twopenny' because of a story that one of her lovers had sent her a purse, filled not with gold or silver coins, but with the cheapest coppers, to show what he thought of her vulgar sexuality.

The speech of Crassus has also vanished. Mercifully.

The speech of Cicero survives. It is one of his most brilliant. Those who are mistaken enough to think of him as a long-winded pompous orator mouthing resounding clichés ought to read the speech *For Caelius*—or, better still, hear it read aloud by a good speaker. It is almost more Italian than Latin. It is more like a Rossini overture than a ceremonial march. Many of its best passages must have provoked shouts of laughter; others are bravura pieces which call for delighted and spontaneous applause. There is very little serious attempt in it to meet Clodia's charges against Caelius—except for the underlying implication that he was a vicious young man, unfit by his associations to be a Roman statesman. Cicero disposes of that very carefully, pleading that youth is the time for sowing wild oats, and promising on his own responsibility that all such erratic behaviour on the part of Caelius is far in the past. The other charges he describes as a tissue of lies, a cheap detective-story invented by a foolish and ill-natured woman.

The most skilful thing in the speech is his gradual demolition of the character and reputation of the woman Clodia. At the opening of the case, she was a formidable personage. She was a woman of great wealth, high rank, and powerful influence. She had a coterie. Even if there were scandals about her, she was far from despicable. After all, she was a Roman matron—related by birth to the proud Claudian house, by marriage to the distinguished family of the Metelli. Cicero sets himself, by one delicate touch after another, to destroy that public façade, and to make a new character for Clodia, a character closer to the truth, which she would never be able to put off.

Obviously Cicero cannot stand up in court—he, a new man from the small country town of Arpinum, the first of his family ever to hold public office—and say, 'Do not believe Clodia, she is no better than a street-walker.' Though she herself has been reckless in flouting conventions, he must still be very cautious in stripping off her noble masks.

In the opening of his speech, therefore, he never mentions her name. He points out that the case against Caelius is so flimsy that it scarcely needs an answer: he will be content with justifying his friend's character and career. Only two bold and shocking phrases are carefully planted, during the first minute, in the mind of the jury. Caelius (says Cicero) is being attacked 'by the influence of a prostitute'; and he adds that any stranger who happened to be in court and hear the evidence would conclude that 'the wantonness of women' ought to be firmly controlled. But even these phrases, as he uses them, are quite impersonal. They serve only to establish an atmosphere.

Then, much later, after completing his laudatory character-sketch of Caelius, Cicero turns to Clodia—with apologies. It would, he says, be absolutely wrong for him to mention a Roman lady (he uses the dignified word *materfamilias*) in court, without every mark of respect, if it were not for the fact that she had been attacking his friend Caelius. And then he slips in a delicate and apparently involuntary allusion to the story that she had been committing incest with her brother. 'I should counter-attack more vigorously than I do, if it were not that I have had grave personal disagreements with this lady's husband—I mean her *brother*. I always make that mistake!' We can see Cicero turning, with a smile of embarrassment, towards the jury, and spreading out his hands in apology for his blunder, while behind him Caelius and the others (who knew the gibe was coming) roar with laughter, and at the other side of the court the woman with the bold flaming eyes writhes in rage.

He goes on to say that it is against his principles to make an enemy of any lady—'particularly of one whom everyone has always considered to be, not the enemy of any one man, but the dear friend of all.' (*Amica* means 'friend', in the feminine, but also 'mistress'.)

Now Cicero exposes her real nature. He himself will not venture to say what he thinks; but others shall. By a fine rhetorical device, he calls up from the dead an ancestor of Clodia, the great statesman of the early Republic, Appius Claudius the Censor. He makes this formidable figure name his own achievements, describe the virtuous women of the Claudian house, and reproach their degenerate descendant Clodia with her folly, her vulgarity, and her vice. Cicero could not in his own person rebuke one of the old aristocracy for being false to her hereditary standards. But, through the mouth of one of her own family, he could speak with all the power of traditional Roman morality, and denounce her as unworthy of her proud name.

After this powerful evocation is over, Cicero turns to show the jury that Clodia is not only wicked but (what is just as bad for a

Roman) light-minded, silly, irresponsible. She lacks gravity. She is not a real person. In fact, she is like a woman in a romantic comedy—and so he quotes again and again from the romantic comedies of Plautus and Terence and other favourite playwrights. It might sound flattering for a woman to be compared to the star of a comedy. But the most prominent women in those plays were nearly always grasping, conscienceless, impudent prostitutes. From then on, by repeated touches on the same theme—usually with a light laugh, often with a quotation from a naughty play to point them—Cicero strengthens the picture of Clodia that he wishes to impress on the jury and the public. She is not a great lady. She is not even an emancipated woman, running the risk of scandal for the sake of an ideal love. She is a *meretrix*—a tart who flaunts her disgrace in public, whose word cannot be trusted, who is both cheap and ridiculous.

A little later, Cicero analyses the charge of attempted poisoning which Clodia had levelled against his friend Caelius. He exposes all its improbabilities, its cynical contempt for truth and logic; and then, after describing its farcical dénouement, he says, 'This is not the final scene of a comedy, it is the end of a farce.' At once his hearers remember that, beneath the courtesans of comedy, there were women still lower and more brazen, the show-girls who played in mimes or farces, who always had to strip naked, who were always involved in ridiculous and obscene plots without even the pretence of ingenuity. Then, with an allusion so discreet that today we can scarcely understand it, he reminds the jury of an obscure and filthy practical joke which a young man—disappointed or disgusted—had recently played on Clodia. It was right for her, he implies. She is not a romantic Camille; she is a vile trollop, a cross between a clown and a whore.

When, at the end of his speech, Cicero turns away from Clodia and gravely asks the jury not to sacrifice a talented and honourable young man to a woman's wantonness—recalling one of the phrases with which he had opened his defence—we ourselves, reading the speech two thousand years after it was written, can scarcely resist the powerful impression which he has created.

Throughout the speech, Catullus is never mentioned. He was not important until after he died. In life he was not quite a serious

figure. During the trial he was still in Asia Minor. He would prob-
ably know nothing of it until it was over. Yet among his works
there is one strange little poem, addressed to Cicero, and thanking
him for his legal skill and eloquence. We do not know its occasion;
it sounds rather forced; but it may have been written in gratitude
and in half-ironic praise as a tribute to the orator who had saved
Catullus's former friend Caelius and destroyed his evil spirit
Clodia.

> You, most eloquent of Romulus' descendants,
> those now living, or dead and gone before them,
> and those still to be born in future ages,
> to you, Cicero, gratefully Catullus
> gives his thanks—he, the worst of living poets,
> just as surely the worst of living poets
> as you, Cicero, are the best of lawyers.[1]

   Was Clodia herself in court? Cruel as a cat (she enjoyed playing
with a captive bird) and bold as a street-walker, she would scarcely
stay away. As we read Cicero's speech and reconstruct his move-
ments during its delivery, we can see him turning, now to the
jury, reasonable moderates like himself; now to the listening
public; now to the bench where Caelius and his supporters are
sitting; and sometimes, with undisguised contempt, towards a
small group of natty young men, perfumed and massaged and
depilated and wearing little oily 'imperial' beards and aristocratic
sneers. In the centre of that group, we can scarcely doubt, sat a
woman who had belonged to them all and believed they therefore
belonged to her; who enjoyed mixing lust either with cruelty or
with courageous degradation; who had thrown away her talents
and her beauty: the woman with the blazing eyes and the insati-
able heart, who spoiled the promise of a man who was a great poet
but might have been far greater. In those few hours she suffered
the searing contempt of her lovers, the suave derision of one of the
most intelligent men in Rome, the mockery of the ordinary

[1] Catullus 49.

citizens. She saw herself as she had made herself, a lady turned into a whore. She suffered something of the torments she had inflicted upon others. Except for the infinitely bitter farewell poem by Catullus, she is never heard of again. She drops out of history. Only her beauty, and her lust, and her fundamental cruelty live on in the eloquence of Cicero and the poetry of Catullus.

IN FAIR VERONA

Verona is a handsome and prosperous little city. It lies within a curve of the grey-green river Adige, a quick-paced stream fed by northern rains and Alpine snows. Indeed, the Adige is one of the longest and strongest rivers in Italy. It has always been an obstacle to armies moving across the huge north central plain. In 1944 the Germans held the Adige line for many weeks. They actually faced the Allies across the river from Verona and exchanged artillery bombardments with them. Before they retreated, they blew every bridge. In the Middle Ages and under the Austrians in the nineteenth century, Verona was a powerful fortress.

It was as a stronghold that the city was established, by the Celts of northern Italy, and taken over by the Romans as they pushed northwards. It became a Roman 'colony' in 89 B.C., shortly before Catullus was born.

He speaks of it without affection. Once, while he was still in love with Clodia (although aware of her infidelities), a friend wrote to ask him for a poem and to warn him to return to Rome. Catullus replied:

Now, when you write 'It is a shame that you, Catullus,
    should linger in Verona: all the élite here
are warming their cold limbs in your deserted bed,'
    it is not shameful—it is miserable.
Forgive me, therefore, if I cannot offer you
    a gift of poetry. My grief prevails.
Here in Verona I have only a few authors,
    because I live in Rome: there is my house,

there is my real home, there the days of my life are spent:
one book-box, out of many, follows me here.[1]

In another poem he begs one of his friends, a young poet like
himself, to make a special trip from Como to Verona to see and
talk with him. Evidently, like many another young intellectual in
a new, raw, provincial city, he found no one congenial in Verona,
and could discover little real interest in literature among its in-
habitants. Occasionally he wrote poems about its local scandals,
but they are sour and clumsy things. For us, who think of Verona
as one of the most romantic of Italian cities, it is curious to realize
that its earliest poet saw it as a remote and dull provincial town,
surrounded and inhabited by bumpkins.

As we see it now, it is mainly a city of the Middle Ages and the
Renaissance. The potent Della Scala family put their stamp upon
it. It was they who built the grim fortress that now commands
Catullus's Sirmio; and in Verona, near the central square, there
still stand their tall austere Gothic tombs. Mediaeval Verona was,
and is, a glorious place.

Within it, however, there are still some remains of the Roman
colony. There is a large amphitheatre, built by Diocletian. There
is a handsome theatre, still, after many invasions and disasters, well
enough preserved. It stands across the river from the main city,
with its back against a lofty hillside, up which climb the tiers of
seats. Many of the finest Greco-Roman theatres are so placed as to
command a noble landscape above and beyond the stage. In
Sicily, the theatre of Segesta looks out over a vast scene of rolling
hills and blue sky. The theatre of Taormina, mutilated and cheap-
ened though it has been, still preserves the magnificent concep-
tion of its builders, a far horizon centred on Mount Etna. Verona
cannot equal these masterpieces, but the stage of its theatre is set
so that the audience can gaze beyond it to the powerful river
Adige, rushing on in a great sweeping curve, and then to the
buildings of the city set within the curve.

Near the centre of the modern city stands a Roman archway,
called the Gate of the Bursars or Moneytakers, perhaps because
the medieval toll-collectors sat there. Its lower storey is good

[1] Catullus 68.27–36.

classical architecture, put up not long after Catullus's death; the cheap and flimsy upper tier was the work of a late emperor. Not far beyond this gate there is a busy and cheerful square called the Vegetable Place, *Piazza delle Erbe*. Nowadays it is usually bright with wheelbarrows loaded with vegetables, flowers, and fruit. There is even one large hand-cart full of singing-birds. This was the site of the forum of Roman Verona: the Roman pavement still lies buried some ten feet beneath the modern square. Now it is surrounded by medieval and baroque buildings, some of them gaily and incomprehensibly painted with weird allegorical figures. Still, it seems to have kept the shape of the Roman forum, and the statue of 'Madonna Verona' which stands in it is originally a Roman work. The sixteen pillars around the piazza remind us of the vanished Roman arcades where strollers could shelter from hot sunshine and sudden rain. It was on this site, and in a little square not unlike this, that Catullus walked, lonely and dissatisfied, despising the Veronese business-men who knew nothing of love, nothing of poetry.

Coarse, Verona may have been in Catullus's time. But it later became a beautiful city, with a tradition of kindly hospitality to poets. During the Dark Ages of illiteracy and barbarism, the poems of Catullus were forgotten: nearly every copy of them perished (save for occasional quotations in anthologies) and only one solitary manuscript survived near his home. In the fourteenth century a scholar discovered this lonely copy. He made it known to his friends, who had it copied for their own use. (Petrarch had a version of it, and used themes adapted from Catullus in his Italian sonnets.) The old manuscript, so long preserved and so strangely rescued, has now been lost again, but we possess two copies made from it or from one of its close kinsmen, as well as others which are later. Through that slender channel flowed the energy, bitterness, and beauty of Catullus's poetry, to inspire hundreds of poets of a later day.

During the warlike Middle Ages another great poet lived in the city. Exiled from his home in Florence, Dante Alighieri spent some time under the protection of the Scala family. Towards the end of his life, when he was within sight of completing his mighty poem on the destiny of man, *The Comedy*, he expressed his sympathy and gratitude to them in an eloquent eulogy; and it was to the young Scala prince who called himself the Great Watchdog, Can Grande, that Dante addressed a long and important letter in which he explained the purposes and methods of his slowly maturing masterpiece.

Almost three hundred years later, one of the very few poets who could be ranked with Catullus and Dante brought Verona into his poetry. Perhaps William Shakespeare actually visited Verona on a brief trip to northern Italy. Certainly he speaks of it with affection; he knows something of its situation and its legends: something too of its chivalrous character. One of his earliest plays is *The Two Gentlemen of Verona*. The hero of another early comedy, *The Taming of the Shrew*, is a gay young Veronese. And the most beautiful romantic play ever written is set in a moonlit garden, a friar's cell, houses, streets, and squares in Verona. Even today it is scarcely possible to hear the name of the city, or to walk through certain of its quiet streets, without catching echoes of Shakespeare's immortal verse and hearing the passionate voices of his star-crossed lovers.

> Wilt thou be gone? It is not yet near day:
> It was the nightingale, and not the lark,
> That pierced the fearful hollow of thine ear;
> Nightly she sings on yon pomegranate tree;
> Believe me, love, it was the nightingale.

> It was the lark, the herald of the morn,
> No nightingale: look, love, what envious streaks
> Do lace the severing clouds in yonder east:
> Night's candles are burnt out, and jocund day
> Stands tiptoe on the misty mountain tops.
> I must be gone and live, or stay and die.

II

VERGIL

LANDSCAPE

ONE of the greatest poets in the world was born near a small village, which has long since disappeared. The date was 15 October, 70 B.C.

His father was a poor man, who married the master's daughter, worked hard, and prospered. The story is that the boy was born in a ditch. His mother's labour pains came upon her unexpectedly during a journey, before she could get to a house; and she lay down in her misery to perform the miracle of motherhood. Yet it would have been wrong for Vergil to be born in a richly carved bed with silken hangings, or even in a warm and comfortable room. Although he became rich and famous, he was always close to the soil. Although he had several houses, he was a wanderer. His first poem and his last both deal with weary exiles travelling slowly through a hostile world in search of a home.

We know the name of Vergil's village, and—roughly—its position. It was called Andes. It was in northern Italy near Mantua. In fact, it was part of the community of which Mantua was the market and the administrative centre. One of the countrymen in his poems calls Mantua

> our city, where we shepherds
> often drive in the tender younglings of our flock.[1]

But he never mentions Andes in his poetry. Instead, he speaks of Mantua as his native place, to which he has brought glory. We

[1] Vergil, *Bucolics*, 1.20–21.

56

cannot now tell with any real certainty where the village was. It has vanished as completely as a Red Indian settlement which has been built over by modern American farms and highways. Although we can try to find it, and with some mild probability, it is not important that we should do so—because Vergil never names it and does not care to describe village life. The farms he loved; but not the villages.

What is important is the general region where he spent his childhood. He describes it several times, always vaguely, omitting and altering details and combining separate effects like a landscape artist, and never reporting with cold exactitude like a surveyor making a map. It always seems as though, when he wrote his early poems, he had thought of the whole countryside around Mantua (up to the neighbouring city of Cremona) as a single unit, and had brought elements from various parts of it into each composite picture. We must remember also that some aspects of the landscape have been altered since his time—new types of crops and of trees have been brought in and the old types abandoned; marshy lands have been drained, rocky fields have been cleared and made cultivable. All this area has been intensely cultivated for many generations. It was fairly good farming land in Vergil's time. It has become much better now. Some memory of this long effort still remains in popular gossip. A taxi-driver points to the lagoons around Mantua, and then to the well-drained fields and the comfortable city, saying, 'The Jews made Mantua. They were all sent here long ago, when it was nothing but marsh. They worked and worked. Little by little, they built it up. There is their cemetery over there, special for them. Yes, the Jews made Mantua.'

However, many of the essentials which Vergil knew still remain.

First is the river he loved, the river he made famous: the Mincio, flowing from Lake Garda to the lagoons around the city of Mantua and finally into the powerful river Po. Milton, who saw it when he visited Italy in 1639, described it in a phrase which evokes its steady unhesitating movement, the whisper of its voice over the stones and among the reeds: 'smooth-sliding Mincius'. Fed by the cold lake water that flows into Garda from the northern hills, it has no sluggishness, no fat warmth, no loads of brown silt. It is a cool river, its almost colourless water tinged with the highland hues of grey and pale green. As it flows under a bridge at Goito on its way towards Mantua, it is about six feet deep even in midsummer, some sixty feet broad, and clear enough to show every stone in its cold gravelly bed.

Yet it is a kindly stream. Beside it, scarcely a foot above its shimmering surface, are rich fields and prosperous gardens. It is lined with pollard willows, pale greyish-green, moving restlessly in the cool air. Now and then a weeping willow, darker in tone, drops its frail mournful streamers into the current. Some young willow trees even grow out of the water. Large clumps of tall reeds, as graceful as the bamboos which the Chinese painters love, rise from the edge of the stream, bending both to water and to wind.

Along the Mincio lie the fields which Vergil knew and loved well. Still extant in them is one specially happy union—the marriage of land and water. For miles and miles along the roads and through the fields run long irrigation ditches carrying water, seldom slow-moving, almost never stagnant, usually in active motion to moisten the earth and feed the roots. At intersections near every farm the long channels of water branch off into the fields. There is usually a watergate at these junctions, a vertical wooden barrier two or three feet high, held in place by a slotted framework on each side of the channel. To water a field, the farmer and his men lift the barrier, and the ditch fills quickly, with a welcome rippling sound. After an hour or two, he can say, like Vergil's father in the *Bucolics*,

> Now, lads, close off the channels: the meadows have
> drunk enough.[1]

The trees of Vergil's time? Some of them still live in his country. His poems speak of ancient beeches and dark oaks standing among the pasture-lands, and describe little herds of sheep and goats moving among them. But now the heavy trees have been cut

[1] Vergil, *Bucolics*, 3.111.

down; the sheep and goats have been shifted to rougher pastures up in the hills. Now that they have gone, the landscape is tamer and more comfortable than it was when Vergil saw it—like most landscapes seen and portrayed by poets. Yet olives still grow plentifully, propagated from generation to generation since the Neolithic age. Strange trees they are, with their gnarled dry trunks splitting with age or twisting with heat, and with their delicately-tinted pale green leaves. Their fruit, full of oil instead of juice, is unlike other fruit. Every tree is an individual. In a grove of a thousand, you will not find two the same in shape, in size, even in yield.

The vines are still there, as they are everywhere in Italy. In his time, Vergil says, they were 'married' to elm-trees—not the tall spreading elms known to Northern Europe, but their younger brothers, trees six or eight feet high, with enough trunk and branches to bear the embrace of the clinging vine, but not greedy enough to suck all the needed nourishment out of the soil. Some of these married couples still stand about the fields near Mantua. They look a little strange, as many couples do at first sight, because their profiles and their complexions are so different. But soon one comes to accept them, and then to enjoy the sight of the broad, flat, pale green leaves of the elm, with clusters of young grapes, darker green, hiding behind them.

The hills are still as Virgil knew them. There are none around Mantua, but he went to school forty miles away in Cremona, and from Cremona we can see both aspects of northern Italy: on one side the fertile plain, on the other the powerful mountains, the lower Alps and the peaks of the Dolomites. People born outside Italy tend to think of it as a soft, heavy, laughing country. But it is not. France, England, Belgium, Holland, even Germany are much more benign lands. In Italy the valleys and flatlands are nearly always productive, and yet one is scarcely ever out of sight of the mountains. They are not merely a backdrop: they are the frontier of life. Nothing will grow on them except wild trees. Few roads cross them; the trails are steep and hard. They send savage floods down the valleys, floods that charge like bulls—a bull was the old Greek symbol of a river-deity—wasting their strength and injuring everything they can reach. Bitter winds blow off them all winter, and they delay the spring. In the north, where Vergil was born and bred, they were the boundary of civilization. South of the mountains, in the basin of the Po and the Mincio and the Adige, the quieter Celtic peoples settled and began to farm. Etruscans, Romans, and others came in, fought them, intermarried with them, organized them, at last merged with them. But beyond that mighty plain stood the Alps, with a few half-savage tribes cowering in the high valleys; beyond them lay the huge areas of northern Europe, only partly explored in Vergil's time, settled by peoples a thousand years or so behind the Italians in civilization. The mountains that Vergil saw from Cremona were a barrier behind which barbarism was still lurking, through which barbarism had often burst.

But a poet is not a photographer. A photographer immortalizes what is apt to be transient and disappear. A poet can create ideal scenery, with a few essential details. He seldom cares to do more. In fact, he gives us, expressed in words, the same delightful memory that we ourselves have of a landscape which has struck us as beautiful, a valley or a coast where we have been happy.

In the first of his poems called *Bucolics*, or *Shepherd Poems*, Vergil paints a little landscape in the manner of Corot. Distant though it is, vague though it is, we can yet love it as the ideal summer scene in a country which is not too hot: where there are no palm trees and scorpions, no dry river-beds and starving wells, no blinding deathly sun at noonday, but a genial summer, almost too warm and yet luxuriously lazy. The painting, however, is not merely a genre picture. There is a story (however disguised) behind it.

Two shepherds talk: one is lying at his ease, making music and singing while his flocks pasture; the other is travelling painfully over the countryside driving a small herd of goats, all that he has saved from a general disaster. The disaster is hinted at, although not described in any detail. A group of ex-soldiers has taken over a whole area of farms, and the farmers, poor enough already, have been turned out on to the high road. One, one alone, having made a special appeal to a powerful, godlike man, has been permitted to keep his farm. The poem—like the *Bucolics* in general— is not simply confectionery: it is not a Toy Symphony or a Marie-

Antoinette idyll. Though elegantly stylized, it is both sweet and bitter. It is like some of Pieter Bruegel's landscapes. Delicately painted, harmoniously disposed, gentle in colours and in forms, they seem to show merely an ideal moment in a vision of country life—until we look closer, and see that there is a gloomy hint of suffering or a touch of sordid debauchery, to keep them from being unreal. The haymakers are happy and sunlit; they make a cycle of sunrays as they lie sleeping; but they are crude, even bestial, in their snoring sleep. The winter scene is exquisitely depicted, all in greys, pale whites, and browns: the children are skating happily on the frozen pond, there is a cheerful fire beside the inn, the hunters and their dogs make a handsome group—but the dogs are starvelings, horribly thin, longing for even a mouthful of meat, and the hunters are carrying back bare poles and nets, unfleshed spears, empty bellies: winter is a hungry time. So Vergil's *Bucolics* are, on the surface, charmingly friendly and exquisitely elaborated poems about the ideally happy life of cowherds, shepherds, and goatherds in a beautiful land which may be northern Italy or a decorative vision of the primitive Greek region of Arcadia; but every one of them has sadness mingled with its charm. To the end of his life Vergil was a melancholy man; behind his heroic scenes, we see and hear the unfortunates groaning and dying, and, as in a late Italian afternoon, his idyllic landscapes are sunny, but they have long sloping shadows and areas of cold blackness.

Here, from his first *Bucolic*, is the idealized north Italian landscape, as described by an exile, a displaced person, who is sadly leaving it and pauses to felicitate a friend who has been able to keep hold of his farm.

> Happy you, my old friend: you will not lose your farm—
> a farm just big enough. Although your pasture-land
> is covered with bare rock and slimy marish reed,
> still, no strange fodder grows to threaten the heavy ewes,
> no foul infection from the neighbour lands will harm them.
> Happy, happy old man. Here, among friendly streams
> and holy springs, you will find dark leaf-shaded coolness.

Here as always the hedge that marks your neighbour's bounds,
pasturing bees of Hybla upon its willow flowers,
will often, whispering, hush you into soft siestas;
under the lofty crag the pruner will sing to the breeze,
while your favourite wood-doves woo in melancholy
and high in the airy elms the mournful pigeons moan.[1]

The friend so addressed was a projection of Vergil himself.
Vergil was not an old man, but, like the happy farmer, he was one
of the few who had managed to keep his land safe from intruders.
In the year 42 B.C., just two years after the assassination of the
dictator Julius Cæsar, Cæsar's heirs took over power in Rome.
Mark Antony, Octavius (later Augustus), and Lepidus defeated
the armies of the republic under Brutus and Cassius. Then they
discharged their victorious soldiers with a bonus, and with gifts of
land. The land was good farming country. It was already settled,
owned, and cultivated by thousands of Italians, but now it was
handed over to the men who had helped the new rulers to win
supremacy. It was as though, after the American Civil War
ended in 1865, the government in Washington had distributed
many of the best farms in the Southern States to the veterans of the
Northern army. The South suffered enough from carpetbaggers
and other interlopers; but at least its farmers were not dispossessed
by tough ex-soldiers from other regions. This act, and the pro-
scriptions which turned hundreds of decent Romans into penniless
outlaws, 'public enemies' who could be killed without trial, were
the two most drastic and brutal acts on the record of the later
emperor Augustus. Propertius lost much of his land near Assisi.
Horace lost virtually everything. Vergil might have lost every-
thing. All the territory of Cremona had been handed over to the
veterans. Greedy for more, they seized land near Mantua also—

Mantua, too near (alas) to poor Cremona.[2]

---

[1] Vergil, *Bucolics*, 1.46–58.
[2] Vergil, *Bucolics*, 9.28.

His land went with the rest. But he appealed to the governor of
the province, Pollio—who was, like many of the great Romans
of those days, not only an able administrator but a man of
scholarly tastes who loved literature. Pollio gave him an intro-
duction (and, no doubt, a favourable letter) to the young Octavius,
and his land was saved. Apparently he first secured a general
restoration of all the land in his district. In another poem, he
makes a shepherd say

> Yet surely I had heard that, from where the hills begin
> to stoop, sloping their ridge gently towards the plain,
> to the water and the ancient broken-crested beeches,
> all had been saved for you by Menalcas with his songs.[1]

Still, the implication is that even Vergil's influence could do little
more than preserve a small area around his home. But thence-
forward he was devoted to Octavius, at once so powerful and so
humane. Victor Hugo and others have called Vergil a miserable
sycophant who accepted a bribe to become the propagandist of a
velvet-gloved tyrant. There are two counter-arguments to this.
One is that Augustus was in fact a very great man, one of the few
foremost builders of peace in the history of the world, who was
accomplishing an all but miraculous regeneration of the whole of
western civilization: Vergil, like many others, recognized his
greatness, and thought himself privileged to expound his ideals.
The other is that Vergil felt in himself the rising power which was
to make him a supreme poet, knew that to be reduced to destitu-
tion and condemned to be a farm labourer for the rest of his life
would mean the murder of a genius, and was therefore grateful to
the monarch who freed not only his body but his soul from
starvation.

In all these early poems, the *Bucolics* of Vergil, fact and fancy
constantly merge. The shepherds have Greek names, but they
sometimes speak of Roman poets and Roman statesmen. They
behave like the Sicilians of Theocritus's *Idylls*, yet sometimes they

[1] Vergil, *Bucolics*, 9.7–10.

are in the half-fabulous Greek land of Arcadia and sometimes near
Vergil's own birthplace in the Italian north. They are almost
exclusively herdsmen, watching their flocks and singing gracefully
stylized songs while the sheep and goats graze peacefully; but the
harder, longer, less romantic work of ploughing, sowing, and
reaping the grain is scarcely mentioned. The *Bucolics* were pub-
lished about 37 B.C., only seven years after the murder of Julius
Cæsar, while Rome was still involved in the apparently endless
civil wars and social revolutions that had begun about a century
earlier. They are vague, charming, and unreal—not (as some
nineteenth-century critics used to say) because the poet was
endeavouring 'to attract the jaded attention of his town-bred
audience', but because he and almost all his friends were sick at
heart, exhausted, nearly maddened, by the worst of all wars—
civil war. The *Bucolics* are poems of escape, from brutal reality
into an ideal blended of the real beauties of nature, the known
graces of Greek imagination, the newly explored charms of Latin
poetic style, and the irresistible pleasure of fantastic dreaming.

We should be wrong to look in such poems for any exact
details which could be used to rediscover Vergil's own home. A
realist like Crabbe will describe a scene as accurately as a surveyor.
Vergil preferred to give a few touches, and to allow the imagina-
tion of his readers to fill out the picture: that is one reason for his
almost universal appeal. He changes each of his readers into a poet
or an artist.

The two paragraphs from the *Bucolics* which are translated
above, on pages 61–2 and 63, give all the important details which
Vergil wished to set down: beeches, a river, the sloping hills; poor
pasture-land, friendly streams, a willow hedge, and an elm-tree.
These are not enough to guide us. Nothing remains to indicate
the home of Vergil, except a faint legend.

THE VILLAGE AND THE FARM

A tradition which seems to have been passed on for many genera-
tions says that Vergil came from a region about five miles east of
Mantua. The whole district is now named after him, Virgilio.

No ancient remains have been found there: no milestones, no inscriptions which might identify any of the Roman settlements.

The strongest claim to be the modern successor of Vergil's birthplace, Andes, is made by the village of Pietole. This claim was recognized by the Italians as early as the time of Dante; in 1884 it was emphasized when the villagers erected a statue of Vergil with Dante's words on its base. Pietole is a quiet unassuming place (and so was Andes). The work of the village goes on; traffic passes through the main street *en route* to Mantua; only an occasional urchin stops to look at the foreigners who have come to visit Vergil's countryside.

Another tradition, more recent, but still going back for four centuries, points to a particular farm as occupying the poet's land. This farm lies about a mile north-east of Pietole. It is a curious place. It calls itself, proudly, La Virgiliana. Once it belonged to the powerful dukes of Mantua, the Gonzagas. Doubtless they used it to raise stock and produce for their household, and broke young horses on it. They laid out a huge open courtyard, ten times the size of any average farmyard, and surrounded it with several rows of solid brick buildings. It must have been a fine sight, with grooms exercising the Gonzaga horses, and perhaps a tilting yard or an archery range over at one side, and the wagons laden with produce for the duke's banquet-tables rolling out of the gate.

Nowadays La Virgiliana is inhabited by eight or ten families of farmers, living in that state of cheerful and sleazy confusion which sometimes makes a peasant look like his primitive ancestors. The children and some of the women are barefooted. The men are small, reddish-brown, and genial. It is a hard life, and yet nobody starves. The people live in the upper parts of the big Renaissance buildings put up by the Gonzaga; they stable the animals and store the farm implements in the lower-floor rooms. Hens pick about the floor, below the elegant sixteenth-century plaster scroll-work. The head of a Gonzaga nobleman, bearded and helmeted, looks proudly out from the wall above carts, and rakes, and scythe-handles. They are very poor, the successors of Vergil. Yet they have a tremendous power of work, a tremendous will to live, a natural sympathy with the land, and a surprising gift of gaiety and good-fellowship. All over Italy we see them, bending over the young crops, trudging long miles out to the distant fields and back again in the evening, driving a few head of cattle in to the weekly market, stooping over the endless rows of vines, and at the critical seasons of the year putting out an extra spurt of energy that carries them from dawn to dusk. Seen from a high ridge in the hills, their work is manifest in the order and thrift of the whole countryside. For miles and miles, each acre of land is carefully, lovingly tilled, there is no waste space, no vacancy: corn-fields, orchards, corn-fields, vine-yards, pasture-land and corn-fields, olives in close ranks, and corn-fields again march along the plain and up the hillside like an army with banners, until the ultimate fertile limit is reached. Italy is a rich country cultivated by poor people.

But Vergil knew the farmers. In his didactic poem, the *Georgics*, he described their work, first corn-growing, then the culture of olives, vines, and fruit-trees, then cattle and horse-rearing, and finally bee-keeping. He showed how complex it was, how much will-power and application it demanded, how many threats from natural disasters and from diseases confronted it. He made it honourable, but not noble. He did not attempt to disguise or glorify the primitive and often sordid life of the farmer. He used words and images that were kept strangers to elevated poetry in his time: dung, spittle, slime, sweat, weeds, pigs, tar. But he emphasized that, with all their difficulty and poverty, the farmers still lived a life of natural wealth, unlike the factitious wealth of city people, and of natural peace of mind. Their chief fault, he said, was that they scarcely realized their own happiness. And at the end of the second book of the *Georgics* he broke out into a splendid paean of praise for the two lives he most admired: the life of philosophy and science, which understands the secrets of the cosmos, and which can rise above the terrors of false religion, and the life of the lover of nature, who can live far from the crowded cities, among the hills and woods and rivers where men are less important than the indwelling spirits that outlive many human generations, but where men are closer to the real secrets of earth, their patient and expectant mother.

Happy—even too happy, if they knew their bliss—
are farmers, who receive, far from the clash of war,
an easy livelihood from the just and generous earth.
Although they own no lofty mansion with proud gates,
from every hall disgorging floods of visitors,
nor gape at doorposts bright with tortoise-shell veneer,
tapestry tricked with gold, and rich bronzes of Corinth,
nor yet disguise white wool with vile Assyrian dye
and waste the value of clear oil with frankincense,
still they sleep without care and live without deceit,
rich with various plenty, peaceful in broad expanses,
in grottoes, lakes of living water, cool dark glens,
with the brute music of cattle, soft sleep at noon
beneath the trees: they have forests, the lairs of wild game;
they have sturdy sons, hard-working, content with little,
the sanctity of God, and reverence for the old.
Justice, quitting this earth, left her last footprints there.

For me, I pray first of all to the kind Muses,
whose votary I am, inspired with passionate love,
that they may welcome me, show me the paths of the skies,
the sun's various failures, the travails of the moon:
how the earth trembles, by what force the deep seas swell,
bursting their barriers, and then return to themselves again;
why the suns in winter hasten to plunge themselves
in the ocean, and what clogs the slowly passing nights.
Yet if I cannot reach these distant realms of nature
because of some cold spiritless blood around my heart,
then let me love the country, the rivers running through valleys,
the streams and woodlands—happy, though unknown. Give me
broad fields and sweeping rivers, lofty mountain ranges
in distant lands, cold precipitous valleys, where I
may lie beneath the enormous darkness of the branches!

Happy the man who understands the cause of things
and treads under his feet all fear, relentless fate,

and the consuming roar of the greedy river of hell.
But happy too the man who knows the gods of the country,
Pan, and old Silvanus, and the sister Nymphs.
Unmoved by the power of the people, the crowns and robes of
    monarchs,
or civil strife that makes a brother betray a brother,
or the northern tribes moving down from the hostile Danube,
or the power of Rome and crumbling kingdoms, he neither
suffers in pity for the poor nor envies the rich.
Fruit offered by the branches, and the generous crops
freely borne by the soil, he can enjoy. He knows not
iron-bound laws, insane mobs, records of state.
Others venture on ships into blind channels, or rush
on steel, or penetrate the palaces of kings;
one storms a town and ruins all its wretched homes,
hoping to drink from jewels and sleep in Tyrian purple;
another hides his wealth, and broods on buried gold;
another gapes with awe at the hustings, stupefied
by loudly redoubled applause from commoners and nobles
along the benches; some bathe in their brothers' blood,
exchange their dear homes for foreign banishment
and search for a fatherland beneath a different sun.
The farmer cleaves the earth with share and curving plough.
There is his yearly work: that makes food for his home
and little ones, for his cattle and well-deserving oxen.
Without delay the year's yield burgeons out in fruit
or in young creatures or in nodding heads of corn,
loading the furrows with the crop, overflowing the bins.
Comes winter: then the generous olive yields its juice;
the pigs come home jolly with acorns; berries flourish.
Autumn too brings forth its various harvests; and high
upon the sunlit rocks the vintage ripens mellow.
Meanwhile his darling children hang upon his kisses;
his chaste home guards its modesty; the cows let down
their generous udders; plump on the luxuriant turf
the kidlings cross their hostile horns, butting and struggling.
And he himself, couched on the grass, keeps holiday
while a fire leaps in the centre and friends crown the bowl;

he pours a cup of invitation to Bacchus, sets up marks
for young herdsmen aiming javelins at the elm,
while others strip their tough bodies for country wrestling.
This was the life which once the ancient Sabines led,
and Remus and his brother; this made Etruria strong;
through this, Rome became the fairest thing on earth
and walled her seven hills into a single city.[1]

This noble picture ends with a short evocation of the central
Italian farming lands, and of Rome itself. It contains some details
which are closer to Italy than to other countries. Yet it is intended
to be, not a local landscape, but a general description of the life of
any farmer in a sunny but temperate country. Vergil could in his
own lifetime see how the once half-savage lands of Spain, and
northern Africa, and southern France had changed into splendid
farming country (not then, as now, half-ruined by deforestation
and neglect of the water supply); he could imagine Ceres and
Bacchus, the gods of grain and wine, marching further north and
west through Europe. Even so, it is scarcely possible to think that
he could have envisaged their later conquests, the broad wheat-
fields of Germany and the vineyards of the Rhineland. Outward
from Europe further and further moved the two divinities, into
regions he had never dreamt of, the huge grainlands of Kansas and
Manitoba, the cattle-pastures of Wyoming and Argentina, the
vineyards of Chile and California and South Africa, the sheep-
runs of Australia and New Zealand—all cultural provinces of the
Roman empire, inheritors of its civilization, transmitters of some
of its finest values and transformers of others. All that movement
was implicit in Vergil's *Georgics*. And through all those lands, the
farmer, industrious, healthy, neither rich nor poor, peaceful, hating
sham and deceit, conservative, simply pious, thrifty but unwilling
to cheat and abominating injustice, devoted without words to
the earth and the animals which he cares for and the family which
they help to support, still continues to sustain the world, with no
important difference from Vergil's description of his life. Good
poetry seizes the essentials and expresses them in permanent form.

[1] Vergil, *Georgics*, 2.458–535.

Vergil could have been content with his praise of the farmer's
life, so eloquently expressed. For some artists, in some countries,
it might have been enough. Some lands, even although they are
beloved, are not beautiful. But Italy is, both to its own sons and to
visitors from abroad, a lovely country. In every region of the
world men have special reasons for loving their own home, even
if it is bleakly cold or bitterly hot or lonely beyond endurance or
beaten by savage seas. The world is full of patriots. But few of them,
surprisingly few, have been able to describe the charm of their
own land—at least in words. Artists have done so in paint. (What
foreigner would have imagined that Holland was an attractive
place, if it were not for the enchanting pictures of Van Goyen and
Ruysdael?) Some have conveyed it very well in music: the power
and the charm of Russia and Spain appear in many fine orchestral
pieces. Scarcely any have made their love of their actual country,
of its physical presence, clear through a work of prose fiction:
there are many novels of patriotic feeling, few of landscape. Poets
have been the most successful in conveying the love of country,
even if they were temporarily embittered or pessimistic. Among
them, Vergil is one of the most eloquent. The emotions which
other writers put into describing the torments and ecstasies of
sexual love, the doubts and raptures of man's approach to God,
the intricate fascinations of explaining one's own personality,
Vergil devotes to the land of Italy and the men who work it.

In a splendid paragraph, he praises Italy as the most temperate
and generous of known lands. Nowadays we should contrast her
with France or England, Germany or Spain. In Vergil's time these
were still frontier regions, not yet cleared of primeval forest. He
therefore compares Italy with the older countries of the Middle
East and the Far East, some of them amazingly wealthy and fertile,
some of them filled with fearsome mythical traditions (like
Colchis, at the extreme end of the Black Sea in *Sacre du Printemps*
country, where Jason sowed the dragon's teeth) or with horrible
animals, but none of them (he says) so natural and kindly as his
own land. The only place where he seems to exaggerate—inex-
plicably to us—is in praising Italy for possessing mines of bronze,
silver, and gold; but perhaps he is contrasting his country with
lands which have no metals whatever. He finishes with a fine brief

eulogy of the tough peasants who in those days produced tough warriors, leads on into praise of the Roman heroes, and ends with a compliment to Octavius, the young Cæsar who was then securing the eastern frontiers. There is something, in this passage, of both the Fifth Symphony, the symphony of will-power, and of the Sixth, the Pastoral.

But neither the wealthy forests of the Medians
nor glorious Ganges, nor the Hermus, turbid with gold,
can equal noble Italy: no, nor Bactria
nor all Arabia rich with incense-bearing groves.
Our fields were never ploughed by bulls snorting fire
and seeded with the teeth of an enormous dragon,
they grew no bristling crop of warrior crests and spears.
Corn heavy with ripeness, the Massic juice of Bacchus,
fill the land, olives and prosperous cattle abound.
Here lives the warrior horse, high stepping through the prairie;
hence come white herds of mighty sacrificial bulls,
washed again and again in Clitumnus' sacred river,
to lead, towards the temples of the gods, the Roman triumphs.
Here spring is persistent, and summer prolongs its stay:
the cattle bear twice yearly, and the trees fruit twice.
Yet raving tigers are not found, nor the savage seed
of lions; and no poisons lurk among our herbs;
nor, with enormous coils covering the ground and rising
vast in scaly horror, appears the monstrous python.
But there are splendid cities, mighty works of men,
towns piled laboriously upon precipitous crags,
and rivers smoothly underflowing ancient walls.
Or shall I name the seas washing both our coasts?
the great lakes? you, Como, greatest of all, and you,
Garda, rising into billows that boom like the sea?
the splendid harbours? the new mole on the Lucrine lake,
where the sea seethes and chafes, furious and baffled,
while from the Julian harbour the roaring main recedes
and into Lake Avernus pours the Tyrrhenian Sea?
Here too are seams of silver, masses of bronze ore

channelled in the earth, and lavish veins of gold.
This land produced the Marsians, the Sabellian stock,
Ligurians, friends of hardship, Volscians with short spears—
hard manly tribes; it bore the noble Roman heroes,
the Scipios, tough in war, and you, magnificent Cæsar,
who now victoriously in the furthest Asian land
defend the citadels of Rome from the soft Indians.
Hail, earthly paradise, mighty mother of crops
and mother of men![1]

THE CITIES

Mantua gave me life, Calabria death. I lie
in Naples—poet of herdsmen, farms, and heroes.

So runs the epitaph which is said to have been carved on Vergil's
tomb. The two sentences (only eleven words in Latin) contain his
whole career and works. He was born near Mantua. He died in
the Calabrian port of Brundisium, far to the south-east. He was
buried in Naples. His three great masterpieces were the *Bucolics*,
about idealized herdsmen; the *Georgics*, ennobling agriculture; and
the *Aeneid*, telling the heroic adventures of the refugee from Troy
who founded the stock of Rome. There is something a little slick
about the epitaph: it is rather a mnemonic for schoolboys than a
reverent tribute to a master deeply mourned; but it does state the
facts.

Vergil was born near Mantua and regarded it as his first home.
It is a curious place—romantic, rather melancholy, not very
healthy, and certainly not busy, common, or workaday. It is
dominated now by the memory of the potentates who held it for
nearly four hundred years—the Gonzagas; by the splendid build-
ings which they caused to be built; and by the presence of several
remarkable artists who worked for them: notably Mantegna and
Giulio Romano. The city really matured during the Middle Ages
and the Renaissance. When Vergil knew it, it was still a rather

[1] Vergil, *Georgics*, 2.136–174.

remote northern town. Something of its melancholy air can still be captured if we pause before entering it, and look at its towers across the wide lagoons, made by 'smooth-sliding Mincius'. A few men, half-naked and dim against the swirling mists, are fishing with hand-thrown nets.

Mantua itself, now Mantova, has no Roman remains, and but a few Roman memories. It suffered in the last war. It suffered also from the dictatorship of Mussolini. In his time, a square in a rather poor quarter of the town was cleared and laid out with gardens; and, in the centre, a statue of Vergil was erected. It is impressive, but it is far too statuesque and 'classical'. The poet was a gentle soul, who hated public appearances, lived mostly in retirement, and was a little awkward in his manner. Still, that was only his physical appearance. In spirit he was, as Dante saw him, a noble and austere being: grace and strength, piety and pity, speak from every line of his poems and are faintly adumbrated in his Mantuan portrait.

In the neighbouring city of Cremona, older and larger than Mantua, Vergil went first to school. For more advanced education, he went further—first to Mediolanum, which is now Milan; then to Rome; and finally, to the most beautiful region of all Italy, the district around Naples. There he attended a small and select college, studying philosophy and the higher aspects of literature. Nowadays, through centuries of foreign occupation and native misgovernment, Naples has become a disreputable and cheap city, gay, but vulgar. In Vergil's time it was very different. It was more Greek than Roman. Its very name, Neapolis, New-City, is Greek. It was surrounded by places which were not only beautiful but historic—Cumae, where Daedalus landed after his pitiful flight from Crete, where the ancient Sibyl dwelt century after century in her cave, and where Aeneas first touched the soil of his new home; Circeii, where the enchantress Circe received Odysseus and failed to turn that wily sailor into a beast among her herd; the rocks where the Sirens sang; Avernus, the mysterious volcanic region, steaming and smoking around its sulphurous lakes, where Aeneas descended into the world of the dead and the unborn. For the Romans, these places and names were almost as evocative, as stirring, as Hebron, Bethel, and Samaria to the Jews. In many dim old legends they were consecrated; in the earliest written Latin poems they were recorded, as links with the prehistoric past when men and gods saw one another face to face. One of Vergil's hardest tasks as a poet was to master all those ancient stories, to harmonize them with one another and with the echoes of distant tribal history, to ignore what was absurd in them, to dignify what was sordid or naive, and to individualize what appeared second-hand or commonplace. He was the one man—poet, or seer—who by the power of his imagination could make that obscure past into a myth known and honoured throughout the western world. We may imagine that an Egyptian or an Assyrian, ancient or modern, might consider the wars of the Hebrews within Palestine, their capture of this town and their sanctification of that hill, to be quite petty, parochial, and distorted as a view of history. But the strength of the Hebrew poets and historians in representing the great Jewish warriors and describing the crucial Jewish battles and rites, was so great that many hundreds of millions of people in the western world have learned to know and respect the characters of Samson, and Jacob, and David. In the same way through the art and the wisdom of Vergil the legends which he created or en-nobled became part of the spiritual inheritance of the west; and the 'noble lie' that the Romans were descended from the stock of exiled Trojans grew into a truth hallowed by both antiquity and poetry.

Vergil seems, after he came to man's estate, to have preferred the south of Italy to the north, and to have loved Naples better than Rome. The modern Italians rather despise Naples for its slums, its immorality, its formidable superstitions; and they are sorry for the south, as a neglected and backward area which needs help. But in Vergil's time Naples and its surroundings were a principal centre of Italy's pleasure, gaiety, and culture, while Tarentum, now little more than a naval base, was a beauty spot as renowned and almost as exotic as Rio de Janeiro. The south of Italy had been settled by Greeks, and civilized by Greeks. The charm of their language, the richness of their culture, the exquisite variety of their art, their proliferating legends, and their cool sophistication were spread over half the peninsula—politically the weaker half, but far the more charming. So also in Sicily, where the modern traveller sees a grim and distrustful populace talking an Italian dialect of its own, living in dismal little medieval villages, and sometimes looking so dark as to be almost Saracen in visage, the Romans of the late Republic and early Empire saw a population largely Greek in descent, talking broad melodious Doric, surrounded by their own incomparable architecture and as much of their art as they had been able to preserve from the rapacious Roman governors, and still embodying a tradition of culture that went back for seven unbroken centuries. Now, one of the most remarkable qualities of Greek civilization was its power to educate; one of the most unexpected and most valuable gifts of the Romans was their readiness to learn from others. Roman civilization was not an original growth, but neither was it a carbon-copy: it was to Greece as the culture of America, North and South, is to that of Europe—a new variety, formed and strengthened by transplantation. And, just as many South Americans think with pride of their Spanish origin, just as many North Americans return in spirit or in body to visit their ancestral homes in western Europe, so those Romans who were most concerned with their past loved not only Roman Italy but Greece, Greece both in the Greek peninsula and islands and in the Italian peninsula and in Sicily. Men like Vergil, and Horace, and Cicero, and Catullus spoke and read and even thought in Greek as easily as in Latin. Their homes were filled with Greek books, Greek pictures, Greek statues. One of the chief aims of their lives was, therefore, to create, in Latin and for contemporary and future Rome, a literature which should equal that created in Greek for the Greeks of an earlier day. They succeeded. But in order that they might receive the full spiritual stimulus they were seeking, it was necessary for them to go to Greece, to see the people, to visit the ancient sites where Plato had taught and the Attic tragedians had been acted, to see the magnificent scenery and those buildings which time and warfare had spared. They made the journey with the same eager excitement which the modern poets of the northern countries were later to feel when approaching the Mediterranean: Byron, Shelley, Goethe, Chateaubriand, and many more. Horace spent some formative months at the university of Athens. Cicero, even after he had made his first success as an orator, passed two years in Athens, Rhodes, and other Greek cities. Catullus's journey to Greek Asia was an important phase in his growth. Vergil died at Brundisium on his way home from a sojourn in Greece, which he undertook while he was still working on his greatest poem—no doubt in order to find additional inspiration for his hard task. And while he was alive, he loved Naples best, the city which, like his poems, was both Italian and Greek.

There were many other reasons why he should love it. He loved natural beauty: Naples lies in what is, without any question, one of the most beautiful sites in the world. The bay is a vast and harmonious curve nearly fifty miles broad. It is marked off by strong promontories, by several boldly and wildly shaped islands, and by the magnificent mountain Vesuvius—which in Vergil's time and for nearly a century afterwards was sleeping peacefully. Its climate is kindly though capricious; its waters are a deep blue, and the sky an arch of the inimitable Mediterranean azure above them. It is easy to live in or near Naples for a long time without doing anything but enjoy the charms of life and nature. For Vergil, it was more than a holiday resort. It was a way of existence. He respected the warriors and statesmen of the past who had built Rome, and those whom he personally knew, Augustus, Agrippa, Maecenas, Pollio, and the others who were then rebuilding it after a catastrophe. But he himself did not feel able to join in their strong and exhausting activity. At best, he could express its ideals in his poems; he himself chose a life devoted to art and to thought. In the little 'seal' or signature-passage at the end of his farming poem, the *Georgics*, he gives his name, and mentions his previous writings; he dates the work by the Eastern campaigns of Octavius; he places its composition in Naples; and he deliberately contrasts his own 'ignoble leisure' with the hard duties of the soldier-prince.

This poem, on the tillage of the fields and the care
of trees, I wrote while mighty Cæsar thundered in war
beside the deep Euphrates, and victoriously
gave laws to a willing world, and built his path towards heaven.

In those years Vergil found the City of the Sirens
a kindly home: I loved books and ignoble ease,
I, who once played at shepherd-songs, and, bold with youth,
sang, Títyrus, of you beneath your beechen shade.[1]

The contrast between Naples and Rome was not merely the
contrast between a Greek and a Roman community, between a
beautiful seaside city and a crowded inland capital, or between
'ignoble ease' and official activity. It was a contrast between two
philosophies, two ways of life. Rome was, and had always been,
the embodiment of Duty, stern daughter of the voice of God, who
compels us to ignore happiness and work till we die, to forget
self and think only of the state or the family or some other supra-
personal entity. To live in Rome, on the upper levels at least, it
was best to be a traditionalist—or a Stoic. But Vergil had begun his
adult life as an Epicurean, recognizing no duty and no standard
except the necessity of tranquil happiness, avoiding responsibility,
caring as little as might be for the future, hoping to 'live in secret'.
This creed he had studied in an Epicurean community near
Naples. He clung to it through much of his life. His earliest
poems, the *Bucolics*, were essentially Epicurean. His poem on
farming, although it celebrates the virtues of hard work and
planning for the future and the surrender of self to duty, still
breaks out into one splendid panegyric of Epicurus himself, in
some of the very words of his Roman follower Lucretius. It is
evident that, although Vergil gradually detached himself from the
Epicurean philosophy, and although the *Aeneid* itself is not in-
fected by it, he always found the creed deeply sympathetic, and
only with a painful effort compelled himself to give it up. Naples
and its neighbourhood embodied the Epicurean ideal. One of the
conflicts in Vergil's soul was the conflict between Roman prac-
ticality and Greek contemplation, between Roman austerity and
the Greek love of what is pleasant and beautiful. Much of the
melancholy that fills his greatest poem, marking it more darkly
and deeply than almost any other epic, springs from the conflict
between his Epicurean self and his Roman ideal, and expresses his

[1] Vergil, *Georgics* 4.559–566, with a quotation of the first line of the *Bucolics*.

sad realization of the fact that one must suffer, in order to create an empire, or a poem.

THE PLACE OF THE TOMB

Vergil spent eleven years on writing the *Aeneid*. The poem, as we have it, is complete in outline, and many of its finest episodes are evidently as perfect as he would wish them. But he intended to spend three years more on removing minor inconsistencies, filling out unfinished scenes, and polishing the whole work. It was to be his last: he said he would write no more, but devote himself to philosophy. Taking his manuscript with him, he left Italy for Greece, the eternal stimulus. Unhappily, the emperor Augustus— on his way home from an official tour of Asia Minor—met him in Athens and persuaded him to return to Italy in his suite. Before leaving, Vergil visited the ancient city of Megara on a burning summer day. He was taken ill. He lived long enough to cross the Adriatic Sea, but died a few days after reaching Italy, in the sea-port of Brundisium. (There is a remarkable novel describing, in the manner of Joyce and Proust, his thoughts and visions during his last illness: Hermann Broch's *The Death of Virgil*.) On his deathbed he asked for the manuscript of the *Aeneid*, so that he might destroy it: it was refused to him. In his will he explicitly directed his executors to publish nothing of his work which he himself had not approved; but his wishes were disobeyed. After he died the *Aeneid* was issued on the authority of Augustus, edited by the emperor's instructions in such a way 'that nothing should be added and that only the superfluities should be removed'. But it is still an imperfect poem: Vergil knew that. We think of the Romans as tough, energetic, practical men, fortunate strong-willed planners, efficient builders whose work has out-lasted many generations of men. But the greatest among them had doubts, disappointments, and an irremovable sense of incom-pleteness. At the heart of the Roman achievement there lay a deep pessimism, and even in their revels a bitterness arose, a pang among the flowers.[1]

The *Aeneid* itself is a poem of doubt, of suffering, of effort almost too great to be endured; its author despaired of it while he wrote it, and, even as he lay dying, wished to destroy it.

He died on 21 September in the year 19 B.C. He was fifty years old.

The stories say that he was buried, by his own wish, not in Rome, but among the scenery he had loved best—between Naples and the little town of Pozzuoli, westwards along the splendid bay. He directed that his ashes should be laid 'outside Naples, on the road to Puteoli, between the first and the second milestones', near a small farm and country-house left to him by Siron, his Epicurean teacher of philosophy. One of his friends had the memorial couplet carved upon his tomb. For a long time the place of his burial was known. It was revered as Shakespeare's grave is now revered. Poets visited it, and almost worshipped at it, as though it had been a shrine. (Indeed, there is something quite saintly about Vergil, which comes through his appearances in later literature and thought.) But apparently, during the Dark Ages, the exact situation of the burial-place was forgotten; the tomb itself was probably destroyed during the barbarian wars. Today, if we measure two miles from the old city-gate of Naples towards Pozzuoli (which is Puteoli), we can find no ancient tomb within that area which might have been Vergil's.

Yet throughout the Dark and the Middle Ages, Vergil was not forgotten. The people of Naples thought of him as their own. The common folk could not read his poems, nor could they understand the ideals of complex and difficult art such as his; but they knew that he had been a great and famous man, that he had seen deeply into the past and dimly into the future, that he had written visions of other-worldly things, and that there was something mystical, something powerful but uncanny, about his mind. So they transformed him from a poet into a wizard, and told scores of

[1] Lucretius 4.1134.

fantastic tales about his powers—how he had built Naples on a foundation of eggs, how he had made a magical fly which kept all real flies out of the Neapolitan meat-shops, and how the only human being to deceive him was a beautiful woman on whom he took a phenomenal revenge.

One of his magical acts, said the legends, was to drive a tunnel through the solid rock between Naples and Posillipo. In fact, the tunnel was constructed by Roman engineers. But, for centuries after the fall of the empire, Roman engineering was equated with magic: hence the numerous Devil's Bridges scattered over Europe, which are really the remains of Roman aqueducts. The highway through the cliff was used for nearly two thousand years, until (in 1885) the modern Italians began to catch up with their ancestors, and built a new tunnel, through which now rolls a ceaseless, relentless stream of traffic. The Roman tunnel is now closed and neglected. Near its mouth there was, for many generations, a large Roman tomb. Because it was beside the magician's work, it was believed by the Neapolitans to be the magician's grave. In 1341 it was visited by that devoted Vergilian, the poet Petrarch, with his friend and patron King Robert of Naples. They found it in ruins. King Robert therefore collected the bones from it, and deposited them in a shrine within the Castel dell' Ovo, the fortified island in the Bay of Naples. Petrarch planted a laurel on the site. As late as the eighteenth century, a large, empty, crumbling building with Roman vaults was visited by tourists on that spot, and was considered to be Vergil's tomb; but not a vestige of it now remains.

When we search for the tomb of Vergil now, we are directed to a little park outside Naples. Beside the gate is a local railway station: Mergellina, named after the beautiful inlet down below on the Bay. Past the gateway, through the tunnel, rolls the main highway. Heavy trucks, motor-scooters, and private cars pour along the road: everything is noise and activity.

Entering the park, we step out of the present into an enclave of the past. It is a tiny place, a few acres, scarcely more—a hillside garden, well cared for, full of winding vistas and surrounded by slopes and precipices. The main pathway winds in Z curves from the gate towards the cliffside. Approaching the rocky face, we see a huge cave receding into black darkness. It might almost be the grotto of the Sibyl at Cumae, where Aeneas learned how to enter the underworld. A cold air strikes out of it, like the chilly breath filtering from the ruins of a bombed house. This, it seems, was the Roman tunnel. But in the seventeenth century, perhaps through a renewal of the volcanic activity which is always present near Naples, hot mineral springs were developed in this area. The wall bears a huge baroque inscription extolling their curative virtues, together with a copy of the epitaph of Vergil.

As the path winds higher, the park becomes a bank of grass and flowers, clinging to the rocky hillside. At one of the turns, there appears a handsome bust of Vergil as a young man, with an inscription showing that it was placed there in 1930 by the Latinists of the State of Ohio. For a moment, the contrast of ancient and modern is surprising; and then we feel the tribute as another proof of the timeless, magical power of Vergil's character.

Higher still, recessed within the rock, is a noble column commemorating the saddest of all lyric poets, Giacomo Leopardi. His short and agonizing life ended in Naples. For many years his body lay in the church of San Vitale, once peaceful, but increasingly surrounded by noisy and dirty slums. At last, in 1939, the casket with his frail remains was brought to this Vergilian sanctuary and reinterred—as though, in that majestic presence, he might find consolation for 'the infinite vanity of everything'.

On a crag above the park, backed against the cliff, stands a Roman tomb, small, unassuming, anonymous. It is the relic of an unknown family: what is called a *columbarium* or dovecot, because of the little niches or nests in the walls, where the urns containing the ashes of the dead were laid. It can scarcely be reached, except by climbing down the cliffside from the street above. There is nothing to be seen. Even the urns have been taken away, by treasure-hunters. On its wall, a scholarly visitor of the Renaissance carved a Latin inscription, which expresses both our disappointment at the absence of any true relic of Vergil, and our sense that here his memory still lingers:

Ravaged the tomb, and broken the urn. Nothing remains.
And yet the poet's name exalts the place.

The ambience is not false to Vergil's character. It is an oasis of
peace close to the busy city of Naples, which he loved. Above it
stands a Roman tomb: frail as it is, looking more permanent than
many of the modern buildings that surround the area. Below the
tomb is a cave through which the forces of the earth once
emerged. Death and the powers of the unseen and unexplored
world are very near. Yet all around is the gold and blue atmo-
sphere of the Mediterranean summer, that rich profusion of energy
that needs only control to be magnificent. Pine trees stand gravely
along the approaches to the tomb, ivy clambers up the hillside,
bright bushes of hydrangea and bougainvillea and Rose of Sharon
smile at the sky. Birds talk to each other in music. The air is full
of life, the earth of history.

III

PROPERTIUS

NORTH of Rome, the land changes. It becomes richer and more fertile, but also bolder and stranger. The rocky Apennine backbone of Italy sends out curving ribs and throws up harsh vertebrae of stone. There are high ridges of hill, with cool glens and forests among them. There are fruitful plains, often commanded by steep spurs of rock which have always made splendid natural fortresses. It is not an easy country to travel through, even now. It was hard for conquerors in the past to unite it, or to dominate and assimilate it. The Romans themselves scarcely succeeded in doing so after centuries of tough fighting. Later, in the Middle Ages, it was broken up among dozens of small feuding communities, each with its own fortress-centre, its own walls, castle, flag, and history. It is not united to this day. But it is full of rich individuality, of glorious traditions, and of noble art.

The land of Italy immediately north and west of Rome is straddled by two provinces. Westward, facing the Mediterranean, lies Tuscany—the mysterious region once settled by invaders from Asia Minor who spoke a language that is still unintelligible. North and eastward, on the central and Adriatic slopes of the Apennines, is Umbria, inhabited by people who spoke a different language from their neighbours—neither Latin nor Etruscan, but a dialect of Oscan. The Romans were apt to think that the Umbrians were rather easy-going and even backward, with their small towns, their fertile farms, and their forests full of game. But several of the finest Roman poets came from Umbria, including one of the most intelligent, sophisticated, and eccentric of all, the elegiac poet Propertius.

He was born in the borderland where Umbria marches with Etruria. His home was near the towns we call Assisi and Perugia. Today Perugia is the chief city of one of the two provinces which make up modern Umbria. In ancient times, although founded by Umbrians, it was conquered by Etruscans: near it there are some splendid Etrurian tombs; and its proud heraldic device, the griffin —a lion eagle-headed and eagle-winged—comes from Etrurian tradition.

The whole region suffered terribly in the civil wars that followed the death of Julius Cæsar. In the 'signature' poem which ends his first published book, Propertius recalls them, and at the same time describes his own origin in enigmatic and melancholy phrases.

What is my home, you ask, Tullus, and where is my family?
    As friend to long-time friend, now let me answer.
You know the doom that civil war brought to Perusia—
    disasters of the years when Italy bled
and Romans harried Romans, raging in bitter conflict.
    My closest grief lies in Etrurian dust:
on that harsh soil was thrown the body of my kinsman,
    his fleshless bones unburied, derelict.
Near that low-lying plain, Umbria—rich in crops,
    a land of generous fields—brought me to birth.[1]

Obscure, bitter, and compressed this little poem sounds in translation; but it is no more obscure and bitter than the original. No poet but Propertius would have thought of the odd and sombre device of describing his birthplace by recalling a disastrous war which had struck a neighbouring city into ruins and had killed one of his own close kinsmen. Yet this oblique and gloomy approach is typical of his work. Certainly no one would ever call him conventional or obvious. He is one of the most difficult of Latin poets.

His central meaning here is clear enough. He was born in

[1] Propertius I.22.

Umbria, near the frontiers of Etruria and the then recently
ravaged city of Perusia. In the fighting, he lost a kinsman, some-
one near to him and probably important to his welfare: an uncle,
a guardian perhaps. In a later poem—less bitter, though as usual
strangely compressed—he gives more details of his home. He
makes a prophetic spirit speak to him, saying:

> Old Umbria bore you on a famous family-tree.
>   I do not lie: the borders of your home
> are these: cloudy Mevánia, among rain-soaked fields,
>   the Umbrian lake, smiling in summer heat,
> and steep Asisium's wall climbing towards the peak—
>   the wall to which your genius has brought fame.[1]

Perusia is now the city of Perugia, proud and warlike still.
Mevania is the town now called Bevagna. The Umbrian lake lay
in one of the basins between the hilly ridges of that country: it
was drained some centuries ago, but we know it was near
Bevagna. Lastly, Asisium is now more famous as Assisi. Pro-
pertius mentions it with special intimacy, as though it were nearer
his heart than the other places. There are Roman stones in Assisi
with the name of the Propertius family carved on them. But it is
ironical that he should claim to have made the little place famous.
Nowadays out of every hundred thousand people who know the
name of Assisi, only one or two would think of Propertius. For
all the others, it is the home of St. Francis.

Propertius's family, then, were rich land-owners in the district
around Assisi. Assisi itself was doubtless the market-town closest
to their farms, and Perugia (before its destruction) the most im-
portant city in the district. After the civil wars had ended, for a
time, in the victory of Cæsar's heirs, Octavius and Mark Antony,
the winners confiscated a great deal of land in central and northern
Italy, to distribute it as rewards to their veterans. At that time
Propertius lost much of his property. He does not particularize;
but we know that some of the veterans were settled in a newly

[1] Propertius 4.1.121-6.

founded town called Hispellum. The town is still there, close to Assisi, on a neighbouring hill-top. It is natural to conclude that some of the land around it once belonged to Propertius. Nowadays it is called Spello: its Roman gateway still stands fast. Its inhabitants sometimes have a bitter and hostile manner, as though they still felt like interlopers. Assisi, loftier and more dominating, seems to look the other way.

ENIGMATIC MELANCHOLY

Sextus Propertius is one of the strangest of Latin poets. I remember that, when I was at college, I fell ill and was in hospital for many weeks. In order to keep my Latin from growing rusty, as soon as I began to be able to sit up and read, I asked my parents to send in a plain text of Propertius—the poems alone, without explanatory notes. I expected to read slowly and meditatively through it, without the interference of any editor, as one might read Keats or Lamartine. Already I knew something about Propertius, and could even repeat some of his most famous lines. The book arrived. I opened it eagerly, and began the first poem—a poem dedicated to his friend Tullus, and telling of his cruel and painful love for the woman he called 'Cynthia'.

> Cynthia first enslaved me with her fatal eyes.
>   I had been uninfected by desire,
> but then love made me lower my proud unwavering gaze
>   and placed his tyrannous foot upon my head,
> remorseless, training me to hate all virtuous girls
>   and lead a purposeless and wanton life.
> Now for a year this madness has afflicted me
>   and still I live like a damned soul in hell.[1]

A fine poem, so far, I thought, and very sympathetic for a young man of romantic inclinations. First love, directed towards

[1] Propertius 1.1.1–8.

a beautiful, arrogant, cruel woman who bewitched Propertius, perverted his mind, and refused to make him happy. The verse, skilful—far more delicate and skilful than can appear in this translation; bold and interesting word-order; powerful images, especially the inter-acting images of evil love as a magical spell which infects men and drives them mad, and as a slavery which makes them kiss the ground and live a life they hate. I moved on to the following couplets.

> Milánion, by accepting every trial, Tullus,
>   broke the hard will of cruel Íasis:
> for now he wandered mindless in Parthenian caverns
>   and roamed among the shaggy savage beasts,
> and further, wounded by the oak-branch of Hylaéus,
>   he groaned and writhed on the Arcadian rocks.
> Therefore he gained the power to tame the lightfoot girl—
>   prayers and service have such power in love.[1]

To me, this meant almost nothing whatever. Tullus (I learnt from other poems in the same book) was clearly a friend in whom Propertius was confiding. But who were Milanion and Iasis and Hylaeus? They were all utterly unknown to me; and I could scarcely see any real connection between this passage and the beautifully strong and vivid opening lines of the poem.

Discouraged, I turned to the second elegy. It began very well.

> My life, why do you love to decorate your hair
>   and move your curves in delicate silk gauze?
> Why do you drench your curls with oriental perfume,
>   and sell yourself with foreign elegance?[2]

Good. A clear situation: the lover complains that his sweetheart

[1] Propertius 1.1.9–16.
[2] Propertius 1.2.1–4.

wants to be too beautiful and to attract other men indiscriminately. But a few lines later I was utterly lost in this:

> Leucippus' Phoebe did not dress to dazzle Castor,
> nor did Hilaira, to catch Pollux' heart.[1]

Castor and Pollux I had heard of: they were the Heavenly Twins in the zodiac; they were guardians of storm-beset seamen; they appeared as the Great Twin Brethren in Macaulay's ballad of Lake Regillus; they had a shared immortality, one inhabiting the world of death while the other lived in heaven, and then exchanging. But who were Phoebe and Hilaira? Merely pretty names? And what had they to do with Propertius and his girl?

Lying in the hospital, between the daily clinical tests and the visits of the doctor and desultory games of chess with the patient in the next bed, I thought about Propertius's peculiar way of writing poetry, and read on slowly through his book, mystified in almost every poem by the jagged ideas and obscure references which nevertheless seemed to accompany genuine experience and intense emotion. No other Latin poet I had ever read had prepared me for this cabalistic type of poetry. His emotions were strange enough—in particular, his blend of strong sexual passion with something like puritanism. His style was bold, elliptical, uncompromising, intended for a small intelligentsia. But the most difficult thing to understand, even to sympathize with, was his habit of breaking suddenly away from violent personal emotion and introducing a remote Greek myth, not even as an interesting tale to be told, but as a decoration, which every reader was apparently expected to understand and appreciate.

For instance, in the first poem, the story behind the enigmatic eight lines which had puzzled me was this. A proud princess called Atalanta, a mighty huntress, was loved by a young prince named Milanion. Like a medieval lady testing her lover's fidelity, she gave him almost insuperable tasks to perform and hardships to endure, hunting in the wild forest and defending her from the attack of savage centaurs: finally, when he had suffered unbe-

[1] Propertius 1.2.15–16.

lievably, she accepted him. (To make it more difficult, Propertius calls her Iasis, 'daughter of Iasos', instead of her own name Atalanta.) So also in the second poem, he brings in two famous beauties who were loved by the princes Castor and Pollux for their beauty, natural and unadorned.

Why does he do this? What poetic purpose does he think it serves?

He does it partly to 'objectify' the themes of his poetry. That is, he does not wish *merely* to write a poem about himself and the girl he loves. He wants if possible to make the theme more dignified by relating it to myth and history, and to understand his own situation more intensely (whether it is love's bitterness or love's doubts or love's happiness) by seeing it in a distant and splendid parallel. Lovers in romantic poetry, heroes in epic and tragic poetry, have often done the same. The best-known example in English is the moonlight scene in the last act of *The Merchant of Venice*, where the young lovers remind each other of similar nights, also filled with intense love, in the past. In such a night, says Lorenzo to Jessica,

> Stood Dido with a willow in her hand
> Upon the wild sea-banks, and waft her love
> To come again to Carthage.

The poetry of T. S. Eliot and Ezra Pound is full of similar abrupt transitions from the present to the distant or mythical past. In *The Waste Land*, among scenes and speeches from contemporary London, the figures of Tiresias, the old blind seer of Thebes, and Philomela, the ravished princess who became a nightingale, appear several times, in order to add dignity to the modern themes, or perhaps, by contrast, to emphasize the squalor of today. A poet like Eliot or Propertius, who is deeply read, and who lives as much in the world of the imagination as in reality, cannot record his own emotions without at the same time recalling the mythical parallels which intensify his experience. So also the great painters often portrayed the women they loved, not simply as contemporaries in the dress of their time, but as saints, goddesses, nymphs, and madonnas.

Partly, also, Propertius does this in order to keep his audience on a sufficiently high level. He does not wish to be understood by everyone. His mistress, 'Cynthia', was highly educated; so were his friends: he wrote for them and for those like them—and for those who (like the youth in the hospital bed) might be willing to puzzle out his meaning and to look up his obscure references. This also resembles the technique of the difficult modern poets such as Eliot and Pound. It has brought them much abuse, but it has made many readers study their poetry with a more earnest attention, and take it more seriously than the work of simpler and easier writers.

One further peculiarity about Propertius's poems is the abruptness and angularity of their movement. He jumps from one subject to another almost without explanation, almost capriciously—while other elegiac poets, Tibullus and Ovid, make a point of gliding smoothly from one theme to another, seldom failing to make the connection clear. This has caused great alarm and despondency among classical scholars. Many professors expect that even highly individual and boldly emotional poetry must follow a logical and predictable plan, or a mechanical pattern. Some of them have actually attempted to rearrange his elegies in regular stanzas of four or more lines—leaving huge gaps, where it is impossible to apply the grid, and blaming the gaps on mediaeval scribes. We have already mentioned Eliot and Pound. Let anyone who believes that poetry must follow a predictable scheme attempt to arrange *The Waste Land* or *The Cantos* in quatrains, or even to account logically for the transitions within these poems as they stand. If he succeeds, he should try Propertius.

The abrupt and angular movement of Propertius's thought does not keep him from being a fine poet. It is one of his chief distinctions. He is the boldest and most original of the Latin elegists. Both his ideas and his illustrations, both his words and the structure of his poems are often recondite, sometimes nearly unintelligible. Yet when they can be understood, they are packed with meaning and emotion, and often filled with delicate and grave music. Even when not fully clear, they have a romantic gloom, an enigmatic melancholy, which is a quality of much distinguished poetry.

CYNTHIA

Propertius was born about 50 B.C., a few years before the assassination of the dictator Cæsar. He moved from Assisi to Rome as a young man, distinguished himself with his first book at the age of twenty, was favoured by Maecenas, published three more volumes, and died in his early thirties. It was a short life. It was a difficult life.

When he died, he was still growing. His powers were increasing steadily. He had always thought deeply about poetry; he had high ambitions for himself—if not to write an epic, at least to rival the most famous of Alexandrian Greek poets, Callimachus; and he was continuing to experiment with new themes, hitherto scarcely touched in poetry by himself or any other.

But his chief emotional experience, the centre of his life as a man, was his love-affair with the woman he calls 'Cynthia'. Her real name was Hostia: she was a well-born Roman lady, unusually beautiful, highly educated, marvellously gifted, herself a poet. She was hard and cruel to Propertius—almost as hard as Clodia had been to Catullus, but with less sordid vulgarity, with a good deal more style and dash, and with something much more like real love in the intervals of anger, doubt, and infidelity. He had days and nights of happiness with her; and although he complains that she would leave him wilfully, or take another lover for a time, he himself was not always faithful. Occasionally she got drunk, and threw wine-cups at him, and clawed his face and tore his hair. Occasionally he got drunk, and left her alone, weeping and dreaming of him. Sometimes she would deny herself to him altogether, on the pretext of some unavoidable engagement; or even—and this infuriated him most of all—promise to be kind, and then shut the door in his face. She was the very embodiment of Roman womanhood, as the old senator defined it: it was 'difficult to live with her, and impossible to live without her'.

If Propertius and Cynthia had had less talent, less money, less of a passion for independence, less of the disease of irresponsibility

that was spreading through Rome like an epidemic, they might
well have married, and lived an irregular but stimulating life.
But marriage, with its obligations and its staid manners and its
regular routine, revolted them. Propertius says that the new em-
peror once introduced a law compelling all bachelors to get
married. He and Cynthia wept together at the very idea . . .
until the law was abandoned as unenforceable. 'Odious en-
deavours!'

Theirs was a paradoxical love. Each of them was frequently,
flagrantly, unfaithful. She would go off with a newcomer—not
necessarily because she had taken a particular fancy to him, but
because he was rich. Propertius himself, fastidious as he was by
nature, would turn to vulgar prostitutes for a change. Yet each of
them would be madly jealous of the other. Propertius never wrote
a serious poem about his love for any other woman. Cynthia
attacked and tried to oust every other claimant to his love; and
even when she was (he thought) deceiving him, she would return
to see if he were deceiving her: she would drive out her rivals,
crush Propertius to the ground as a rebel, and then fall into his
arms.

He tells such a story himself. Cynthia had left Rome, he says,
on the pretext of attending an important religious ceremony, but
really in order to pursue another possibility of love. He determined
to retaliate.

After so many insults offered to my bed,
    I moved to the offensive, led the charge.
There is a girl called Phyllis on the Aventine—
    when sober, unattractive; charming, drunk.
Then there is Teia—lives near the Tarpeian Park—
    a lovely thing, but hard to satisfy.
These I invited to relieve my night alone,
    and, with strange lovers, start a new intrigue.
A single couch was set for the three in a private garden,
    and I had one fair charmer at each side.
My Lygdamus served drinks in lightweight summer glasses,
    the pure juice from Methymna, rich and strong.

A Nile boy played the pipes, Phyllis the castanets;
    we scattered simple roses for our scent.
The Mighty Mite, with all his dwarfish limbs contracted,
    tossed his short arms in time to the flageolets.

Yet, though the lamps were often filled, the light kept sinking;
    the table tottered and fell upside down;
and while I diced and played always for double sixes,
    I threw the miserable double ace.
The girls sang: I was deaf; showed their breasts: I was blind;
    I felt alone and wretched, far away . . .
when suddenly the house gate opened, grating slowly,
    confused murmurs were heard out in the hall,
and in a moment Cynthia burst open both the doors,
    her hair not elegant, but neat—and furious!
My fingers lost their grip. The wine-cup clattered down.
    My lips, though loose and hot with wine, grew pale.
Her eyes were thunderbolts; she raged like a woman;
    she looked as frightful as a captured city.
She hooked her furious nails into Phyllis's eyes,
    while Teia cried 'Help! Fire!' to all the neighbours.
The lights went on all round, the sleeping Romans woke,
    the whole street raved—midnight delirium!
The girls, with hair torn and with all their dress disordered,
    dashed through the darkness to a neighbouring bar—
while Cynthia raved triumphant over the loot they left,
    then turned to me, slashed a fist in my face,
left a scar on my neck, sank bloody teeth in my shoulder,
    and in particular bruised my guilty eyes.
After her muscles had grown tired with thrashing me,
    next Lygdamus, cowering beside the couch,
was dragged out prostrate, begging mercy in my name.
    (Lygdamus, I was a helpless captive too!)
At last I offered unconditional surrender
    and grovelled. She *just* let me touch her foot,
and said, 'If you wish absolution for your sin,
    here are the firm conditions of my pact.

You shall not dress smartly to stroll the avenues,
　or linger round the entrance, at the fights;
never look up and backwards towards the gallery,
　or stop to chat beside a lady's chair.
And, item one, let Lygdamus, my chief complaint,
　be sold in fetters on the auction block!'

Those were her conditions. 'I accept,' said I.
　She laughed, arrogant with victory.
Then, each and every spot touched by the visiting girls
　she disinfected; washed the threshold clean;
directed me to change my clothes, not once, but twice;
　and touched my head three times with burning sulphur.
So, after she had changed each separate sheet and blanket,
　I kissed her. We made peace, all over the bed.[1]

They were, quite obviously, in love. But, equally obviously,
they would not endure any constraint whatever. They refused to
get married and be legally bound to each other for ever. (It has
sometimes been said that Cynthia was technically a prostitute,
and that it was therefore legally impossible for Propertius to
marry her; but this appears to be quite mistaken.) They refused
even to remain faithful to each other outside marriage—not
because they had lost their interest, but because any sort of fidelity
appeared to them to have something forced in it: it changed love
from a passion into a duty; it hung as heavy on their necks as a
chain binding two prisoners in the same narrow cell. We might
almost say that the two always loved each other, but could never
truly enjoy their love unless they were stimulated by some priva-
tion, some guilt, or some danger. They loved most ardently when
she had to steal out of another man's house through the window
to meet Propertius; when she had just caught Propertius in a
naughty escapade; after a bitter quarrel; or when they were kept
apart by many miles of highroad or sea. Propertius had something
in common with Marcel Proust, whose male characters are usually

[1] Propertius 4.8. 27-88.

unable to experience love to the full while they are happily in the arms of the women they adore, but can feel it only when they are separated from them by change of place, by inexorable time, or by the painful hallucinations of jealousy.

THE SPRINGS OF CLITUMNUS

During one of these short separations from his mistress, Propertius wrote a poem which shows the complexity of his love for her, the deviousness of his character, and the bizarre, tangential movement of his poetry. It is strange to see how he can take a theme which might seem deeply romantic, and turn it into something coolly realistic and cynical; and, nevertheless, leave within its bitterness a few hints of sincere love for the simple, the innocent, the beautiful. This elegy contains one of the few references in all his work to the surroundings of his own home. Cynthia is going to spend a short holiday in the countryside where he was born—not far from Assisi, and close to the source of the river Clitumnus. Propertius admits that it is lovely and peaceful; but he adds that it is boring. He prefers Rome, with its adventures, its late revels, its brilliant conversations, its sensuality and its glitter. Yet, as he thinks of Cynthia, he feels irresistibly drawn to her. Rather than confess that he cannot bear separation, he suggests that he will try a short hunting trip in the same neighbourhood; and then, as his jealousy grows, he cries like Orlando to Rosalind 'Tongues I'll hang on every tree', so that no other lover shall dare to approach her. This might have been a charming idyll; and yet its cynical tone and its slangy words make it the reverse of true romance.

I hate your leaving me in Rome. Yet, Cynthia,
    I am glad you will be buried in the country.
The farm-lands are quite chaste. They harbour no seducers
    to flatter you and turn your mind to vice.
No rivals will be fighting under your bedroom window
    and you will lose no sleep from importunate calls.

Alone, without me, you will gaze at the lonely hills,
   the cattle, and some peasant's poor domain.
There you will find no theatres to corrupt your morals,
   no temples (where you have so often sinned).
There you will watch the bulls ploughing, hour after hour,
   and see the vines barbered by skilful hands.
At the rude shrine you will burn an occasional candle
   when, at the rural altar, falls a kid,
and then shorten your dress to join the dancing chorus,
   but catch no possible lover's roving eye.

I myself shall go hunting—changing my allegiance
   from Venus to Diana, chaste and fair.
I quite look forward to the kill, hanging up antlers
   on pine-trees, telling hounds just what to do.
Of course I shall not try to challenge horrid lions,
   or, face to face, encounter rustic boars.
No, I shall think it very bold to catch a delicate
   hare, or neatly shoot a sitting bird,
among the woods where the Clitumnus hides its lovely
   springs, and white oxen bathe in the cool stream.

Whenever you have any wild ideas, darling,
   remember, in a few dawns I'll be there.
Neither the lonely woods will be enough to keep me
   nor all the streams wandering through moss-grown rocks,
but I shall make them constantly cry 'Cynthia!'—
   for every absent man has enemies.[1]

It is a sophisticated poem to a sophisticated lady. It is full of dry
humour—no remote and barren cliffs, no sea-haunting halcyons
here. There is something very funny about the notion of the
elegant Cynthia dancing the tarantella along with the nut-brown

[1] Propertius 2.19.

country girls, and the passionate Propertius going on safari after bunnies and nightingales. There are scarcely more than two lines of sincere poetry in the whole elegy. These are the description of Propertius's hunting-ground:

among the woods where the Clitumnus hides its lovely
springs, and white oxen bathe in the cool stream.

This brief sentence takes us to one of the most delightful places in Italy: to the springs of the river Clitumnus.

The Clitumnus (now called the Clitunno) rises about ten miles from Assisi, on the edge of a richly fertile plain. It is a mild and graceful little stream. Meandering slowly among fields and vineyards, it waters the whole flat valley until it falls at last into a tributary of the Tiber, after a brief but happy life.

Its unique charm is its springs. In the days of pagan Rome they were sacred. A temple was built to do them honour. The cattle which fed in the surrounding fields and were bathed in Clitumnus water made the most perfect sacrifices at solemn religious festivals. In his praise of the beauties of Italy, Vergil singled them out:

Hence come white herds of mighty sacrificial bulls,
washed again and again in Clitumnus' sacred river,
to lead, towards the temples of the gods, the Roman triumphs.[1]

The Roman lawyer and statesman, Pliny the younger, visited them early in the second century A.D., and wrote a pleasant letter to a friend, describing the springs and the river, and the naively religious atmosphere that enfolded them.

[1] Vergil, *Georgics* 2.145-8.

MY DEAR ROMANUS,

Have you ever seen the Clitumnus spring? If not (and I think not, or you would have told me), do see it. I have just visited it, and am sorry to be so late in doing so.

There is a fair-sized hill, dark with ancient cypress-woods. Beneath this the spring rises, gushing out in several veins of unequal size. After the initial flow has smoothed out, it spreads into a broad pool, pure and clear as glass, so that you can count the coins that have been thrown into it and the pebbles glittering at the bottom. From there it is borne onwards, not by any slope of the ground, but by its own volume and weight—one moment it is a spring, and the next a copious river, large enough for boats to navigate. When they are trying to move upstream, it carries them downwards, pushing so vigorously that although the channel is perfectly level, the boats can steer downstream without oars, while upstream they can scarcely make their way with both oars and poles. It is delightful to alternate the two kinds of sailing, and to change from effort to ease, from ease to effort. The banks are clothed with many an ash-tree and many a poplar, which, imaged in green, the translucent river includes as though sunk in its depths. Both the chill and the colour of the water are equal to snow.

Near it there is an ancient and venerable temple. In it stands Clitumnus himself, clothed, and draped in a crimson-bordered robe: the oracular lots around him show that his divinity is present and can foretell coming events. Around this temple there are several smaller shrines, each with its god. Every one has its own cult, its own name, and some even their own springs. For besides the largest, which is as it were the parent of the rest, there are smaller springs starting in different places; but they mingle with the river. It is crossed by a bridge—the frontier between sacred and profane: in the upper reaches it is permitted only to sail, bathing too is allowed lower down. The inhabitants of Hispellum (to whom the emperor Augustus presented the place) have formed a corporation to maintain the bathing station and provide lodgings for visitors. There are also country houses, planted along the edge of the river to enjoy its charms. In fact, everything will delight you. You will even be able to do some research: there are many inscriptions written by different hands on all the pillars and walls, commemorating the spring and its god. You will admire most of them, and laugh at some; but no, kind as you are by nature, you will not laugh at any of them. My greetings to you.

PLINY.[1]

Nowadays, in a world where different conceptions of sanctity prevail, the springs of Clitumnus are no longer sacred; but they are still hallowed by their exceptional beauty. The painter Poussin admired them deeply. Byron paid tribute to them in *Childe Harold's Pilgrimage*. One of the finest poets of modern Italy, Giosuè Carducci, wrote a long lyrical meditation upon their quiet waters. They are hauntingly lovely.

The river Clitumnus does not emerge from a rock, in a cascade; nor, like most rivers, gather itself together from several small streams; nor is it the overspill of a lake constantly renewed by rain. It arises as though by a miracle, out of the flat earth, just where the smooth plain strikes upwards into a range of hills. The hills themselves are stone, covered with a thin surface of earth and terraced to carry vineyards. In earlier times the hillside above the source was deeply wooded: the trees were protected by the sanctity of the spring. But now they are bare and hot; their surface is dry all summer long; their pebbles bake in the sun; their soil is crunchy and arid. Even in the plain beneath there is no sign of moisture—apart from the little Clitumnus: no lake, no canal, no brook, not even a well visible. Yet between the parched hills and the hot plain, a river rises out of the ground.

The springs of Clitumnus lie a few yards off the main highway to Assisi, just where it passes under the shoulder of a sun-browned hill. There is a little farm beside them, and all around them lie other farms, with groves and fields. The springs themselves are private property. They have not become a national monument: it is necessary to get permission to visit them: the owner is wise enough to wish to discourage crowds, but courteous enough to allow anyone with genuine interest to be admitted. It would in

[1] Pliny, *Letters* 8.8.

fact be a disaster if bus-loads of tourists were deposited in this place every day throughout the summer. Apart from the inevitable noise, hurry, and disorder, apart from the cigarette-stubs they would throw into the water and the film-containers they would drop on the grass, they would treat the springs chiefly as a curiosity, demand both less and more than the little sanctuary can give, go away disappointed, and yet diminish the cool repose which is essential to that place. When we saw the springs, no one else was there, except four other visitors, behaving quietly and decently. Even so, it was depressing to see, in one of the fountain-beds, half a dozen Coca-Cola bottles set to cool for possible sale to tourists. Only the charm and quiet of the scene made us forget the profanation.

All that one sees at first, after walking through the farmyard, is a chain of pools of water lying calmly under sunlit trees. But, as soon as one looks into the water, one sees that it is moving: it is alive: it is being born, moment by moment, continuously. This might at first glance be a little lake or a cluster of lakelets—except that a lake is nearly always still; it is water held in a cup of rock or a depression of the earth. These pools constantly flow upwards out of the ground, and onwards. One sees in them the birth of a river—or rather, perhaps, the gentle emergence into sunlight of a pure stream which has long flowed underground. The pools are not deep. They are not rock-rimmed or boldly angled or bitten far into the ground. They simply appear, among the trees. On a dark night one might well go out of the farmhouse to call a dog, and walk straight into them. They are not deep enough to drown anyone: it might be a delightful experience, like feeling a pair of cool arms around one's neck in the darkness.

The springs are about three feet deep. Their bed is creamy white gravel mixed with fine sand. Even in the smallest inlet, a pool the size of a little table, the gravel is constantly stirring, and the surface quivers every fifteen seconds with a tiny explosion of water. The clear fluid is coming up out of the earth. Although the springs are quite shallow, it would scarcely be possible to stanch them or to stop them. If one filled them up with earth and planted sacrilegious trees above them, the trees would subside and topple, the earth would be carried gently away. If one bedded them with concrete, it might last six months or six years, and then it would crack and give way; or, conceivably, the quiet little river would reappear elsewhere, creating new springs and a fresh sanctuary. It seems evident that the water flows by thousands of tiny dark channels through the hills, and gathers here, to emerge into the daylight. All water in motion is wonderful. Cool copious fresh water, absolutely clean, rising out of dry earth under a hot sun, is very wonderful.

Gazing into the larger pools, we see wells. The bottom sinks away, here and there, into a conical recess about five feet broad and six or eight feet deep, filled with equally clear, though darker, water. Into this well, below the surface, gush stronger springs of the subterranean miracle.

The springs are more than gravel, sand, and water. They are filled with delicate water-plants, all in motion. It looks as though a garden had been overrun by rising floods. There are starlike green flowers; ferns, or so they seem; sphagnum mosses; tender bright moss, streaming lightly just beneath the surface; long elegant leaves which might be the leaves of narcissus flowers; thin filigree fronds like 'baby's breath'. The clean liquid nourishes and reveals many different kinds of green, some youthful and tender, some brilliantly iridescent, some old and autumnally dark. Tiny fish flit in and out of the foliage, like birds of the water.

The surface of the springs can never be still. It breaks and breathes as new water is born from below, and the whole streams incessantly towards the river bed. Delicate waterflies ply above it in the sunlight, and white butterflies. Birds chirp in the tranquil branches. Hens drink, thoughtfully. In the farmyard, its roots fed by the underground water, a huge old figtree grows. Beside the springs are edges of blossoming thyme, and big bunches of canna reeds. Willows hang over the wells, gazing into them with a soft narcissus melancholy. Poplar trees, lifting heads and arms to the sky, disdain their own reflections. Between their trunks we see the glinting sides of white oxen, and the timbre of church bells drifts faintly over the water. There is no noise; but there is, in the water and in the air, a ceaseless happy whisper, as though kind spirits inhabited the place.

DEATH AND TRANSFIGURATION

Another poet might have written exquisite poetry about the springs of Clitumnus. Not Propertius. Throughout most of his life love appeared to him the only thing worth writing of. Cynthia (he said) was his beginning and his end. He rejected suggestions that he might choose some larger and more permanent theme; he almost ignored the splendid historical and moral subjects which his contemporaries Horace and Vergil were attacking, In his mind there was an agonizing conflict between the Roman sense of responsibility, between respect for a long-established moral code which had produced many magnificent men and women in the past, and his own personal wish to be free, emancipated, non-moral. To the end of his life he represented himself as being careless and selfish, dissipated, weak, and oversexed. Yet in his later years he began to recognize the value and the power of older and stronger ideals. This conflict is admirably shown in two of his final poems.

One of these is a macabre elegy worthy of Poe or Baudelaire. It describes the last visit of Cynthia to her lover—on the night after her dead body had been cremated and the ashes entombed near her home at Tivoli.

Ghosts do exist. Death does not finish everything.
    The pale phantom lives to escape the pyre.
Yes: bending over my pillow, I saw Cynthia—
    interred that day beside the highway's roar.
Still sleepless, brooding on my mistress' funeral,
    I loathed the chilly empire of my bed.
Her hair was just the same as at her burial,
    her eyes the same; her dress scorched down one side;
the fire had eaten at her favourite beryl ring;
    her lips had tasted Lethé, and were pale.

She spoke, in a voice panting with life and passion: her hands
    quivered meanwhile, the frail knuckles snapped.
'Cheat! Liar! false to me and every other girl,
    can sleep have any influence on you?
Can you forget those wakeful nights in the Subura?—
    the well-known window, open for my escape,
through which I dropped the rope, night after night, and dangled
    climbing down hand by hand into your arms?
Even at street-corners Venus brought us together: often
    we warmed the paving-stones as we embraced.
Gone now, gone, our secret promises! The wind,
    deaf and unfeeling, scattered all our vows.

Yet, as my eyes were closing, no one spoke my name:
    I could have gained, at your call, one more day.
No watcher sat beside my body with his rattle;
    my head was gashed, propped on a broken pot.
Then were you seen sadly stooping above my coffin
    and sobbing passionately, clothed in black?
If you would not escort my bier beyond the gates,
    you might have made it walk slowly till then.
And why, ungrateful dog, did you not call the winds
    to fan my flames, perfume my pyre with spice?
Was it too much to break a jar of wine upon
    my ashes, strew them with cheap hyacinths?

Lygdamus must be burned: that slave needs white-hot iron:
    I saw his treachery in my pale wine.
Or else let cunning Nomas hide her secret potions—
    the glowing pot will soon convict her hands.

And she who once was cheap for public sale each night
    but now trails gold embroidery in the dust—
who gives the servant-girls cruel new loads of spinning
    if any chance to chatter about my face—

(because old Petalé hung garlands on my tombstone
   she lies imprisoned in the filthy stocks;
Lalagé was hung up by her twisted hair and beaten
   because she asked a favour in my name)—
that woman now has melted down my golden statue,
   to get a dowry from my blazing pyre!

Propertius, you deserve it, yet I shan't reproach you.
   I was the queen for long years in your books.
I swear, by the irrevocable spell of Destiny
   (and so may Cerberus let me gently past!),
I kept my faith to you. If not, let hissing vipers
   slide through my grave and coil upon my bones.
For, in the hideous stream of death, there are two currents
   whereupon the phantoms move, some here, some there.
One channel carries Clytemnestra, proud and vicious,
   and her whose wooden monster charmed the bull.
But on the other, in a barque whose sails are filled
   by winds rose-scented from Elysium,
to music rich with strings, gay with the sounding cymbals
   of Cybelé and the rapid Lydian lyre,
Andrómeda, and Hýpermnéstra, loving wives,
   show the soft bosom of their faithfulness:
how one was bruised in chains, and, through her mother's guilt,
   bound innocent upon a sea-wet crag;
how, while the other's sisters dared a mighty deed,
   she found her heart too kind for such a crime.
Sharing our tears in death, we comfort life's love-sickness,
   while I conceal your many treacheries.

But now, hear my injunctions—*if* you can still obey
   and are not all benumbed by Chloris' magic.
First, let my nurse, Parthenié, in trembling age
   lack nothing: in your need, she was kind to you.
And let my darling Latris, named for faithful service,
   not hold the looking-glass for your new love.

All the remaining poems you have made for me,
    burn them; and henceforth praise my name no more.
Tear off the ivy from my tomb when its fighting tendrils
    twist softly with their tresses round my bones.
Where fruitful Anio broods among its branchy fields,
    where Hercules' power keeps the ivory white,
there on a pillar write a phrase worthy of me,
    but short, to catch the Roman traveller's eye:
Here in the earth of Tibur golden Cynthia lies,
    a glory added, Anio, to your banks.

Remember, do not scorn dreams from the gates of the good:
    when good dreams visit this world, they have weight.
At night we fly up, phantoms released from prison,
    and Cerberus himself wanders unchained;
at dawn the law compels us to revisit Lethé,
    all counted by the ferryman while we cross.
Though others may possess you, later I shall hold you
    alone and clutching closely, bone to bone.'

After this speech of harsh complaint and anger ended,
    the ghost melted away from my embrace.[1]

The whole elegy is less than a hundred lines long; yet it contains as much material as would make a striking novel, although it is obliquely presented. There are the first stages of the love-affair of Propertius and Cynthia—stolen meetings beneath the windows of a house in the Subura where she was living, apparently with another man; his accomplice, the old nurse Parthenié, who carried messages for him without demanding bribes; the poetry he wrote to glorify her; his infatuation with a new mistress, Chloris, once a prostitute but now sumptuously dressed and arrogantly dominating Propertius's household; there is the suspicion that Cynthia was poisoned by the agency of his pert body-servant Lygdamus

[1] Propertius 4.7.

and a cunning old Berber woman ('Nomas' = Nomad); and
finally her assertion that, in spite of his infidelities (and hers?) she
has never loved anyone else. Here also are all the stages of
Cynthia's death and burial—all marked by Propertius's neglect:
the closing of her eyes; the wake-night, when no one guarded her
corpse, with a rattle to scare away the witches, and when she had
only a broken pot to prop her head instead of a soft pillow; the
funeral procession moving to the gate of Rome and then down
the long highway towards Tivoli; the burning of the body; and
the tomb, still lacking its inscription. What Propertius leaves out
is just as interesting as what he tells us. Why did Cynthia have to
climb out of the window to meet him? Probably because she was
living with a rich and arrogant lover whom she liked to cheat;
but we are not told. Once again we think of the modern poets
who also use the art of omission. We hear Eliot speak of 'the awful
daring of a moment's surrender', and vainly ask ourselves what
secret lies behind that phrase. For all its energy, the poetry of
Propertius depends on obliquity and understatement. Like his life,
it was a harsh blend of superficial vice with an underlying love
for the ideal good, faintly perceived, seldom acknowledged, often
defiled, never forgotten.

After that sardonic and sensual vision, it is strange to read
Propertius's final elegy. It is almost diametrically opposite to the
poem about Cynthia's phantom. That is macabre, but as light and
frail as the ghost's crackling knuckles: it is a poem of hopeless
remorse, in which Propertius admits his own weakness and implies
that it is incurable. There is even something horribly comical
about the ghost's opening its long speech with Cynthia's usual
denunciation 'Cheat! Liar!' In death the two were still divided.
But the final elegy is utterly different. It deals with a subject of
central importance, in a tone of sustained nobility. It has been
justly named 'the queen of elegies'. Within a hundred and two
lines, it contains the whole life, and death, and hope for immor-
tality of a noble Roman woman.

Her name is Cornelia. She comes from one of the greatest
families in Rome, and is the step-daughter of the new emperor,

Augustus. Her husband, Lucius Aemilius Paullus, is a distinguished statesman. But she has died an untimely death (we are not told how), leaving him a widower with three young children. Now, a few hours after her funeral, she speaks to him—the plan of the poem is a strange counterpart to that of the elegy on Cynthia's ghost—and gives her spiritual testament to her husband and family. The poem is therefore, technically, a 'consolation'. (That was one type of literature in which the Greeks and Romans far excelled us: the speech, or letter, or poem intended to relieve the pain of someone who had just suffered a terrible loss.) But it has—like almost all Propertius's poems—a peculiar yet natural twist.

Cornelia died young, long before her time. Why was she taken away? Perhaps she was guilty of some secret sin? Perhaps her death was intended as a punishment? Or might she be condemned to wander for ever in some limbo of the imperfect souls who died before their time? This is not altogether a pagan superstition. Many of us, when contemplating the untimely deaths of certain 'inheritors of unfulfilled renown' like Keats, have asked whether there were not some injustice, even some guilt, behind the death, and have wished to be reassured. Cornelia therefore speaks in her own defence. She addresses the severest judges of the dead; she calls for the Furies to listen, and for the most famous inhabitants of hell to pause in their punishments: she says she will accept damnation if it can be proved that her life, although cut off early, was not both virtuous and complete. She surveys it all, and with fine logic proves that nothing was lacking to its purity, nobility, and glory. That being admitted, she will not linger among the untimely dead, nor see the abodes of the damned, but become, like other good women, a 'late espousèd saint'. The consolation, by changing to a complete justification, has become perfect.

Cease, Paullus, to harass my sepulchre with tears.
    No prayers will unlock the gates of night.
As soon as we have entered the frontier of death,
    the road behind is barred with adamant.
Your pleading may be heard by the god of the gloomy palace,
    but all your tears sink into soundless sands.

Heaven is moved by prayers. But once Charon is paid,
   the smoke-dim gate shuts off the grassy tomb.
So sang the mourning trumpets, when the hateful torch
   touched my head on the pillow, and destroyed it.
My Paullus could not save me, nor my family's triumphs,
   nor all my children, pledges of my honour.
Still I, Cornelia, found the Fates implacable;
   and now I am a frail handful of ash.

Nights of the damned, slow stream of hell, and sombre
     marshes,
   and you, dark river coiled about my feet,
although I come here early, I am innocent:
   the lord of Death cannot condemn my soul.
Or if there is a judge of spirits, an Aeacus,
   let him try my skeleton by his laws.
His brother Minos, with one more, shall sit in judgment,
   and in the hushed court let the Furies watch.
The stone of Sisyphus, Ixion's wheel, must pause;
   let Tantalus for once drink his mirage;
keep savage Cerberus from snapping at the ghosts
   and let him lie quiet, with loose chain.
Hear my defence. If I deceive the court, my shoulders
   shall bear the Danaids' eternal urn.

My father's house will guarantee that I am noble:
   they conquered Africa with its wealth and power.
My mother's ancestors are the renowned Libónes.
   Both houses stand secure in old renown.
Then, when I passed from girlhood to a happy wedding,
   changing lilies for roses on my hair,
I entered your bed, Paullus: only now I leave it:
   write on the stone that I was one man's bride.
Witness, you ashes of my noble ancestors,
   who set their mark on conquered Africa,

and, Perseus, you who aped the courage of Achilles,
   and him who smashed the proud Achillean house,
that I upheld the censor's standards, and that never
   misdeed of mine caused my own home to blush.
Cornelia brought no shame to those ancestral triumphs:
   no: she herself became a precedent.

There was no shadow of change. My life was spotless always,
   pure from the wedding torch to the torch of death.
Nature gave me a code of laws drawn from my blood;
   terror of justice could not better them.
However harsh the standard, I can meet its test.
   No woman could be sullied by my touch:
not you, Claudia, servant of the tower-crowned goddess,
   who pulled reluctant Cýbelé ashore,
nor you who once revived Vesta's hallowed fires,
   making the hearth blaze up beneath your robe.
And you, Scribonia, dearest mother, have I shamed you?
   What would you change in me, except my fate?
My mother's tears, the city's sorrow, honour me;
   my corpse is sanctified by Cæsar's sobs:
grieving that I, a sister worthy of his daughter,
   should die, the god was human, and shed tears!

Nevertheless, I earned the matron's robe of honour:
   the home I left was not barren and cold.
You, Lepidus, you, Paullus, are my consolation:
   in your embrace I closed my dying eyes.
I saw my brother hold his second chair of office:
   when he was consul, I his sister died.
My daughter—emblem of your father's censorship—
   like me, marry one husband, one alone.

And give our family strong successors: I shall gladly
   set sail, leaving a growing crop of lives.

This is the final glory in a woman's triumph—
    when frank tongues honour her even in the tomb.
Now, Paullus, cherish all the pledges I have borne you.
    Even in my ashes breathes my love for them.
You must be both their mother and their father: all
    my darlings' weight now clings around your neck.
Kiss them when they weep, and add their mother's kisses:
    now all our household rests upon your arms.
And if you grieve for me, they must not witness it.
    When they embrace you, cheat them—dry your eyes.
Enough for you, Paullus, to wear the nights with longing,
    to dream of phantoms with Cornelia's face;
and, when you talk in secret to my portrait, speak
    and pause a while, as though I might reply.

Yet if the centre of our family should be changed,
    and a wary stepmother enter my bed,
then, children, praise your father's marriage—and endure it:
    your kindly ways will take *her* prisoner.
And do not praise your mother overmuch: your frankness
    will seem like insults to the newcomer.
Or if he still remains contented with my phantom
    and thinks my ashes worth a lifelong faith,
meet his approaching age, before it comes too near;
    fend off a widower's gloomy loneliness.
You must add to your lives the years lost from mine:
    though old, let him be happy in my sons.
Yes, it is good. I never mourned for any child.
    They stood united at my funeral pyre.

I have made my defence. Rise, witnesses, and weep,
    while the kind earth pours blessing on my bones.
Heaven itself makes virtue welcome: let me enter,
    borne on the tranquil tide of innocence.[1]

---

[1] Propertius 4.11.

Magnificent though it is, this poem makes a strange end to Propertius's elegies. They began with Cynthia, beautiful, talented, cruel, 'emancipated', and bad. It was she who taught him 'to hate all virtuous girls, and lead a purposeless and wanton life'. Yet his poems ended with the death of Cynthia, and with the death and apotheosis of a Roman wife and mother, who was the exact antithesis of Cynthia in almost every detail. Cynthia was not faithful to one lover, and actually refused to marry him; Cornelia was the bride of one man, one alone. Cynthia was a public scandal throughout Rome; Cornelia called on all the city to witness her chastity. Cynthia got drunk and kicked over the table and threw wine-cups at her lover; Cornelia denied herself these naive excitements in order to bring up her sons decently and be an example to her daughter. Even so, she did not appear to be stuffy and conventional. Although she boasted of her distinguished ancestry a little too much for modern taste, she did show that it is a difficult and admirable achievement to be a great lady and still to be a good woman.

Propertius began his life and his poetry with a series of drastic conflicts. Fire and ice contended in his soul (as in that of one of his modern admirers) beneath the suffocating night. At first it seemed as though he would be wholly given over to sensual pleasures and sensual pains, accepting the woman's domination over him and complaining weakly about its harshness, submitting with relief, like Tibullus, or fighting the obsession, like Catullus. His friends invited him to write of greater and nobler themes than love: of the history of his country, which had just reached one of its many tremendous climaxes; of the recent triumph of young Cæsar over Antony and Cleopatra with the forces of the East; of *any* topic wider than his bed. He refused again and again. But Vergil was his friend; and Vergil was engaged on a mighty poem, 'something greater than the *Iliad* was being born'. Horace was not his friend; but Horace was writing majestic poems on patriotic and ethical themes. Partly through watching them at work, and partly through growing older, Propertius grew stronger. The power of the woman diminished. He began to see the hollowness of a life devoted to sensuality, its fragmentation and its waste. In his later volumes, he produced poems which were more than personal adventures decorated by mythical allusions. He thought of the past and the future. He created visions of the prehistory of Rome, brilliant etchings worthy to be put near the huge canvas of the *Aeneid*. Instead of dwindling bitterly away like Catullus, he wrote two major poems, one saying goodbye to his obsession, Cynthia, and the other extolling a good woman as a real and vital ideal.

Conversion is a difficult process. It is not always explicitly recorded in poetry, or even completed in a lifetime. How Propertius's brief and passionate life closed, we cannot tell. The Roman poets of the great generations died young. They found their ardent lives and their subtle tasks as exhausting as the operating table or the torturer's dungeon. We cannot now know what carried off Propertius in his early thirties. We only feel that —like the woman whose life he praised in his final poem—he died too young, and asks for understanding.

Twelve centuries after his death another well-to-do young man who resembled him in many ways was born in Assisi. Francisco Bernardone was handsome; he was talented; he had money enough; he had a passionate nature; he appeared to think only of pleasurable adventure. But something changed him. He abandoned pleasure. He gave away all his money. He renounced his family. He thought of sickness and death more than of life. He thought of others, never of himself. He led a strange, simple, almost mad existence. But it flowered out both in virtue and in poetry, and, as his eyes were closing for the last time, he could say, like Cornelia,

> Heaven itself makes virtue welcome: let me enter,
> borne on the tranquil tide of innocence.

In Assisi today almost everything belongs to the world of St. Francis. Apart from a few inscriptions and details, there is only a small and elegant Capitoline temple (dedicated to the trinity of Jupiter, Juno, and Minerva) above ground to remind the visitor of the world of Propertius, and, below ground, the relics of the Roman Forum. High above them soar the immense walls and towers of the churches of St. Francis. His presence, the unique presence of the young man who tried to become like Christ and all but succeeded, is everywhere. Yet it is difficult to visit Assisi, and to read the poems of Propertius and the life of Francisco Bernardone, without seeing the two men as spiritual kinsmen (in the same way as Vergil and Dante, although at a far greater distance from each other). Around the towers of the church of St. Francis, the doves which once were the messengers of Venus now rise, the emanations of a loftier and purer spirit.

IV

HORACE

H E was not a slave, but he was the son of a slave, and was born in one of the poorest, most remote and miserable parts of Italy. It was remembered that he had no family, no descent, that his father had been a freed slave. It was remembered both by Horace and by his enemies, for a time at least; but it was forgotten by his friends, who loved him for his remarkable talent and his pleasant personality. Many loved him—Vergil, best of them all, most of all. He was offered one of the posts of greatest power in the whole world: the post of private secretary to the emperor Augustus; but he refused it, because he saw it would somehow convert him into a slave. Instead, he became the poet laureate of Rome, and remained a free man.

As a poet, he has been much admired and much disliked. 'Then farewell, Horace—whom I hated so,' cried Byron, because at school he had been compelled to translate, sometimes to learn by heart, Horace's lyric poems—which are extremely difficult in language and in rhythm and in structure, and which are not youthful and ardent in tone, but cool, sophisticated, mature, so that they are among the Latin classics least likely to appeal to adolescent schoolboys. Byron's loathing of them was repeated later in Tennyson, Swinburne, Thackeray, and many others, who, even if they later realized what a master Horace was, nearly always felt something of the early revulsion come over them when they opened his book. Even apart from this instilled dislike, there are few readers who enjoy *all* of Horace's poetry. This is because he is so versatile, so elusive, and because his character and poetic outlook altered so strikingly while he was still writing. His earliest works are short bitter satirical and pessimistic lyrics (the

Epodes) and satires which are nearly always witty, but sometimes very cruel and sometimes very dirty. In middle life he produced three slender volumes of lyrics, followed later by a fourth—the 103 Songs, or Odes, which more than all the rest of his work make him an immortal. Finally he turned to poetic letters, suave and intelligent little essays on morality, literature, and the conduct of life. It is unusual for a bitter satirist to turn to writing lyric verse; it is unusual for a lyricist to abandon his songs entirely and take to writing little discourses which, but for their easy jogging metre, are almost prose. Horace himself knew that he was a changeable man; he enjoyed his own inconsistencies; but they make it hard for his readers to see him steadily and see him whole.

His personal character and the meanings of his poetry are difficult to elucidate—partly because he believed that easy straight-forward poems were bound to be cheap and superficial, partly because his eccentric career gave his mind many strange quirks which he himself found hard to manage, and partly because the times through which he lived tried men's souls, and changed them to the depths. Inconsistent he may have been, and in some of the most important areas of decision, but he emerged from all his trials as a sane, sensible, well-adjusted man with a blessed gift for happiness.

Quintus Horatius Flaccus, whom we call Horace, was born in 65 B.C., just twenty-one years before Cæsar, having attacked his own country with a specially trained army and seized the dictator-ship, was stabbed to death. Horace came from the town of Venusia, in a rocky, thirsty area near the heel of Italy, but he left it early. Although he was certainly not ashamed of his birth-place, he speaks of it comparatively seldom. His father had been a slave. No one knows whether the man was born free in some other land, and then kidnapped and sold in a Roman market; or captured in war and brought back to Italy as a prisoner; or enslaved after the rising of the Italian peoples against the central domination of Rome. The last possibility sounds rather more likely than the others. He was, it seems, not the slave of an indi-vidual owner, but of the township of Venusia, and took his name

Horatius from the Horatian tribe, under which the voters of that region were registered. Flaccus, 'flap-eared', may have been his name as a slave. Attempts have been made to prove that he was a Celt, a Jew (there were many Jews in the town), a Greek (it was full of Greek-speaking people), and so forth. Horace never speaks of his racial origin; and he never mentions his own mother. But by the time he was born, his father had been set free, and, with admirable resolution, had determined to make enough money to give Horace the education of a free man and a gentleman.

What sort of capital would a freed slave possess? How could he start an independent life? When he gained his liberty, he must still have been like a man coming out of prison or a concentration-camp. It was hard for him to make a living. Many freedmen stayed on with their old masters, as accountants, secretaries, land-agents, and the like; some borrowed money and started in business for themselves. Horace's father was at first (as the poet himself says) 'poor on a meagre farm'—perhaps a derelict place he took over, perhaps a piece of land given him as a gratuity by the town-ship in recognition of good service. But he knew, as most Italians have always known, that there was no money in farming. He went to the city. Doubtless he sold his place and used the price as capital. He became a dealer in general merchandise, buying here and selling there as opportunity offered. Those were troubled times in Rome. Rich and powerful men were often endangered by in-trigue, impoverished by outlawry; many families with great estates were still land-poor and needed money; some speculations grew and prospered in a few months. In such a time of economic disorder, a wise and thrifty man can make a small fortune, or even a great one. So, it seems, did Horace's father. With the pro-ceeds he gave the boy the best education available. And he did not, like some newly rich parents, merely buy him a string of dip-lomas; he gave him a sense of social security, and a strong moral training.

> My clothes, and the servants following me,
> would seem to anyone, passing in the crowd, so rich,
> they must have come from an old and proud inheritance.
> And he himself, most incorruptible of guardians,

escorted me to all my teachers. Thus he kept me
pure—the first reward of virtue—not only in deed,
but pure even from the slightest shadow of disgrace.[1]

This may sound snobbish. It is not. It is typical of Horace's
compressed and highly intelligent psychological poetry, where
less is said than is left to the reader to discover. If the boy had not
been well dressed and equipped, he might have felt he had no real
right to his education and grown into one of those social misfits
who are always on the outside looking in. (And later, though the
father could scarcely foresee such a splendid fortune, Horace
would have found it far more difficult to meet the greatest men
in the world on friendly terms and win their unembarrassed un-
constrained affection.) These four lines about his father's guardian-
ship cover a great deal. The Romans did not trust a man who had
once been a slave: Augustus, usually so liberal, would not admit
such people to his table and his confidence. This is because he
thought slavery was a kind of brain-washing, which made the
unfortunate victim permanently unreliable and utterly unscru-
pulous, so that he would do anything to get an advantage or avoid
a blow. Further, the Romans were apt to distrust the son of a
slave in the same way as some people in an established country
distrust recent immigrants—because they feel the immigrant must
have been brought up with different moral standards and be less
sensitive to fine shades of right and wrong. By leaving his business
and personally taking his young son to his classes—not for vulgar
display, but in order to keep him from making evil acquaintances
or incurring bad habits—Horace's father showed that he prized
intellectual and moral discipline above money or everything else.
That lesson became one of the chief themes of Horace's mature
poetry. By pointing out that he himself not only contracted no
bad habits, but was never even suspected of them, Horace shows
that the household of an ex-slave can be a pattern of high moral
conduct. Both negatively through his *Epodes* and *Satires*, and
positively in his lyrics, he became one of the principal moralists of
the Roman world.

[1] Hor. *Serm.* 1.6.78–84.

After his schooling in Rome, Horace went on to the centre of culture—Athens. There he studied philosophy: or rather began his lifelong study of philosophy, and deepened his knowledge of Greek so far that he actually began writing poems in the Greek language. While he was still a student, Brutus and other haters of dictatorship killed Julius Cæsar, and then moved through Greece and the Near East, raising an army to oppose his successors. Horace joined the republican army under Brutus, fought in the decisive battle at Philippi, and, with others of his defeated comrades, ran away, 'dropping his poor dishonoured shield'. As a republican, he was considered a rebel against the new order set up by Cæsar's heirs. Returning to Rome, he found that almost all his property had been declared forfeit and confiscated. (His father must have died.) With what he was able to salvage, Horace bought a clerkship in the civil service. Rather like A. E. Housman slaving in the Patent Office during the day and working in the British Museum at night, he began to write new poems, polish those he had already planned, and, with a characteristic mixture of resolution and diffidence, to publish his first attempts.

These, the *Epodes* and the early *Satires*, were cruel pessimistic poems. They earned him some enmity. But they were so original and so intelligent that they brought him into notice. Horace became a friend of young Vergil and of other rising poets. Through them he met one of the richest and most influential men in the group which centred on Cæsar's heir Octavius. This was the clever, sensitive, indolent, infinitely tactful, brilliantly evocative Maecenas. In the same poem in which he praises his own father, Horace describes his meeting with his patron.

> I cannot call it mere good fortune
> that chanced to give me you, Maecenas, for a friend.
> Coincidence did not bring us together: Vergil
> (the best of men) and Varius had told you what I was.
> Facing you first, I spoke a little, hesitating—
> for silent shyness stopped my tongue from saying more.
> My father was not noble; I myself could not
> ride over my estates on a pure-blooded nag—

I told you; told you all. You answered (in your manner)
little. I left. Nine months passed. You recalled me, and
made me one of your friends.[1]

To be one of the friends of a rich Roman gentleman at that
time was not merely a matter of sharing a few interests and meet-
ing occasionally. It was a much closer link. It implied that the
richer man would do all he could to further his new friend's
career; advise him on personal problems; raise his whole standard
of living; listen sympathetically to his poems if he wrote; take him
into his confidence on state affairs, as far as possible; relieve his
financial difficulties, within reason; both stimulate his ambition
and show him how to satisfy it. Horace now could, if he wished,
dine at Maecenas's house every night. It is implied that he gave up
his boring civil-service post, and got from Maecenas a modest
income—nothing sumptuous, nothing dazzling, but enough to
allow him to read and write and think in peace: enough, even if he
did not care to call on his patron, to live in modest leisure. It looks
like a good way of helping a young writer without killing his
initiative and originality. Horace describes his life in Rome under
this dispensation, and praises it, as a tactful way of saying that he
owes it to Maecenas, and is grateful.

                    Wherever my fancy leads,
    I walk alone. I price flour and vegetables.
    I wander past the tricky Circus, and through the Forum
    at evening; I watch the fortune-tellers; then I return
    to eat my dinner—a dish of polenta, leeks, and peas . . .
    I sleep till ten a.m.; then take a stroll, or read
    or write something I can enjoy; then have my bath . . .
    My frugal luncheon just prevents my passing the day
    with an empty stomach; then I lounge at home. This is
    a life unharried by the tortures of ambition;
    and it assures me that I'll live more pleasantly
    than if my ancestors had all been senators.[2]

[1] Hor. *Serm.* 1.6.52–62.
[2] Hor. *Serm.* 1.6.111–5, 122–3, 127–31.

His early poems are nearly all about Rome and Roman society
—the Rome which was being magnificently rebuilt by the mag-
nificent heir of Cæsar, the Roman society which, shaken and dis-
ordered by the revolutions of the past decades, was a wonderful
sight for a satiric poet. Like Juvenal after him, like Dickens in
nineteenth-century England, Horace spent much time wandering
the streets of the capital; he watched the crowds, he photographed
the eccentric individuals in his mind, he tried over his verses in his
head, and he was infuriated when a social climber interrupted him.

> Walking along the Sacred Road, as is my habit,
> I was reflecting on some trifle, quite engrossed,
> when up comes somebody known to me only by name,
> and grabs my hand . . .[1]

Nowadays Rome is not so crowded, nor so rich and splendid, as
it was in Horace's time. Yet it is often recognizably the same city.
As one wanders through its busy streets, one occasionally sees a
plump little man strolling vaguely along, eyeing the shop win-
dows, glancing at the pretty girls, pausing to buy a lottery ticket,
reading the headlines in a newspaper-office window, and at last
sitting down to drink a glass of bitter Campari and to watch, with
apparent complacency, the noisy traffic swirling past. One puts
him down as—well, what? A Milanese business-man, who has just
concluded a successful transaction, and is enjoying Rome before
returning to his desk and his wife? Or a small landowner from
central Italy, on his annual visit to the capital? He may be either
of these, the plump little man with the watchful eyes; he may be a
metropolitan lawyer, taking the air after a difficult day in court.
But it is still possible that he may be an artist, a philosopher, or a
poet.

[1] Hor. *Serm.* 1.9.1-4.

TIVOLI

Rome is intolerable for several months every summer. All those who can, escape. The Pope himself goes to one of the old towns set in a ring around the city, like protecting reefs round an oceanic island. It is called Castel Gandolfo now. Once it was Alba Longa, the town founded by the son of Aeneas three centuries before the birth of Rome.

Another of these little cities is Tivoli. (The Romans called it Tibur: Tibure, Tibori, Tivori, Tivoli—so hard Latin changed into soft Italian.) It lies about eighteen miles east of Rome, on the top and the slopes of a dramatically steep hill. It is a beautiful place. Often, when we see a town which was once Roman and has since become Italian, we find that it has lost some of its early spaciousness and repose, while becoming more cruel, feudal, grim, and constricted. Not so Tivoli. It was lovely when the Romans enjoyed it. The most sensitive and imaginative of the emperors, Hadrian, built a huge rambling summer palace there, and many men of taste had country houses on its steep slopes. During the high days of the Renaissance, Cardinal Ippolito d'Este put a magnificent mansion on the slope of the hill that supports the town, and decorated it with gardens and fountains that would have delighted even the fastidious Hadrian.

Because the Este garden is so beautiful, it is a little difficult to realize at first that Tivoli itself is beautiful. It is full of powerful relics of antiquity (particularly the remains of the temple of Hercules) and of fine medieval and Renaissance buildings. Its site is marvellous. It stands on steep rocky spurs which fall away in abrupt cliffs to the plain, hundreds of feet below. Down these cliffs falls the river Anio. Its cascade was always picturesque, but endangered the city during floods; therefore, early last century, the stream was diverted through a tunnel, from which it now emerges to drop sheer down the cliff for over 350 feet, which is more than twice the height of Niagara. Far below the falls, in a cavern filled with the sound of water, there lived the river spirit, a prophet nymph. Her name was Albunea. Later she was called the Sibyl of Tibur. Long afterwards, when the artists of the Renais-

sance painted the seers of ancient times, they would group the
Hebrew prophets together, and opposite them range the pagan
visionaries—the Sibyl of Cumae, who met Aeneas when he
landed in Italy, the Sibyl of Tivoli, and the others. High above the
chasm, on the edge of the cliff facing the town, stands the temple
of the Sibyl. Near it is another temple dedicated to another vener-
able feminine divinity, the goddess of hearth and home, Vesta.
Both these lovely buildings existed in the time of Horace; they
survived the Middle Ages by being converted into churches.

Horace loved Tivoli. As his friendship with Maecenas ripened,
as the two men (both of them rather sensitive and difficult) learnt
to know each other better, as his poetry became more subtle and
more confident, he spent less and less time in Rome. It was a good
place for a satirist, and he had enjoyed it while writing his first
satires; but as he grew towards maturity he began to plan poetry
which would be far higher and more difficult than satire, which
would require more reflection and more solitude, which could
best be written when he was in close touch with nature. As
he himself was to say later, in an imaginary argument with a
friend:

> Do you think I can write poetry in Rome,
> harassed by all its labours and anxieties?
> A begs me 'Bail me out!' B asks me 'Hear my poems,
> and drop all other duties!' C is ill, D also,
> in different parts of the city: I must visit them both:
> you know the long distance between their homes. 'Yes, but
> the streets are clear, they have no obstacles to thought.'
> Steaming with haste, a builder hurries on mules and men;
> a mighty crane swings out with a beam or a block of stone;
> sad funerals cross the paths of huge lumbering trucks;
> a mad dog bolts this way, a muddy sow that way:
> now go and think of poems rich in melody!
> The choir of poets all loves woods and shuns the city.[1]

[1] Hor. *Ep.* 2.2.65–77.

To avoid these labours and anxieties, Horace stayed in little towns or quiet cities, in the country or near the sea. Tivoli was one of his favourite spots. Once, scolding himself humorously for his fickleness, he wrote of the two extremes between which his inclinations wavered:

In Rome my fancy blows me to Tibur, in Tibur to Rome.[1]

Even when he had a country house of his own buried in the hills, he still enjoyed the charm and grandeur of Tivoli. We know from his own words that he lived there often, and considered it as a home. He never tells us exactly where he stayed. Perhaps he merely took lodgings, or put up with friends: Maecenas himself, lover of beauty and luxury, may well have had a villa in or near the town. Still, the enthusiasm of those who love the poet has persisted in identifying one particular house in Tivoli as the home of Horace. There is no positive proof. Yet it is unmistakably the remains of a pleasant Roman house built in, or just before, his time; it is in the particular region where, after his death, his house was pointed out; and it commands just that aspect of river and hillside, grove and lofty town, which Horace often mentions in his poems. When we see it, we must reflect that, if it was not his, at least he dined there and sat on the terrace with one of his friends.

Discreetly, it turns its back on the highroad leading into Tivoli. Over gardens and vineyards, terraced at each side of it on a steep slope, it gazes towards the town, across the rocky canyon where the Sibyl once lived, 'the home of echoing Albunea', as Horace calls it. Although the house looks over a dark gorge, it has a view filled with air and light. For many yards, there is nothing in front of it but the moving breezes of the valley: the birds swim about in them like graceful winged fish. Beyond, there appear 'the green steeps whence Anio leaps in floods of snow-white foam'. Opposite the falls are the temple of Vesta and the temple of the Sibyl herself. Behind and above the house are steep slopes, their fields patched with sunlit rock, clothed with olive-trees and sparse grass; there

[1] Hor. *Ep.* I.8.12.

are occasional cypresses, and even a palm-tree. Higher up, the hill
is darkened by pines.

The house believed to be Horace's has several layers of history
in it. Today it is a private residence. (We were allowed to visit it
by a courteous English couple: they told us that the owner, an
Italian lady, intended soon to return and live in it permanently.)
For many years it was owned by a Harrow schoolmaster called
C. H. Hallam, who loved Horace dearly (schoolmasters are apt
to enjoy him better than their pupils) and spent the years of his
retirement in it. He succeeded in convincing Thomas Ashby,
director of the British School at Rome, that it might well have
belonged to Horace or been used by him. Living in the villa, with
Horace's poems always at his elbow, Hallam observed many little
details which made him love the place more and more, and con-
vinced him of his theory. For instance, Horace speaks of 'the home
of echoing Albunea'. Now, waterfalls do not usually echo. But at
night, when the air was still, Hallam and his friends often heard a
peculiar sound-effect coming from the chasm, a clear clangour
like the chiming of bells—the very sound, they concluded, that
Horace had heard and described.

Before it was transformed into a modern house, it was a
monastery of St. Anthony of Padua, the eloquent Franciscan. In
the uppermost part of the building, facing the highway, there still
remains a small church, containing about a dozen pews—each
named after a family. It is open, and is apparently used for regular
worship.

Beneath the modern house and the monastery are the remains
of the Roman villa. On the basement floor we can see fragments
of Roman walls, wedges of tufa laid in the unmistakable network
pattern. In the huge old kitchen, above the stove, is a large chunk
of Roman masonry. The cellar, on a still lower level, is a big
vaulted room which anyone with an eye for such things will
recognize at once. It is part of a Roman bath. Every Roman
house which pretended to be comfortable had its private baths—
not simply a bathroom, but a small suite of rooms arranged to
provide hot water, steam bathing, massage, cold showers, a pool,
and so on. This chamber (we know from other examples) is the
'nymphs' room', the cool hall where natural running water

poured out in sprays and fountains, and where the owner and his friends could relax and chat, however hot the Italian sun might be outside. The shape of the pool remains, the arch above, and traces of the decorations on walls and ceiling. Hallam found part of an altar there, and believed that the room had been preserved by being transformed into a little Christian sanctuary.

In one of his best lyrics, Horace described his own art by contrasting it with that of the superb poet of triumphs, Pindar. Pindar, he said, was impossible to rival, for power, energy, inspiration. Pindar was like the great swan which, almost without effort, conquers the higher air on its long migratory flights, while Horace himself, although winged, was much more humble, much more fragile.

> Borne by strong winds, Pindar the Theban swan soars
> high above, Antonius, through the lofty
> realms of cloud: while I, in another fashion—
>   just like a small bee
> sipping each sweet blossom of thyme and roving
> through the thick groves, over the slopes of Tibur
> rich with streams—so, cell upon cell, I labour
>   moulding my poems.[1]

This is the famous comparison of the thoughtful poet to the bee, which does not claim to be original, which takes something from every flower, which does not soar high but keeps within a narrow compass, and yet (in Swift's phrase) produces, in honey and wax, sweetness and light.

Across the Sibyl's valley there is a quiet place. We can sit there and look over at the house which may have been Horace's. In the gorge beneath, the trees talk to the gentle wind blowing through them. Even at hot summer noon the birds sing cheerfully in the branches. The sound of falling water cools the sunshine. We sit in

[1] Horace, *Carm.* 4.2.25–32.

a garden, gazing now at the temples of the forgotten divinities, now at the little house of the poet. Beside us there are beds of carnations and petunias. A large brown and black bee moves among them, first tasting the outer petals, then entering each blossom to drink its nectar, then passing on to another, and at last flying quietly away to its home—there to preserve, like a poet, the beauty of a flower which is soon to die.

THE ODES

Except to schoolboys, the Odes of Horace have been, for nearly two thousand years, one of the best-loved books of poetry ever written. They are one of the few absolutely central and un-challengeable classics in Latin and in the whole of western litera-ture. For many generations, a man was not considered educated unless he knew them. Certain scholars and poets (e.g. Tennyson) have had them all off by heart, in the same way as good musicians know Bach's Forty-Eight Preludes and Fugues. They have been quoted by thousands of distinguished men in unimaginably different contexts; imitated in Latin; imitated in other languages; set to music; parodied; studied by the greatest classical scholars; translated, usually with resounding lack of success; and, even by those recalcitrants like Byron who hated them, reluctantly remem-bered. Just as the first duty of a composer is to write memorable melodies, so the first duty of a poet is to write phrases which, after being read two or three times, imprint themselves on the memory and can ever afterwards be recalled, without effort, but with pleasure and with savour. This is one of Horace's greatest gifts.

It would be easy to fill a five-hundred-page book with tributes of gratitude to Horace. One of the strangest appeared only recently, in a biography of Rudyard Kipling by C. E. Carrington. Kipling's own verses were mostly in the style of folk-poetry: chanties, music-hall songs, dialect songs with a coarse simple rhythm, and the like. Nevertheless, he had been taught to under-stand Horace at school, by a forceful master who showed him much of the power and some of the grace of the Odes. Recalling that event, he produced one of the few good short stories ever

written about the experience of teaching and being taught
('Regulus' in *A Diversity of Creatures*). He collaborated with the
Oxford classicist A. D. Godley in producing a 'Fifth Volume of
Horace's Odes', combining good Latin imitation of Horace's style
with comically schoolboyish English versions by Kipling himself.
In his later years, when he suffered cruelly from nervousness and
sleeplessness, he passed many dreary night hours by repeating
Horace's lyrics to himself. And once at least, in a poem which
blends the phraseology of the Bible with the restrained and
meditative tone of the Odes, he produced a ceremonial hymn,
'Recessional', of which Horace would scarcely have been
ashamed.

The word 'classic' has a monumental sound. Surely (we think)
a classic must have been long expected, easily recognized, and
instantly acclaimed? But—no. Some books which were to become
'classical' were neglected when they appeared; many were
opposed; some greeted with surprise and even bewilder-
ment. There was an element of surprise, of the unexpected and
even unwelcome, about many of the classical poems produced in
Horace's lifetime. To appreciate them fully, we ought to try to
realize this. Indeed, it is valuable to try to do so in studying many
great artists. After reading Shakespeare's *King John*, stop, and try
to imagine that the same man is going on to write *King Lear*.
Play an early Beethoven sonata—say the sixth, in F major—and
then look forward into the mists out of which will emerge the
Seventh Symphony and the late Quartets. In the same way, it is
difficult to read Vergil's little bucolic poems and imagine that the
same man could produce the *Georgics*; impossible to forecast that
he would compose the *Aeneid*.

So, when we read Horace's first work, the Epodes, usually
bitter, occasionally downright disgusting—as when he describes
his discarded sweetheart as making up her complexion with 'wet
chalk and crocodile dung'; when we read his early Satires, deft,
amusing, sometimes wise, but not infrequently cruel and vulgar—
then we find it impossible to forecast that the same man will write
the Odes. It is not usual for a satiric poet to turn to lyrics in middle
age; it is highly unusual for lyrics so graceful and skilful to be pro-
duced without much preparatory work—of which there is

scarcely any trace in Horace's career except the seventeen Epodes. When Maecenas gave Horace his friendship and encouragement, he knew that he would get *some* return from it; but even he may have been astonished by the Odes.

They appeared in 23 B.C., when Horace was forty-two. There are only eighty-eight of them in all, covering about eighty-five pages of text.[1] Yet, in the last of the main group, Horace looked back on his lyrics and called them, frail as they were, 'a monument more durable than bronze'. In this proud boast, he was proved right. They are, as far as anything in this world can be, immortal.

Let us see what they look like. They are a series of short lyrical pieces in a variety of Greek metres, most of which Horace was the first to bring into Latin. (Catullus had written two or three poems in one of those patterns, the Sapphic, but there was no large body of work like Horace's new production anywhere in the Latin language.) They are mood pictures. There is very rarely any continuity of thought between two successive poems, and there is only one group which can be read together, without a pause and a change. A few are long, even grandiose. Many are less than a page in length. There are some delightful pieces of only eight lines.

Their subjects vary widely: that is one of their chief charms—for few lyrical poets have ever had such a wide range. There are many poems about love, both heterosexual and homosexual; many about drinking, music, and merry-making; some about religion and superstition; some about patriotism, national discipline, and war; some about morality and the conduct of life; many about the inevitable and shockingly speedy approach of death. They are the poems of a philosopher who is also a sensualist: of a passionate man who feels he has passed the zenith of his life and is growing old.

Their greatest distinction is the extreme subtlety, compression, and variety of their thought. Most lyric poems—from Sappho's songs through Shakespeare's sonnets to the most modern lyrical utterances—are predictable, in that they take a single thought and develop it along a single line. They are the poems of a single

---

[1] There is a fourth volume, which appeared some ten years after the others, as a late gleaning. It contains only fifteen lyrics.

moment, intensely realized. But Horace's Odes are more like the lyrics of Gerard Manley Hopkins or Dylan Thomas. The eminent scholar A. Y. Campbell tells a good story about this. He went through a copy of the Odes which had belonged to Walter Savage Landor, himself a fine lyric poet; and he was astonished to find that Landor had repeatedly struck out the concluding stanzas of Horace's poems, writing in the margin '*What trash*' or '*Stuff*' or '*Better without*'. This puzzled Campbell. But in time he realized that it was the natural reaction of a simple and direct poet criticizing a complex and indirect poet. The easiest example is the famous ode (1.9) only twenty-four lines long, which begins with a picture of a mountain covered deep in snow, and ends with a picture of a girl laughing in a corner, while her new lover takes off her ring. To pass from one image to the other is difficult, almost impossible except for a witty poet; and yet the central theme is clear, and the sequence of thoughts is fairly simple: *snow —winter—the death of the year—resist death—enjoy life—enjoy love.* In something of the same fashion, Bach will begin one of his fugues with a deceptively simple statement, a little dance-theme or a casual air, perhaps not even his own; and then, in only two pages, he will extract from it a truly incredible number of intellectual permutations, developments, and complexities, raising it into another dimension of music, and yet all without losing the initial rhythm. So Horace takes common themes, even shallow themes, and then thinks about them, deeply.

The second virtue of the Odes is their phrasing. One expects to find lovely images in a collection of lyric poetry from any language: 'I wandered lonely as a cloud', 'my love is like a red, red rose', 'les sanglots longs des violons', 'bare ruined choirs, where late the sweet birds sang'—and such images Horace pours out. One expects also to find poignantly sweet and powerfully wise utterances: 'Come kiss me, sweet-and-twenty', 'O saisons, ô châteaux!', 'the most ancient heavens, through thee, are fresh and strong'—and these too can be found in Horace. But specially he is a master of meditative phrases, those which Tennyson called

> jewels five-words-long
> That on the stretched forefinger of all Time
> Sparkle for ever.

Often Horace's phrases are deceptively simple—like Shakespeare's
'The rest is silence'. Yet they linger in the memory. The bride
who broke her oath to murder her husband on the wedding-night
was 'magnificently false'. The heroes of prehistoric times are
recalled in a few words: 'brave men lived before Agamemnon'.
After death, 'we are dust and shadow'. The anxious girl who tries
through astrology to foresee the future is told, almost untrans-
latably, to 'pluck today'—as though it were a flower. And in a
remarkably apt epigram Horace describes the character of a
nation he scarcely knew: 'the British, cruel to strangers'.

In translation these phrases look less good than they are. This is
because in Latin they are given additional authority by Horace's
gift for rhythm and music, and by the delightfully complicated
metres which he employs. Ultimately they were developed from
Greek song-and-dance rhythms. But Greek dancing was infinitely
subtler than our own pounding three-to-the-bar and four-to-the-
bar dances. It contained many more half-steps and cross-rhythms,
and, with its complex interweaving movements of arms and
draperies, it would make even our classical ballets seem naive.
Therefore the best Greek and Graeco-Roman lyric metres are
much more intricate and subtle than any rhythms we are accus-
tomed to in the lyric poetry of English, French, German, Italian,
and other modern languages. For instance, most of our lyrics are
simple iambics: ♪♪ ♪♪ ♪♪ ♪♪ But even the simplest of Horace's
lyric metres (imitated on page 125) is based on a nine-beat line
arranged like this: ♪♪♪♪♪ ♪♪♪♪♪ His Alcaic stanza is far more
complex; and he has many other variations within what looks
like a simple pattern of two-line or four-line stanzas. This subtlety
was another of the surprises in Horace's Odes. Until he published
them, hardly any Roman (and surely no Greek) would believe
that Latin—originally a coarse, loosely-textured, roughly-
accented language—could ever be persuaded to produce rhyth-
mical effects of such extreme delicacy. It is also one of the many

qualities which make his Odes the despair of all translators in all languages.

In another way also, Horace was a bold innovator. This was in his experiments with word-order. Unsophisticated students nowadays are usually accustomed only to plain, rather naive lyric poems like this:

> I wandered lonely as a cloud
> That floats on high o'er vales and hills.

When they first see the peculiar order of the words in Horace's lyrics, they are apt to think either that all Latin authors were bound by the perversity of the language to arrange their words 'unnaturally', or that Horace's metres were so difficult that he could not write straightforward Latin. Only if they have read a good deal of the more sophisticated modern poets (Eliot, Thomas, Hopkins, Auden) can they see the truth: that Horace is a meditative poet who wishes to be read slowly and thoughtfully, and who ventures on bold distortions of the 'natural' prose word order so as to achieve the tone of high intelligence and subtlety of emotion that he desires.

The simplest example of this is one of Horace's light comic effects. It is the beginning of an anti-love poem. Ode 1.5, only sixteen lines long, is addressed to a beautiful blonde called Pyrrha. Horace himself was once in love with her, and just escaped shipwreck—for she is dangerous, her bright smile and her golden charms are as treacherous as the summer sea that may suddenly blacken in a fearful storm. Horace (recalling his own experience) asks her who is now wooing her—poor fellow. The first sentence, translated literally, runs like this:

"What slender youth, among many a rose, drenched with flowing perfumes, is now urging you, Pyrrha, within a pleasant grotto?"

Horace could have written this sentence or its equivalent in virtu-

ally any metre he chose, so as to speak perfectly straightforwardly
more or less in the utterance of every day. But what he actually
wrote was this:

> What many slender you boy among a rose
> drenched with flowing urges perfumes
>   pleasant, Pyrrha, within a grotto?

Now, this is not deliberate perversity. It is wit. Horace can be
humorous and cynical even in the placing of his words. So here,
in the first line, the girl ('you') is central. The 'slender . . . boy'
enlaces her. Both are surrounded by 'many . . . a rose'. In the
second line, the boy is gently satirized. Like many Italian youths,
he loves hair-dressings and perfumes and overdoes them: so his
wooing ('urges') is surrounded by 'flowing . . . perfumes'—so
that we can almost smell the mixture of real roses and artificial
carnations in the little grotto. In the third line we are reminded
that, in spite of it all, the love-scene is charming, and Pyrrha is at
its centre.

Later in the same poem, Horace speaks—with sympathy,
not with envy—of the young lover 'who now credulously
enjoys golden you'; but he sharpens the antithesis by writing
'who now you enjoys credulous golden'.

Many modern readers who do not know Latin may well think
that this is *too* subtle, that no poet in any language could ever
have intended such tiny and delicate effects. But beginners in the
classics are always convinced after they have read, not one, but
fifty of Horace's lyrics and have observed effects of equal subtlety
in them all. Other readers may do well to think either of con-
temporary English and French poetry or perhaps of music. The
care with which Horace placed words and managed rhythms
reminds me most frequently of the extreme, the all but incredible
grace with which Chopin or Brahms will touch and develop a
single cadence, or Bach vary a deceptively simple theme, or Wolf
create a piano setting which is actually more expressive than the

poem it is intended to accompany. Similar effects are being attempted by modern poets, although none has so far reached the mastery displayed by Horace. He was writing for people who already knew all the best poetry in their own language, who had been prepared for his work by the boldly imaginative departures in word-order and syntax achieved by his predecessors, and who also knew the poetry of another language so intimately that they were prepared to accept bold extensions of their native poetry which were intended to rival it.

Here are two English translations of the poem. The first is by Milton—who loved the ode dearly, and thought of it when he described Adam and Eve happy in their bower in Eden:

> These, lulled by nightingales, embracing slept,
> And on their naked limbs the flowery roof
> Showered roses.[1]

Milton says he has rendered the poem 'almost word for word without rhyme according to the Latin measure, as near as the language will permit'.

> What slender youth, bedewed with liquid odours,
> Courts thee on roses in some pleasant cave,
>   Pyrrha? For whom bind'st thou
>   In wreaths thy golden hair,
> Plain in thy neatness? Oh, how oft shall he
> On faith and changèd gods complain, and seas
>   Rough with black winds and storms
>   Unwonted shall admire,
> Who now enjoys thee credulous, all gold;
> Who always vacant, always amiable,
>   Hopes thee, of flattering gales
>   Unmindful! Hapless they

[1] *Paradise Lost* 4.771–3.

To whom thou untried seem'st fair! Me, in my vowed
Picture, the sacred wall declares t' have hung
      My dank and dropping weeds
    To the stern God of Sea.

In a metre closer to the original and in less heavily Latinized language, I have attempted to keep the gay humour which fills Horace's poem full of rueful amusement.

What slim elegant youth, drenched in effusive scent,
now sits close to your side, Pyrrha, in some recess
      rich with many a rose-bloom?
    Who loves smoothing your yellow hair,
chic yet daintily plain? How many gods profaned,
what indelible vows he will lament, and oh,
      what dark hurricane-lashed seas
    he will watch with a pallid cheek!
Poor fool, golden he thinks you will for ever be,
heart-free always, he hopes, always adorable—
      yet knows not the deceitful
    off-shore squalls. To a novice, you
shine too temptingly bright. Here on the temple wall
one small tablet of mine, offering up my clothes
      (all I saved from a shipwreck),
    says Thank God, that I just escaped.

Fifth and greatest among the major virtues of Horace's lyrics has always been ranked their wisdom. For centuries readers have praised their ripe mellowness, their gentle urbanity, the cool balanced contentment which is always a valuable lesson, but was exceptionally valuable in Horace's own day, when after nearly three generations of civil war and violent emotional stress the Romans had to be shown the virtues of simplicity, calmness, and spiritual order. The same wisdom would make his poems important for our own time, were it possible to translate them adequately.

His admirers usually point with particular admiration to the six great poems at the opening of the third book, known as the Roman Odes, because they deal with the ideals of Roman morality and the reforms which it needed. Here are some stanzas from one of them—lines which say (as other Roman moralists were to say after Horace) that the decline of Rome began with a collapse in familial, and particularly in sexual, morality.

Our generations, fertile in vice, defiled
first marriage, first the family and the home;
    from that defilement foul corruption
  flowed to infect both the rich and humble.
Now girls compete in learning voluptuous
dance-rhythms, forget simplicity, learn to lie,
    still young and still fresh, plan and practise
  vicious adventures, disgraceful passions.
Soon such a girl looks out for a younger love,
leaving her husband over his drinks, and gives,
    in furtive darkness, any stranger
  casual pleasure, without distinction;
yes, she will rise quite openly from the table
watched by her husband, leaving to meet a huckster
    or some insistent cargo-skipper
  rich with the price of her degradation.
Such parents did not foster the men who once
dyed deep the sea with blood from the Punic fleet,
    struck down the powerful Pyrrhus, conquered
  Hannibal, routed the eastern sultans.
Those were the sons of farmers and soldiers too—
tough males, accustomed, mattock in hand, to break
    hard clods, and bring home logs for firing
  under the eye of a mother stern and
strong-willed, when sunset lengthened the growing dark
under the mountains, lifting the heavy yoke
    up from the ox-team's weary shoulders,
  bringing repose and the friendly evening.
Time's long corrosion, what does it not infect?

Our fathers' epoch, worse than our ancestors',
    brought forth our own race, steeped in vice and
soon to give birth to a viler offspring.[1]

These are grave charges. They are not Horace's own invention.
They were believed by many of the greatest men in Rome. The
emperor himself endeavoured, by an ingenious series of laws, to
arrest the moral decay of his people; and failed. He could scarcely
have wished for a more eloquent advocate than Horace. In these
and a few other Odes we hear the stern voice of Horace's country-
bred father speaking through the skilfully measured syllables, and
behind the rhythms of the Greek dance-song, for a moment, rises
the heavy tread of the yeoman legions of Roman Italy.

But when we read the Odes of Horace as a complete work—
and so they were published—we find it harder to believe, or even
to remember, his moral preachments. These ethical utterances are
stern and traditional, Roman and rustic. Most of the Odes are
light, voluptuous, sophisticated, urbane, and Greek. If they have a
pervading morality, it is Epicureanism, tempered by superstition.
Live for yourself, they say, think only of today, enjoy love and
wine, ignore wealth so long as you have enough to live on, and
despise ambition, which merely makes you miserable. They are
light and touched with humour, or frail and touched with melan-
choly. Again and again their lesson is one of evasion and com-
placent languor. Heroism, purposeful work, high moral standards
are seldom mentioned. Tactfully Horace declines to write an ode
in praise of the mighty emperor Augustus: he suggests that a
younger poet, more daring and more competent to equal Pindar,
might do so. With mild deprecation he refuses to write an ode in
praise of Augustus's marshal, Agrippa: he explains that, not being
Homer, he cannot write of battles—except the battles waged
against young men by girls, armed with their pointed nails. In
most of the Odes, marriage and family life (which the emperor
was trying to reinforce by law, if not by example) are scarcely
mentioned.

To this criticism it may be objected that Horace was writing

[1] Horace, *Carm.* 3.6.17–48.

light poetry, and should not be reproached for doing so. True; but he professed in the most serious of his Odes to be doing something more—and then contradicted it by the rest of his lyrical utterances. And it is useless to suggest that lyric poets cannot or must not give moral advice. Milton and Wordsworth and many others wrote sonnets which had deep moral significance, and which, when taken together with their other poems, made a serious and consistent whole. Horace himself constantly gives his readers moral advice; only it is usually inconsistent with the principles of conservatism, patriotism, duty, and self-sacrifice which he preaches in his greatest poems. It is generally counsels of enjoyment and relaxation: love while you can, dance and drink, sing and be merry, live for today alone, pay no attention to threats of war from Spain and Russia, drown care in wine, invite the coquettish whore Lydé to join us, spring will not last for ever. In fact, Horace's Odes teach at least two different and incompatible lessons: energy and retirement, morality and voluptuousness, Roman toughness and Greek frivolity, religious conservatism and carefree Epicureanism, social and ethical reform and mild unabashed hedonism. Aesthetically they are very nearly perfect; but morally, through them as through the work of every other poet of Horace's time, there runs a fundamental, an insoluble conflict.

THE SABINE FARM

Tivoli is delightful. But there Horace was never quite free. He could not be entirely alone. He was surrounded by important people who had claims on him. A messenger from Rome could arrive, to disturb his meditations, in a single day.

With fine tact, Maecenas saw that, in order to produce his best poetry and live his happiest life, Horace must be wholly independent, inaccessible, invisible. Also, the little poet's health was not strong: he had to take care of himself. Therefore, when Horace was thirty-two, Maecenas gave him an estate buried among the Sabine hills, seven or eight miles further away from Rome than Tivoli: not a large and pretentious domain, but a country home where, if he wished, he could live entirely free of

worry about money, about social duties, about everything except
the three things which absorbed him—his character, his health,
and his art.

It is a little difficult to describe Horace's place in the country.
It is usually called his 'Sabine farm'. But that implies that it was
virtually a subsistence farm from which he was constantly at work
extracting crops and a living. If it is called an 'estate', that makes us
think of an imposing mansion set among manicured lawns and
landscaped woodlands, utterly out of touch with the real life of
the countryside. In fact, it was a farm, in so far as it carried stock
(cattle and goats), contained an orchard, produced corn, olives,
and wine, and was worked by a foreman with eight slave-
labourers—occasionally assisted by Horace himself. It was an
estate, in that Horace did not have to exist on the produce of his
own fields: he rented much of his land to five tenant-farmers,
whom he did not 'exploit' but treated as friends; and their rents
assisted him in making his place truly independent. There are still
some estates like this in Italy, although not many of the landlords
will do as Horace did, and 'move stones, shift clods'. This was
enough for him to live on all the rest of his life, on a modest but
comfortable standard. He had enough to buy books, to travel, to
leave the farm in the dead winter season, to visit Rome occasion-
ally, and reluctantly. The word 'patronage' implies dependence.
Surely this was patronage at its very best. Maecenas deliberately
gave Horace the power to disappear into the country, to cut the
bonds between them, to ruin his talents if he wished, to work as
slowly or as eccentrically as he chose. This was not patronage, but
friendship: Maecenas made his friend free.

Horace was too proud, Maecenas was too tactful, to make the
arrangement formal and public. There is no poem in which
Horace explicitly thanks his patron for the gift of the Sabine farm.
Instead, there are several genial poems in which he describes his
country home with the utmost delight, calls it heaven, and mani-
fests both complete happiness in its possession and spiritual energy
renewed by his new freedom. From these poems we can recon-
struct it, imagine Horace's life upon it, and even, in imagination,
visit it. Perhaps the earliest of these is a satire in which he con-
trasts city life with country life, and begins:

This was one of my prayers: a little space of land,
with a garden, near the house a spring of living water,
and a small wood besides. Heaven has fulfilled it, better
and richer than my hopes. It is good. I ask no more
now, Mercury, but this: make it for ever my own.[1]

He goes on to describe the torments of greed for money, the drive
of ambition, the hot glare of publicity which has been beating on
him for the last seven years, ever since he became one of Maecenas'
friends. Everyone calls him a lucky man to be the favourite of the
famous statesman, but he sighs to himself:

My country home, when shall I see you, and be free,
now reading the books of the ancients, now sleeping through
    long hours,
to hide this anxious life under sweet oblivion?
Oh, when shall I enjoy your beans (Pythagoras' kinsmen)
and vegetables, served with a fine hock of ham?[2]
Oh, heavenly evenings, heavenly banquets! my friends and I
dine in my home at peace, feeding the cheeky slaveboys
with morsels from our table . . .
We don't discuss the mansions and estates of others,
nor the latest ballet-star's technique. No, we examine
more vital subjects which it is wrong to neglect: whether
happiness comes to men from riches or from virtue;
what motive makes men friends—profit or rectitude;
what is the true nature of good, and what its essence.[3]

Horace scarcely implies that the Sabine farmers engaged in
abstract philosophical discussions—he himself had been educated

[1] Hor. *Serm.* 2.6.1–5.

[2] Not a refined city dinner, but a healthy country banquet; pork and beans
were the food of the common people in Italy, and Horace ennobles them by
a sly joke about the philosopher Pythagoras' reverence for beans.

[3] Hor. *Serm.* 2.6.60–67, 70–76.

in Athens, the centre of philosophical subtlety, and he would not attempt to impose such an exaggeration upon his readers. He means that his country friends were not inarticulate boors, as townspeople often believe farmers to be; and that they did not merely gossip over their meals, as city people are apt to do; but that they talked about problems of morality—doubtless illustrating their talk by proverbs (like Sancho Panza), by examples (like his own father), by anecdotes, and by fables. He ends this particular poem with the fable of the town mouse and the country mouse. The town mouse, after being entertained in the country, persuaded its country friend to come up to the city, took it to a great mansion, gave it a seat on a sumptuous couch, brought in an exquisite feast, surrounded it with luxury—until suddenly the doors burst open and a pack of huge dogs rushed in, barking savagely. Then—

the country mouse said 'Not for me
this life. Thank you. Good-bye. My woods, my little burrow
(alarm-proof) will console me, with a frugal heap of vetch.'[1]

This charming poem was written when Horace was about thirty-three, soon after Maecenas had given him the Sabine farm. Nine years later, in 23 B.C., he published the lyrics which made him one of the greatest poets in Rome. Some of them we know were written in his Sabine home, for they praise it and describe its beauties, and many of them breathe the reflective tranquillity which he found there at its purest and sweetest.

Three years after the Odes, Horace issued a collection of poetic Letters to his friends. Some of them describe his farm; some do not mention it; but its presence is implied in most of them. He uses it, and his happiness in it, as a moral to teach young men to be moderate. He invites people to visit him in it. Yet even the fact that he writes letters from it implies his wish for seclusion: one does not write a poetic letter to a man living less than forty miles away if one hopes to see him next week. Selfish? Perhaps. But

[1] Hor. *Serm.* 2.6.115-7.

creative writers have to guard themselves against people who, with the best intentions in the world, will try to suck their blood. Sometimes I think Horace prudently chose to have his country place in a secluded spot, far from any town, difficult to reach, delightful but inaccessible. Here is his own picture of it.

My dear friend Quinctius, you might ask about my farm—
if it enriches its master with ploughland or with olives,
with fruit or pastures or with elm-trees clothed in vines:
so let me lovingly sketch its shape and situation.
Unbroken hills, just once divided by a dark
valley: the sun approaching looks on the right side,
departing, warms the left with the rays of his vanishing chariot.
You'd praise the temperate air. And think of this!—the kindly
bushes bear wild plums and cherries, the oak and ilex
delight the cattle with their acorns, me with their shade.
Tarentum might have been brought north with all its foliage.
There is a spring besides, worthy to name a river:
Hebrus, wandering through Thrace, is no purer or colder.
Its flow will cure distempered heads and sickly stomachs.
That is my hidden home: dear, yes, and beautiful.[1]

Perhaps the Roman intelligentsia were surprised at Horace's passion for country solitude. Certainly the Roman aristocrats were. They loved huge luxurious mansions, with dining-rooms built far out above the sea, and many swimming-pools. Rome of the early empire looked rather like certain parts of California.

Meanwhile some of the people on his estate thought him mad for preferring the country to the city. Like the Italian in Browning's poem, they cried

Had I but plenty of money, money enough and to spare,
The house for me, no doubt, were a house in the city-square.

[1] Hor. *Ep.* 1.16.1–15.

Ah, such a life, such a life, as one leads at the window there! . . .
Bang-whang-whang, goes the drum, *tootle-te-tootle* the fife.
Oh, a day in the city-square, there is no such pleasure in life![1]

On this theme, the theme of discontent, deliberate maladjustment,
Horace wrote an amusing letter to his foreman—the man who
worked the home farm and perhaps collected the rents from the
tenants and certainly kept the servants in order, and equally
certainly grumbled whenever the master returned, hot and sticky,
from the city.

You who manage the farm that restores me to myself—
the farm you despise, with its five smoking cottages
and five good fathers marketing at Varia—
let's have a match: can I pull weeds out of my soul
harder than you from the ground? Who's better, I or my land? . . .
I love the life of the country; you call the city heaven.
Each man admires the other's fortune, loathes his own.
Fools, both of us: each blaming a place which doesn't deserve it;
the mind, the mind is to blame, which never escapes from itself.
Once, a labourer, you prayed heaven for the country,
and now, a foreman, you long for the city, the baths, the circus.
You know I am consistent. I always leave with a sigh
whenever loathsome business drags me back to Rome.
Our ideals differ, then. That is the real dissension
between us. What you think are lonely cheerless wastes
everyone like me would call delightful, and hate
what you judge beautiful. Brothels and steaming taverns
make you long for the city—I see it: also the fact that
your patch would grow exotic spices sooner than grapes,
and there's no neighbouring inn which can supply you with wine,
and no accessible girl to play the pipe for dancing
while you lollop clumsily around. Yet you must work
land untouched by the spade for years, and curry the ox
after unyoking him, yes, and pull down leaves to fill him;

---

[1] Browning, 'Up at a villa—down in the city'.

unwillingly, too, you must cope with the stream, after rain,
and teach it with massive effort to spare the sunny field.
Now see what breaks the harmony between us two.
I, once handsome in delicate clothes and sleek hair,
once (even without a gift) favoured by greedy Cinara,
addicted once to rich wine as early as noon,
I now love brief dinners, and naps in the grass by the stream.
I'm not ashamed of my fun: the shame would be not to have
 stopped it.
Now here no envious rival squints his evil eye
upon my bliss, or poisons it with furtive fangs.
My neighbours merely laugh at me, digging and heaving rocks,
while you would rather eat with the slaves in a city mansion.
Your prayers make you one of them; but townbred drudges
envy you your free firewood and stock and garden.
The slow ox longs for a saddle, the lazy horse longs to plough;
but each should be content to practise the skill he knows.[1]

 This Letter shows Horace almost at his best and his worst. It is
full of good phrases, neat paradoxes, amusing antitheses. The
rhythm is a skilful blend of light verse and natural prose. The
subject is one Horace loved and often discussed. There are some
pleasant touches of autobiography—for instance, Cinara, famous
from one of the odes; and there is a charming play of humour
throughout. On the other hand, the thought sometimes verges on
platitude; and there is something cold, almost repellent, about
Horace's lack of sympathy for the foreman who has to work hard
and stay on the farm year in, year out, without either Horace's
own prospect of change, or the two things an Italian peasant must
have: wine and a woman. The poem is particularly harsh when we
remember that it is addressed to a man who was almost what
Horace's own father had been.

 But indirectly it tells us quite a lot about Horace's country
place. The nearest market town was Varia. There were five
tenant-farmers. There was no village close by big enough to have
an inn. The surroundings were rocky, neglected, and desolate.

[1] Hor. *Ep.* 1.14, omitting lines 6–9.

There was a stream which was apt to flood one of the best fields.

The Letter to Quinctius (translated on page 141) tells us also that the little estate was surrounded by hills with only one thickly wooded valley piercing them, but that it got full sun morning and evening. There was a fine spring of pure cold water.

Elsewhere in Horace's poems there are other details. Once he dates a letter to a friend from 'the crumbling temple of Vacuna'. Once he says

Whenever I am refreshed by the cold stream of Digentia—
the stream drunk by Mandela, that village wrinkled with cold[1]

—from which we gather that the little river running through his property, and occasionally flooding it, was called Digentia; and that a near-by village was Mandela.

Ever since the sixteenth century, scholars have been piecing all these and other hints together, and endeavouring to pin-point Horace's farm on the map. His description of the landscape—like most Greek and Roman descriptions of landscape—is pretty vague; but he does give a few facts and some useful names. Early in the seventeenth century a German scholar combined these, and placed the house in the exact region where it was later found. In the eighteenth century, working independently, two Italian scholars and a French abbé located the actual site; and preliminary excavations revealed the outline of a small but pleasant dwelling, long buried beneath tons of soil, with fields and vineyards growing above it. It was often visited thereafter, and at last in 1911 the Italians began to excavate it thoroughly. Fifteen years later, in 1926, Dr. Lugli published the results in an exhaustive treatise. In 1930–31 a young scholar attached to the American Academy at Rome did some more digging, made the plan of the place still clearer, and produced a handsome and convincing reconstruction of the buildings and the area as they had appeared during Horace's lifetime. Of course we have only the outline of a house. The walls and the roof have gone long ago, except for the lower courses which indicate the size and style of the place; the fragmentary

[1] Hor. *Ep.* 1.18.104–5.

works of art and small utensils found during the dig are in a museum near by. Yet the floor-plan is clear, and some of the mosaic floors are still in place. As Horace himself says, it is a modest enough house. But anyone who has had the pleasure of visiting it will never again call it a farm. It was a charming country house, inhabited by a man who had good taste and loved both comfort and seclusion.

To reach the 'Sabine farm', we leave Tivoli: an elegant place, rather prosperous, rather luxurious. We drive into the hill country where once the Sabines lived, an ancient people, brave, frugal, deeply religious. In this land there are few flat plains. Everything slants. The olives grow in plantations terraced out of the hillsides, the vineyards march up the slopes, on one side of the road there is a deep glen, on the other a range of high curving hilltops. Many of the villages seem to have been planted in the warlike Middle Ages; they cling to the high crests, like frightened animals retreating from a forest fire or a flood.

In time we reach the market town where Horace's five tenants went for their supplies. Perhaps their wives went with them, as many Italian farm-women do now, carrying chickens and fruit in baskets on their heads, to return with flour and vegetables and salt. Horace knew it as Varia. Now it is called Varo Village, Vicovaro. Apart from its ancient name, it has (as Baedeker would say) 'little to commend it to the visitor'.

Further on we enter a long valley watered by a small river. The river is now called Licenza, a name which has changed very little. Horace called it the Digentia. Soften the initial D, and soften the -tia: you have Licenza. Across on the other side we see a poor village, where life must be hard, deathly hot in summer and 'wrinkled with cold' in the winter. It has two names, Bardella-Cantalupo. The second seems to mean Wolfsong, a cold wintry name indeed; the first is the one which Horace knew, slightly changed into Bardella from the original Mandela.

High on the left as we drive on, there is another poor village. Sometimes one wonders if the modern Italian farmer lives even as well as his ancestors in Roman times. The soil has grown no richer, the hills and valleys have lost so many of their trees, the medieval villages are so tiny and cramped. This place is now called Roccagiovine. In it there is a Roman inscription saying that the emperor Vespasian (about a century after Horace) 'restored the temple of Victory'. This was 'the crumbling temple of Vacuna'—for Vacuna was not the deity who presides over committees, Our Lady of Vacuity: she was the Sabine goddess of victory. The temple is gone now; but the inscription reminds us that Horace once sat there in its shade, and composed a poetic letter to one of his friends.

The road along the valley of the Licenza winds higher into the hills. A mile or so ahead, across the stream, appear two small villages, clinging to their peaks in millennial terror. Both are called Licenza: or rather, one is Licenza, and the other is Licenza Township, Civitella di Licenza. They look tiny, and bare, and comfortless. Horace does speak of a little hamlet near him called Haedilia, which might, at nearly seventy generations' remove, be one of these.

Within sight of them, we stop. The highroad rises away into the hills ahead. On our right is the river Licenza; beyond it the villages, perched uneasily on their craggy sites. On our left is a steep hillside deep in woods. A discreet notice says VILLA D'ORAZIO, 'Horace's villa'. There is no gatekeeper, no roll of tickets, no turnstile, no guides: simply a path, outlined with stones, leading through the trees.

The path leads steeply upwards from the highway, in S curves and sharp angles. But the climb is not exhausting, since we walk among cool ferns and are shaded by ample trees. Birds talk among the branches. After about half a mile, we emerge quite suddenly on a level plot of ground, covering an acre or so—almost the only level patch within some miles. Here in the sun lie the remains of Horace's country home. All around, almost unbroken, rise the steep hills.

In a sunlit spot among the trees, we see the ground plan of the house, outlined by the lowest courses of the walls, built in brick. The excavations have been done with such care and detail that it is not difficult to see how Horace lived.

The villa itself, with its garden, faced almost exactly due south.

It covered an area of 142 feet by 363 feet altogether. It had twelve rooms, six on the eastern side and six on the western, grouped around two central courtyards open to the sky for light and air. (The rooms are quite small, but so was Horace.) One of them was a little summer dining-room, built out among the flower-beds. There was a roomy hall, and on one side, towards the west, a suite of bathrooms with an indoor pool. The main buildings appear to have been two storeys high, but not more than that. To the south lay a big formal garden covering nearly 3,000 square yards, surrounded on all four sides by a corridor with large windows opening in upon the garden, where Horace could stroll in comfort when the weather out of doors was inclement. In the centre of the garden was a fish-pool. Graceful statues stood here and there; fountains played; and Horace's favourite trees grew near by.

The site for the villa was chosen with great care. It was a shoulder of the hill which Horace called Lucretilis and his successors now call Monte Gennaro; and it was artificially levelled to take the villa and the garden. Towards the north the land falls away abruptly, down to the river Licenza, with views across the valley toward the two little hill towns. To the south a more gentle slope leads to the ancient Roman road. The house and garden are screened from the river valley and the road by a fine chestnut wood. There is plenty of water, summer and winter, coming from the hills.

But besides the house and garden, Horace had a reasonably large farm. To begin with, we know he had livestock: sheep and goats, and cattle for ploughing. Naturally he had a vegetable garden. He owned a vineyard: the wine was not very good, but it was sweetened by being his own. He had an orchard and an olive grove. Down near the river he owned cornfields; and finally he had a private wood for timber and shade. The place was worked by eight slaves under a foreman, but we know from Horace himself that the discipline was far from strict. Outside his estate there was a lot of wild country to wander through. As he walked about the city of Rome, he was subject to annoyance from social parasites or heavy commercial traffic; but here different emergencies were apt to confront him. Once a tree fell near him unexpectedly and nearly killed him; and once, when he was alone and unarmed, he met a wolf in the forest. He was composing poetry—one of the Odes—and with rare good taste the wolf forbore to interrupt him.

The house itself was rather elaborately decorated. We should never forget that today we live comfortably enough, but usually in a state of aesthetic starvation which would have horrified a Roman or a Greek. We have plenty of machines and mechanical appliances in every room; but our floors are usually plain, our walls are plain except for a few copies of paintings hanging on them, our furniture has bare austere lines, and hardly one of us in a thousand owns a piece of sculpture. During the excavations of Horace's country house many fragments of its decorations were found, enough to show that he was surrounded by pleasing shapes and colours. There is a bold and rather comic mask of Silenus, the attendant of Bacchus, which was used to decorate a fountain. There are many fragments of frescoes from the walls: a young Bacchus, a dancing girl, a poet with his lyre. And on the floors of the villa there were cool elegant mosaic patterns, different for every room. Some poets like bearskins or Islamic prayer-rugs, or even rough pieces of sacking, upon their floors. Horace wrote neat, economical, fanciful, yet beautifully controlled poems; beneath his feet he liked to see close, varied, abstract patterns. What Piet Mondriaan did as framed 'pictures', Horace's decorators put on his floors.

The custodian of Horace's villa, whether he knows it or not, is remotely descended from the foreman who once managed his 'farm'. The foreman used to tell Horace how he longed for relaxation and gaiety, and the life of the city. Here, among the ruins of his villa, we are met by a beautifully-mannered guide with white hair framing his red face. He can do what Horace's foreman certainly could not attempt: quote Horace's best poems, in mellifluous Latin, every syllable clear and melodious. But just as Horace's foreman envied the slaves in the city, so the custodian of his relics finds his job, although important, a little less than perfect. It is not unpleasant here, in the sunshine; this official is much more dignified than many guardians of works of art in Italy (the furtive starved figures in the Naples museum, the officious and ignorant guides in Pompeii); yet he suffers from the two torments which might be pleasures in other countries, but are agonies in Italy—regular day-by-day routine, and isolation from his fellow-men. 'Even on days of festival, think of it, I must be here,' says he—although a festival might be the only day on which a visitor from abroad could get a car and drive out to the poet's home. Perhaps he longs to live in the city, with the caffès, the roaring motor-cycles, and the bright lights; and perhaps we are just as wrong in criticizing him as Horace was in rebuking his discontented foreman.

Good buildings last a long time. Horace's country house, along with all his other property, was left to the emperor Augustus—the man against whom he had once fought and whom he (like so many others) had come to revere. (Maecenas was already dead.) The villa became part of the imperial domain. Doubtless it was preserved for some time as a relic of a great poet, but (as it is today) unvisited except by scholars and antiquarians. Then in the second century of our era it was bought and inhabited by a rich man of simple tastes. He added an elaborate set of baths, and a fish-pool which had special wall-niches in which the fish could lay and hatch their eggs. The fish-pool was entered by a subaqueous passage, with windows through which the guests could watch the fish at play.

After that stage of luxury, the villa passed through three characteristic changes. First, it was occupied by a family who 'winter-ized' it and made it fit to live in all year round, by adapting the heating system of Horace's baths to supply warmth to the whole house. (This is a common mark of the poverty-stricken later Empire—the country house and estate taken over and made into a subsistence farm.) Then it became a little Christian monastery, with a church dedicated to Saints Peter and Marcellinus. (The fish-pool was changed into the burial crypt, and when excavated was found to be full of bones.) Finally it was abandoned, silted over, and forgotten. Vines were planted above its remains, and only the vines preserved a faint memory of one of its avatars, for they were called the Vines of St. Peter.

The estate of Horace is even now a charming place. When laid out more for comfort and less for cultivation, it must have been delightful. On their lower slopes, the hills are rich with vines and vegetable gardens, interspersed with trees—fig, alder, and hawthorn. Higher up they are terraced, clothed in grey olives and brown pines. The moving air is full of voices: chirping of crickets, crowing of cocks, singing of birds, chatter and ripple of water. The house itself is a suntrap; yet only twenty paces away are cool ferns and green shades. It is a place of peace.

The lands which Horace owned doubtless lay along the river Licenza, down below. We cannot see them from his house, and indeed he must have kept away from them. He does speak of two things near by—a hill called Lucretilis, and a cold clear spring of water. The guardian says he can show us these. He takes us up a steep and little-used pathway among rows of cultivated plants and beneath vine arbours. This is the slope of Horace's hill, Lucretilis, rising a good thousand feet above his villa. In a vine arbour just like one of these, he sat on a small bench in autumn, and drank peacefully, and composed one of his most graceful and amusing little songs, in praise of pleasure and moderation.

> I detest all luxury Oriental:
> bring me no fat leis of frangipani,
> boy, and don't search every forgotten nook where
>   lingers a late rose.
> Nothing but one plain little crown of myrtle
> need you weave me. Myrtle is no disgrace to
> you as page-boy, nor to your master, drinking,
>   shaded by vine-leaves.[1]

At last, about ten minutes from the house, we come to a steep slope, from which rushes a stream of clear water, absolutely clear and transparent, and—even in July, under the burning Dog-star—deliciously cold. This is the Bandusian spring. Once Horace promised, although it was only a small unknown source far in

[1] Hor. *Carm.* 1.38.

the remote hills, to make it famous. He treated it as divine, by sacrificing a kidling to it, and giving it libations of wine, and throwing flowers into it; and he wrote a poem which indeed made it famous through many centuries when its very site was forgotten.

Hail, Bandusian spring, clearer than crystal pure,
fountain worthy of sweet wine and of wreaths of flowers.
    Take my gift of a young kid
   whose head, swelling with early horns,
even now promises love, promises battles too—
vain forecasts: for he shall, after tomorrow's dawn,
    dye your coolness with red blood,
   he, once gayest of all the herd.
Untouched, even in the fierce hour of the blazing Dog,
unwarmed, you with your streams offer delightful cold
    to bulls tired with the heavy plough
   and to wandering herds of kine.
You too shall be among fountains of high renown,
when my song celebrates this overarching oak,
    this dark hollow of rocks whence
   leaps your chattering waterfall.[1]

This little place, because of Horace's eloquence, became one of the ideal spots in the imagination of thousands of readers. It is not wildly romantic: not a savage place, holy and enchanted, beset by demoniac presences; nor even hallowed by the memory of a thirsty hero or a benign nymph or a saintly hermit. It is merely a spring, quiet and beautiful. But the voice of the water still sounds, as it sounded to Horace, selfless and enduring and almost human: merry, wordless, and alive.

As we leave Horace's home and make our way down through the chestnut groves, unseen birds are calling in the green shade. One of them says a single note over and over again, in a soft hoarse

[1] Hor. *Carm.* 3.13.

meditative repetition like a primitive prayer. But deeper in the woods, we hear for the first time a perfectly unmistakable voice, a rich pure utterance which is all melody. Among the cool ferns we pause, and listen, and answer it. It sings again, a phrase of four descending notes. When that is answered, it sings once more, and again, in an inexhaustible wealth of soft music. It is the nightingale. Invisible among the trees, it sings like no other bird, speaking of passion, beauty, and immortality. As it sings, phrase upon phrase, cool and refreshing as the Bandusian water, we remember that once in an English garden young John Keats sat under a tree listening to the same music, with a volume of Horace's poems open upon his knee. He read the opening lines of the fourteenth Epode:

> Why a soft numbness drenches all my inmost senses
> with deep oblivion,
> as though with thirsty throat I'd drained the cup that brings
> a sleep as low as Lethe . . .[1]

And then he wrote:

> My heart aches, and a drowsy numbness pains
> My sense, as though of hemlock I had drunk,
> Or emptied some dull opiate to the drains
> One minute past, and Lethe-wards had sunk . . .

It was the opening of his *Ode to a Nightingale*. That sweetness, translated back into wordless music, meets us at the end of an exquisite movement of Respighi's suite, *The Pines of Rome*. To hear it, and to drink from the Bandusian spring, is to feel, even for one hour, something of the perpetual flow of music and poetry which moves through the souls of great artists—though nearly always, whilst this muddy vesture of decay doth grossly close it in, we cannot hear it.

[1] Hor. *Epod.* 14.1–4.

THE LETTERS

It is terribly exhausting to write difficult and controlled lyric poetry. A. E. Housman, the poet of *A Shropshire Lad*, called his second book *Last Poems*: in a brief preface, he explained that he did not expect to be revisited by the continuous excitement under which he had written his earlier book, 'nor indeed could I well sustain it if it came'. In the same way, after constructing his 'monument more enduring than bronze', Horace was exhausted.

Also, he was disappointed with the reception of his three books of Odes. He knew that they were something unequalled in the literature of his country, something which—because it gave the Romans a body of poetry equal in precision and grace to the lyrics of Greece—had made him a classic; still, he was distressed by their unsympathetic reception. He was rather bitter about it.

> Now shall I tell you why the ungrateful reader praises
> my work and loves it at home, but disparages it in public?
> I do not whistle up the winds of popularity
> by giving lavish parties, handing out trashy gifts.
> I cannot hear and criticize distinguished authors
> on lecture-platforms and in meetings of professors.
> 'Hence these tears!'[1]

Horace may have been perfectly right in his diagnosis. His lyrics were—like the poems of Eliot and Auden and Thomas in our own time—much too difficult to be understood and accepted at once. If he refused to court publicity by giving large parties to welcome his book into the world, by reciting them at specially arranged public assemblies, and by engaging in lively critical discussions with eminent littérateurs, but simply launched the Odes, sink or swim, small wonder that they were not an immediate success. They have never been an immediate success. Like the Preludes and Fugues of Bach, like the poems of Rilke and Donne, like the

[1] Hor. *Ep.* 1.19.35–41.

etchings of Callot, Horace's lyrics depend on a taste which must be acquired, and acquired with time and effort.

Later, the Roman public—now sensitive enough, and favoured in one generation with more fine poetry than most nations are given in an entire millennium—came to understand and to enjoy Horace's lyrics. Soon enough—too soon for his own taste—they became a schoolbook. Horace thought that was a terrible fate, but he knew it was better for schoolboys to read poems like his than to read the old-fashioned stuff which his own teacher had beaten into his brain through his bottom, the two-hundred-year-old translation of the *Odyssey* into an obsolete metre by Livius Andronicus, in Latin which was so archaic as to be comical.

But Horace was tired. The effort of creating a classical literature is enormous. Virgil died at fifty. Propertius wrote nothing after forty. Horace gave something like seven years, from his thirty-fifth to his forty-second year, to the Odes. Then he rested. It was not his mind that was tired: he could still think, perhaps better than ever. But he could hardly make music any more, nor indeed sustain the emotion of making it.

Nearly ten years later he produced a fourth book of lyrics. Significantly, it opened with a protest, the cry of an ageing seer against the returning god, the protest of an elderly lover against the revival of passion.

So hostilities are renewed
once more, Venus? Oh, no! Spare me, for Venus' sake![1]

But these last lyrics are touched by the cool breezes of autumn, the first hints of frost, the partial resignation of approaching age.

Alone and thoughtful, Horace wrote letters to his friends. Lonely people write letters, so that they can communicate even with those whose eyes are turned elsewhere. Often such letters are merely negative, calls for sympathy, cries of despair. Often

[1] Hor. *Carm.* 4.1.1–2.

they are dreary personal reports, tedious self-analyses, lists of minuscule happenings within one tiny system. But Horace was one of the great letter-writers—as, we may judge from his other poems, he had been one of the great talkers and charmers. He gave positive and winning advice. He sketched, in these poetic Letters, both his own character and the personalities of his correspondents. He gossiped without rambling. And into some of his Letters he distilled the thought of a lifetime—on ethics, on literature, on social life. His Letters are virtually essays in verse—skilfully informal verse which compresses much thought into small space and a gracefully unobtrusive style.

Some of Horace's letters are obviously dated from Rome. A few were written at his house in Tivoli. Four at least are from his dear home in the Sabine hills—enough to show how highly he prized it.

One of these letters is exceptionally interesting. It is to Maecenas, the rich, powerful, and sensitive Maecenas. As his patron, Maecenas might have insisted that Horace should dine with him every week, spend a few months every year staying with him, aid him with his correspondence, advise him about young poets who deserved help, attend his grandest parties, join his suite on important occasions, supervise the building of his library, and so on. Horace spent some energy and some tact on evading these tentacles. Once, for example, he and Vergil and Varius, all good poets, were privileged to accompany Maecenas on a highly important diplomatic mission. But later, Horace showed what he thought of his useless journey by describing it, stage by stage, in a satire which listed one boring or trivial incident after another—like the diary of an inefficient reporter—and entirely omitted both the purpose and the climactic meeting and the results of the conference. Like most good Roman satires, this is double-edged. It satirizes not only the powerful politicos who wanted the poets to attend on them and then gave them so little to think about, but the inquisitive public which wanted so desperately to know what went on in the secret conferences.

After he had acquired his Sabine home, Horace wrote a delightful letter to Maecenas, thanking him indirectly, explaining that the house and his own independence were too pleasant to leave,

and justifying his own self-reliance, his refusal to be either a client
or a parasite.

I promised I should spend only a week in the country—
liar! now you have missed me all through August. Yet
if you wish me to remain healthy, thoroughly fit,
Maecenas, please give me (afraid of illness) the leave
which you would give me were I ill. Let the first fig
and autumn heat bring out the slow black funerals,
while every father and mamma worries about the children,
while business occupations and social observances
result in burning fevers and quick obituaries.
Later, when winter plasters snow on the Alban fields,
your poet will come down to the seashore, watch his health,
keep warm, and read; and, my dear friend, revisit you
(if you permit) with the warm west winds and the first swallows.

You made me rich, Maecenas, but not like the southern farmer
feeding his guests on pears, urging them 'Eat up!'
'I've had enough.' 'Take more; take all you want.' 'No, thanks.
'Surely your children will enjoy a few as presents?'
'Your kindness means as much as though I'd gone home loaded.'
'Very well. What you leave will go straight to the pigs.'

Only a foolish wastrel gives gifts that he despises:
that seed produces a crop of ingratitude, always will.
A good and wise man is ready to help the deserving,
yet knows well enough the difference of dross and gold.
I shall show myself worthy of all your distinction;
but if you want me never to roam away, you must
make my lungs strong again, turn my hair black and curly,
restore my pleasant talk and my power of laughing gaily
and lamenting over the wine the escape of stubborn Cinara.

A slender fox once slid through a thin delicate crack
into a bin of wheat, and fed full, and then
vainly endeavoured to extract his bulging body.
Looking on, a weasel called 'If you want to escape,
you must be slender to slide through the hole that you slenderly
    slid in!'
If faced with this parable, I'll resign all I possess . . .
A little man needs little. Today imperial Rome
attracts me less than empty Tibur, peaceful Tarentum.[1]

This and a few other such poems make Horace's declaration of
independence. Also, they announce his retirement. Once he was a
Roman. He meditated his 'trifles' while he walked along the
busiest streets; he loved wandering round the market-place in the
evenings, he enjoyed dropping into shops and chatting, and watch-
ing the fortune-tellers. Now in his forties he has become a country-
man, as he was born. Except for a few rare and great occasions, he
will return to imperial Rome no more. His friends, who loved the
smoke and wealth and noise of Rome, quizzed him about this.
To one of them, the sophisticated Aristius Fuscus, Horace wrote
a letter explaining his resolution.

Greetings to you, Fuscus, lover of the city,
from me, a lover of the country. In this alone
we are unlike. In everything else we might be twins
with kindred souls; each of us may reject a trifle,
but we nod acceptance to everything else, like a pigeon pair.
You keep your nest in the city. I praise the charming country—
its brooks, its rocks painted with moss, its quiet woods.
You see? I live like a king, ever since leaving all
you and your friends describe as heavenly happiness.
Now, like a temple-slave escaped, I hate fat cakes
and long for bread, as better than rich honeyed confections.
If we must live in perfect harmony with nature

[1] Hor. *Ep.* 1.7.1–34, 44–45.

and first discover a site on which to build our home,
what place is better than the heavenly countryside?
Where are the winters warmer? Where does a kinder air
temper the furious Dog, control the raging Lion
when once the climbing sun has entered his grim cage?
Where does distressful care less often break your sleep?
Does grass smell worse, or shine less bright, than Libyan marble?
Is water streaming through the city pipes much purer
than that which chatters and ripples, slanting down the brook?
Among variegated pillars, woods are planted;
the most admired mansions command huge landscapes:
toss Nature out with a pitchfork, still she will return,
and conquer unobserved your false fastidiousness.
The bogus expert who cannot tell local dyes
from fine Phoenician wool richly steeped in purple
is not more deeply, not more painfully misled
than he who cannot well distinguish true and false.
Whatever anyone enjoys too much, will crush him
by disappearing. What you love most, you must lose
against your will. Avoid big things. In a poor cottage
you may live a better life than kings and the friends of kings.

Once a hard-fighting stag drove a horse from the common
pasture. After losing many a bitter battle,
the horse begged man for help, agreeing to wear the reins.
But after conquering his enemy in triumph,
he could not drop his rider, nor shake off his bridle.

The man who, fearing poverty, abandons freedom
(a dearer thing than metal) is carrying a rider—
a permanent master—because he cannot live on little.
A discontented man is like an ill-shod walker:
a big shoe trips him up, a small shoe pinches him.
My friend, you will be wise if you can live contented;
and do not let me get away unpunished, if
I seem to accumulate and to go beyond the limit.

Capital can be either a master or a servant:
it ought to be the donkey, not the man with the stick.

This, dictated behind the crumbling shrine of Vacuna,
from me—happy, except that I miss your company.[1]

When Horace published his first book of Letters, he was about forty-five. During the next few years he produced two longer Letters, on literature; a peculiar essay on writing for the stage, which is now known as *The Art of Poetry* and is still imperfectly understood, chiefly because much of it looks far too naive and obvious for the meditative and subtle Horace to have set down seriously; also an official hymn for a great state celebration; and his last volume of Odes, fifteen in all. His life's work was done.

He died in 8 B.C., at the age of fifty-six. Once he described his career, character, and appearance, at the end of his first book of Letters. 'Go, little book,' he wrote—

say I was born in poverty of a father once a slave,
but stretched my wings far beyond that humble nest:
what you subtract from my descent, add to my virtues;
say that I pleased the greatest Romans, in war and peace;
say I was small, and early grey, and loved hot sunshine,
swift to anger and yet easy to pacify . . .[2]

He did indeed 'please the greatest Romans'. Vergil was his friend, Maecenas, on his deathbed, commended Horace to the emperor, saying 'Think always of him as you do of me', and Augustus offered to make him his private secretary, not being offended when he refused. These were only the first of many thousands who have admired Horace for the temperance and wisdom which enabled him to rise almost from the very depths to almost the very

[1] Hor. *Ep.* 1.10.
[2] Hor. *Ep.* 1.20.20–25.

summit, and then, deliberately, rather than become a much-courted celebrity, to retire into modest independence; who have delighted in his deft and exquisite poetry; and who, for his urbane humour, his fine tact, and his essentially civilized wisdom, have loved him.

V

TIBULLUS

STYLE

STYLE is an extraordinary thing. It is one of the subtlest secrets of all art. Through a sensitive appreciation of style, we can actually understand a creative artist more deeply than through weighing his subjects, dissecting his themes, or reading his biography. In painting, it is composition, colour-sense, and brush-work. In sculpture, it is the treatment of depths and surfaces and the choice of stones and metals. In music, it is surely the melodic line, the tone-colour, and the shape of the phrase—who could fail to recognize the four hammer-blows in C minor as the very voice of Beethoven? In prose and poetry, it is the choice of words, their placing, and the rhythms and melodies of sentence and paragraph. The work of a really good writer can be subjected—from this point of view alone, almost without reference to his meaning and message—to long and subtle analysis, which does not deform or deaden our appreciation of his art, but increases it more than we should have thought possible.

For example, when Bernard Berenson estimated a newly dis-covered picture, which might be by a master such as Botticelli, he used to arrange, first of all, to see it rapidly and all at once, without preparation. Next came the detailed study. And in that, one of the most difficult and rewarding investigations was his examination of the brushwork. In those two movements, by which he first subjected himself to the total impression of the picture, and then reconstructed the very movements of the artist's hand, the very quality of his paint and brushes, Berenson pene-trated as close as possible to the soul of the painter.

In the same way, students of music can spend months of profit-able work simply on analysing a single composer's use of the varied instruments of the orchestra—how he loves groups of horns, with their strange muffled distant voices, how he will balance them with clear high violins, shimmering like fountain-spray at the top of their range, how he maintains command over his audience by recurrent and insistent drums. It is possible, similarly, to learn much about Plato by studying something apparently so insignificant as his use of particles—the little almost-meaningless words of emphasis and qualification like 'of course', 'certainly', 'at least', in which the Greek language is so rich, and which (in written prose) perform the same function as gestures, voice-tones, and facial expressions in conversation. Much can be told about the date and the emotional tone of any play by Shakespeare, simply from an examination of the endings of the lines. A great artist impregnates every detail of his work.

Not only a man's art, but his temperament, is reflected in his style. Any intelligent reader of Ezra Pound's *Cantos* would know, without further information, that Pound had led a life of spiritual and intellectual excitement, disorganization, intermittence, and conflict. The random quizzical ethos of Laurence Sterne, and even his rather frail health, are reflected in his punctuation. Chopin's music gradually becomes tubercular.

One of the rewards of reading good writers, not in translation but in their own languages, is that we can learn to appreciate their styles. Translations are deformations, disguises; an original gives us the man's voice as his friends and his first readers heard it: almost as he himself heard it. Only if a Frenchman understands English well and has read much English poetry with ease, can he appreciate Shakespeare. A good Greek scholar can read a Greek poem, explain its meaning, discuss its beauties of rhythm and tone, analyse its structure and its models—and still be left with an important residue of experience which he is usually powerless to explain unless in hints, but which is none the less a vital moment of his enjoyment, which is indeed one of the chief reasons he devoted himself to the study of Greek.

This is much more true of Greek and Latin poetry than the average man realizes. The Greek and Roman poets did not write very much. But they spent a great deal of thought and effort on their styles. Although they worked within a limited range of metres and handled a comparatively small collection of subjects, every one of them who has any claim to be called good developed an entirely individual style—so unmistakable that no careful reader could confuse it with the style of any other poet (even with a poet writing in the same metre on the same subjects), so expressive that it conveyed meanings and nuances of emotion which supplemented and deepened the themes of his poems. Tennyson in his ode on the anniversary of Vergil's birth speaks of

> all the charm of all the Muses
> often flowering in a lonely word.

Without exaggerating, any lover of the Greek and Roman classics will accept this, and go further. He will point to a single syllable, a single cadence, even a single vowel, and say truly that it could have been placed only by one poet, and that it expresses many years of his meditation on life and art, as many centuries of the turbulent history of our planet are expressed in a single diamond.

All this comes home to anyone who reads Tibullus in his own words. He might easily be called a decadent. He flaunts his own spiritual weaknesses. He admits that he cannot resist temptation, even when the object is utterly unworthy of him. He cries and complains of small disasters in a surprisingly un-Roman way. All the traditional ideals of his nation he rejects: courage, self-control, self-sacrifice, energy and a planned career—he boasts that they are all quite meaningless to him, and that he is ready to accept the scorn of others if he can just live his own inert and sensual life. He sounds like a thoroughly despicable young man.

And yet his style proves that at heart he was not. There is a positive sweetness in his elegies, there are a gentleness and grace which can only have inhabited a good and sensitive soul. The movement of his thought is calm and orderly, and if his epithets are sometimes a little obvious, even vapid, his verse is always delicately melodious. When read slowly, sympathetically, and meditatively, he is quite clearly an admirable poet. In music, he might be compared to Mendelssohn or Fauré. A gentle, soft-hearted man, he had an exquisitely subtle taste, and the spirit of a fine artist.

CONSOLATION

We know very little about Albius Tibullus, beyond what he himself tells us in his poems. The only biography of him which has survived is seven lines in length. It is confused and obscure, and tells us only that he died young, and that he was remarkably handsome and elegant in person. But we know how he appeared to one of the most intelligent of his friends. Horace wrote him this letter:

Albius, candid judge of my satiric poems,
what is your way of life, there in the district of Pedum?
Writing poetry which will outdo the recent success,
or strolling silently among the healthy woods,
thinking of themes which good and wise men ought to cherish?
You were never a brainless, heartless body. Heaven
gave you good looks, and wealth, and the art of enjoying them.

A nurse could ask no more for her darling foster-child
than common sense, and the power of saying what he thinks,
pure and good repute, and admirable health,
and a decent livelihood, without holes in his purse.
Tossed by the passions—hope, anxiety, fear, and anger—
believe that every day which dawns will be your last,
and let each extra hour become a welcome bonus.

Now come and see me, fat, well-tanned, and glistening,
and laugh at a sleek pig from Epicurus' herd.[1]

Genial as it is in tone, this is a curious and basically rather sad letter. In fact, it is a 'consolation'. It is intended to shake Tibullus

[1] Horace, *Ep.*1.4.

out of a melancholy which had become habitual, to encourage him to enjoy his life.

Horace begins with the young poet's name and address (near Pedum, in a wooded countryside) and a compliment to his acute critical sense. Then he goes on to ask whether Tibullus is writing poetry (he specifies it as the best type of elegiac poetry, by mentioning a recent success in that line) or thinking of philosophic subjects. This, by delicate implication, is an exhortation to him not to waste time on cheap pleasures or vague aimless brooding. Girls—who seem from Tibullus's own poems to have been his chief interest in life—are not even mentioned. Then Horace lists all the enviable advantages which Tibullus enjoyed; and in three very succinct lines reminds him that life is short and full of emotional crises which cannot be avoided but must be faced: so that his duty is to live fully and gratefully. Finally, Horace adds a tactful invitation to visit him in his home, and a reminder that he himself, practising the philosophy of calm enjoyment, has been able to find happiness—although (he adds with a smile) the opponents of Epicureanism call it the happiness of a pig in a sty. The last couplet contains a discreet comparison of Horace's own short figure to the amorous and graceful elegance for which his biographer says Tibullus was distinguished. All this, you observe, is done by light touches. There is no direct pressure. Even the hint that Tibullus is slightly spoiled ('no fond nurse could wish more blessings for her pet baby') is very delicate, and suitably humorous. The whole letter, only sixteen lines long, gives us a remarkably clear picture of Tibullus—as well as of its author Horace.

The picture is strengthened by another little poem, one of Horace's lyrics. Here it is. (The names are modernized to correspond to the elegant Greek pseudonyms in Horace's verse.)

Now don't overindulge grief for your lost coquette,
my poor comrade, and don't publish lugubrious
dark-blue dirges of love, endlessly asking why
      she broke faith, took a younger man.
See how Audrey—a rare beauty with clustered curls—
burns for David; but he yearns for the arrogant

Eileen; yet we shall watch slavering mountain wolves
      mate with delicate fallow deer
far, far sooner than Eileen will indulge his lust.
Cruel Love always conjoins two inappropriate
hearts, minds, bodies with one pair of unbroken chains:
      Love does relish a savage joke.
I too, though a liaison with a kinder girl
was quite possible, still clung to my cruel Sue—
slum-bred woman, and wild, stormier than the waves
      wind-whipped, lashing Atlantic rocks.[1]

This poem also is a consolation to a weak and emotional man.

Slight as it seems, it is beautifully constructed. The first stanza shows a girl turning from one man to another. The second shows a man turning from one girl to another—and then being frustrated. The third contains Horace's general advice about love, to regard it as a subject for wry laughter rather than bitter elegiac complaint. The fourth shows Horace himself between two girls: committing the same folly in clinging to the cruel sweetheart as Tibullus is committing in yearning for the beauty who has deserted him. By implication, therefore, it says 'Be glad you have escaped: turn to someone gentler and more loving than your lost coquette'. Even in the style, with harsh phrases such as 'indulge his lust' and 'slum-bred woman' (which are no gentler in the Latin), there are reminders that the whole business of sexual love has something violent and coarse in it, which a wise man will take not with tears or shudders of horror, but with an indulgent smile.

Horace's picture of Tibullus is confirmed by Tibullus's own poems: both by their themes and by their style.

He was a gentle, sensitive soul. He was a skilful artist. He was happiest and most truly himself when he was alone in the quiet countryside. But he was unable to resist the fascination of pretty women—even when they were ruthless, even when they were worthless. They dominated him, and wrecked a life which might have been better spent.

And it is clear that, physically, he was not strong. Horace hints

[1] Horace, *Carm.* 1.33.

at this in the phrase 'strolling among the healthy woods', and again in the implied contrast between his own plump epicurean body and the frail drooping frame of his friend. Although Horace could scarcely have divined it, his letter to Tibullus was published only a year or so before the young poet died.

RITE OF SPRING

Catullus's love for the hateful and beautiful Clodia was intense and disastrously foolish. Tibullus—who was born about 54 B.C., just when Catullus's life was coming to an end—went much further into folly.

He had been a soldier. He had even earned a decoration for courage. By the time we meet him (in his poetry) he loathes war, wishes only to live tranquilly in the country, and does not object to being stigmatized as a sluggard and close to a coward. He had been quite rich. Although he says he was poor, the truth probably is that, in the troubles of the long Roman revolution, he had lost some property, but still had enough to keep him in comfort. (Horace says that he had no holes in his purse.) But he would not attempt to make more money, or even to recover his losses. He was a passive character.

He was passionately devoted to at least two mistresses: Plania (whom he disguises in the poetic manner as 'Delia'), and a woman with the sinister name of Nemesis. The second was a greedy, conscienceless creature who loved nothing but herself and cash. The first was not much better. Neither brought him much happiness. Yet what is most striking in his life is his almost entire subservience to them. Rich, handsome, talented as he was, with the world at his feet, he preferred to be dominated and tormented by two tramps.

> I do not care to win renown, my Delia: let me
> be called a lazy coward, only be with you.[1]

[1] Tibullus 1.1.57-58.

He tried without much success to get Delia to live with him on his country place, and promised her she could be the mistress, in every sense.

> A farmer I shall be. Delia will guard the harvest
>   in hot sunshine upon the threshing-floor;
> or she will supervise the grapes heaping the wine-vats
>   and watch the white must trodden by nimble feet . . .
> Let her direct the work, and govern all the workers,
>   while I love being nothing in my home.[1]

Curious, is it not, to see such weakness, such self-surrender, in a Roman, in one of the race that had conquered the western world? This is not 'the desire of the moth for the star', the selfless devotion of the troubadour to a distant princess, the adoration of an almost unattainable beauty, which has in it something of ideal goodness. This is not even the unwilling subjection of a man to a strong and dangerous woman, as was the passion of Catullus for Clodia. This is something more like masochism, deliberate self-torture, the humiliation of a man before a woman who is not even strong, but merely cheap and bad. It is close to the death-wish. In fact, we notice that when Tibullus speaks of his love for Delia or Nemesis, he often mentions his own death. After saying

> I do not care to win renown, my Delia: let me
>   be called a lazy coward, only be with you . . .

he immediately goes on:

> And when my last hour comes, let me still look at you,
>   and, dying, clasp you with my feeble hand.

[1] Tibullus 1.5.21–24, 29–30.

Then you will weep, when I lie on the pyre, my Delia,
then you will give me kisses mingled with tears.[1]

He did in fact die young—apparently in his thirties. It is impossible for us now to determine whether he was physically delicate, worn by the troubles of his time and by the efforts of soldiering; and, because he felt a premature death approaching, clung too eagerly to any woman who would give him the semblance of affection together with the authority a sick man needs—like George Sand—or had some psychical weakness on which ruthless women fed until they wore him out. Certainly he is a new moral phenomenon in the social history of Rome.

Yet we do notice one thing about his poems. This is that he equates country life with health, and equates eager love, war, greed for money, and other passions, with madness or illness. To be well—he says again and again directly or by implication—is to live among the fields and the trees, to work on the land or at least to enjoy its presence; and yet so many powerful forces call us away—away from life towards sickness and death.

Horace, inimitably tactful, felt this too. In his short letter to Tibullus, he pictured him hopefully as 'strolling among the healthy woods'—he uses an odd word, *reptare*, which implies very slow cautious movement like that of a grazing animal, a plant, a reptile, or a sick person: 'stroll' is too jaunty to convey its full meaning. Towards the end, he reminded him that all human beings are subject to the cardinal passions, and encouraged him to enjoy life day by day. The implication is that Tibullus was not doing so.

The style of Tibullus's poems is a clue to the secret of his life. They are not disorderly, half-crazed, disorganized: they are neither frenetic nor psychotic. But they are weak, filled with anticipations of death, confessions of spiritual invalidism, fascinated examinations of his own moral impotence. The Romans all loved drinking, but Tibullus's second elegy is the first poem in

[1] Tibullus 1.1.59–62.

which any Roman says he is planning to drink himself into un-
consciousness to forget an unhappy love-affair.

Still, the poems are carefully designed and beautifully phrased.
Although the man who wrote them was in grave psychical
trouble, he was a well-balanced artist. In his early youth—if his
brief biography is correct—he had been a gallant soldier, decorated
for courage; but there is not a trace of that in his poems. There
he appears as a defeated man: scarcely hale; seldom happy, except
in the quiet countryside.

Here is the best-balanced, healthiest, and most successful of his
elegies. It is a description of a charming Roman religious festival:
the Ambarvalia, held every spring to purify the fields from evil
influences, and to beg the deities of corn and wine for their kindly
protection and favour. In it, stage by stage, we see the rite com-
pleted: the invocation of the divinities, the worshippers attending
in ritual purity, the prayer, the sacrifice, and then the feast and
rejoicing—during which Tibullus sings a song praising country
life as the root of all civilization, and then a second song praising
his other devotion, naughty sexual adventures. He was really two
men.

> Keep holy silence. We must purify the fields
>   with rites passed down from early ancestors.

> Come, Bacchus, with the sweet grape-clusters hanging from
>   your horns. Come, Ceres, garlanded with wheat.

> This is a sacred day. Ploughman and earth must rest,
>   the heavy ploughshare hang at rest on the wall.
> Unharness all the yokes: let the oxen stand and feast
>   at the full manger, wearing crowns of flowers.
> Everything must keep holiday: no spinster girl
>   must touch the heaped-up wool with skilful hand.
> You too, stand far away, do not approach the altars—
>   you who last night enjoyed the pleasures of love.
> Purity pleases heaven: all must wear clean garments
>   and purify their hands with running water.

Now see, the sacred lamb moves towards the burning altar,
　　with worshippers white-clad and olive-crowned.

Ancestral gods! We purify the farms and farmers.
　　Do you repel all evil from our limits:
let not the crop, with lying shoots, deceive the sower,
　　let not the tottering lamb fear the quick wolf.
Then shall the countryman, beaming from a fat harvest,
　　heap mighty logs upon the blazing fire,
while crowds of children (signs of a farm's prosperity)
　　build cottages of sticks before the hearth.

My prayer will be fulfilled—see there! the sacrifice,
　　perfect and whole, proclaims the gods are pleased.

Now fetch me out the smoky casks of old Falernian,
　　open the jars of fragrant Chian wine.
Let good drink bless the day, for it is no disgrace
　　to souse and stagger at a festival.
But everyone must shout a toast, 'Health to Messalla!'
　　and in his absence let us cheer his name.
Messalla, conqueror of the Aquitanians,
　　whose triumph glorifies your ancient race,
be with me now in spirit, inspire me, while my song
　　gives thanks to all the gods of the countryside.

I sing the country and its gods. They taught mankind
　　to turn away from acorns (their first food),
and they first taught us how, by joining beams together,
　　to make a little home roofed with green leaves;
they too (the legend says) first trained to servitude
　　strong bulls, and first made rolling wagon wheels.
Then barbarism vanished; then orchards were planted
　　and fertile gardens drank the nourishing streams;
then golden grapes were trodden for their generous liquor,
　　sober water was mixed with careless wine.

The country brings full harvest, when in blazing summer,
    year after year, the earth lets fall her golden hair.
The frail bee, in the country, gathers up the flowers
    laboriously, to fill sweet honeycombs.

It was the farmer first who, tired with constant ploughing,
    sang rustic poems in a steady rhythm,
and, after a full dinner, first played country music
    on a dry oat-stalk, to the festive gods.
A farmer, red-besmeared with lees of Bacchus' wine,
    first, though inexpert, led the dancing choirs,
and won a memorable gift, best of the herd—
    a he-goat, to increase his scanty wealth.
A country boy was first to weave wreaths of spring blossoms
    to decorate the antique gods of the home.
The handiwork of dainty girls comes from the country—
    the soft fleece grown by a pure white sheep:
that is the work of women too, who turn the distaff
    and whirl the spindle round with agile thumbs;
meanwhile some busy indefatigable weaver
    sings, as the swinging loom-weights clash and ring.

Once in the country too, among the cattle, Cupid
    was born, among the fierce untamable mares.
There first, untrained, they say he practised archery—
    but ah! how skilful now he has become!
He aims no more at animals. Girls are his targets,
    and he enjoys shooting down gallant men.
He wastes the youngsters' money. He compels old fellows
    to talk like fools at an angry woman's door.
It is Love who guides the girl, stepping in secret silence
    over her guards in the dark, to meet a youth,
breathless with fright, trying each step ahead on tiptoe,
    feeling her midnight path with outstretched hands.
What misery to be tyrannized by Love! but ah!
    bliss, to enjoy his soft and favouring smiles!

Come, holy spirit, to our feast. But leave your arrows,
  I pray you, hide away your blazing torch.

Now, friends, sing praise to Love's great godhead: summon him
  to help our herds—and, secretly, ourselves.
No, openly and unashamed. Our prayers are drowned
  by jolly shouts and squealing clarinets.
Sing, dance, hurrah! Already Night is harnessing
  her chariot: dancing golden stars appear;
and after them will come, silent on wings of darkness,
  Sleep, and black Dreams on hesitating feet.[1]

And so, with fading chords like those which conclude Mendelssohn's music for *A Midsummer-Night's Dream*, closes one of the finest elegies in the Latin language.

The Romans did not have a very high conception of godhead, but they had a strong sense of religious duty. It is touching to see how even this rather sensual and frivolous young poet becomes earnest and responsible, feels himself to be both master of the household and priest of the gods, on this solemn occasion. The cult of the fields, one of the oldest in Rome, was one which lasted long after others had become mere formulae. Walter Pater, in the first chapter of his Roman novel of conversion, *Marius the Epicurean*, has an eloquent description (based partly on this poem) of its power to hold and to charm even a youth more thoughtful than Tibullus.

Yet even in this admirable elegy we can see traces of the conflict which was fatal to him. Most of it is about country life, a healthy and happy existence, with simple love-affairs leading to simple marriages and 'crowds of children'. The paean of praise to the life of the farmer as the origin of poetry, music, drama, and other arts may be a little artificial, but it was in line with contemporary theory about these matters, and it was a valuable offset to the idea of Italian townsfolk that all peasants were half animals and half plants. But then Tibullus drags in Cupid (with a rather

[1] Tibullus 2.1.

forced transition), and in a moment he has left nature and the
healthy fields far behind, and is in the city, where old men court
arrogant courtesans and rich men's mistresses elude their guards at
midnight: themes of sophisticated love-elegy, and wholly in-
appropriate to the atmosphere of naive piety and healthy jolli-
fication which fills the rest of the poem.

The country meant health and peace for him. But the city
meant excitement and passion, the lure of the forbidden, the
delights of sophisticated naughtiness. Could he have tasted all
those pleasures without allowing them to wear him out, could he
have returned in time, like Horace, to the natural life of woods
and streams, fields and gardens, reading a little, talking to his
neighbours, and writing, he would have been a healthier and a
happier man. If our estimate of his style is correct, he would have
become a finer poet. To read the whole of his work, sixteen
elegies, is to see a constant conflict in a soul too delicate to endure
it. It is like watching Thomas Gray trying to write Baudelaire's
Flowers of Evil.

THE DARK WOODS

Tibullus never tells us where he lived. 'In the country,' he says,
rure, and no more. His biography does not say. Only Horace's
little letter tells us: 'in the district of Pedum'.

Pedum was an ancient city on a strategic height near Rome,
which was captured by the Roman general Coriolanus in 488 B.C.,
struggled to keep its independence, and was at last destroyed by
Camillus in 338. The survivors became Roman citizens (more or
less) but the city disappeared. Nothing remained of it except its
name as applied to the district which it had once ruled: the district
of Pedum. But we know roughly where it was—on the road from
Rome to Praeneste (now Palestrina) about nineteen miles from
the capital. (Strange to think of those savage and bloody wars
between little cities only a day's march away from one another;
and yet these wars were part of an enormous and important
historical process.) Those primitive settlements were almost all on
steep hills strongly defended by nature. Pedum probably lay under

one of the little Italian towns which are now perched on hills in the same neighbourhood—perhaps Zagarolo, or Gallicano. There is nothing very Roman about them today, but the country near them has changed very little.

It is a strange region. It might be in the heart of a distant and isolated province, although it is less than twenty miles from a great city.

Around Rome itself stretches the broad, noble, gently undulant Latin plain with its ring of hill-towns. It is full of long spacious views. There, when the sun goes down,

> the quiet-coloured end of evening smiles
> Miles and miles.[1]

But take the road which runs south-eastward towards Palestrina, and after ten miles or so you suddenly find yourself in different territory. The views close in. Hills rise steeply on all sides. Pathways twist and recurve along cool glens and down sloping valleys. All around there are dark shadowy woods.

You reach Gallicano by taking a side road into this region. Deeper and deeper the narrow highway works into wooded hills. Glimpses of the town can be caught through thick trees. Finally you drive into a cleft cut through sheer rock for some fifty yards. It is like entering a fortress.

Gallicano is a poor place, which looks frightened and hostile. For many centuries its inhabitants tilled the fields and the vineyards lower down in the valleys, and climbed the steep hill at night to sleep in safety from disease and marauders. They still have a wary look. The town is only six or eight narrow streets, rising steeply up a rocky crest. The houses themselves are like outcrops of stone, hard, small, forbidding. On the way out, you can stop and look up to houses perched bird-high on a cliff above, and down to a field a hundred feet below the wheels of your car.

Outside Gallicano, the country, although secretive, is more genial. It is a fertile land, full of groves, massed with powerful

[1] Browning, 'Love among the Ruins'.

chestnut-trees, rich with green shade and the sound of water, quiet and shadowy. The peasants in the fields are red men—as red as American Indians; as red as the paintings of their ancestors on the Greek and Roman vases. Huge white oxen graze in the lush grass, with their backs to the sun, and long horns gleaming. And now and then a pair of them, yoked together, drags a slow wagon along the dusty road. In their strong handsome faces and their steady lurching walk there is something of Roman determination.

'Healthy forests,' said Horace in his letter to Tibullus. They are healthy in summer. On a day when the plains around Rome bake like the floor of a huge oven, when the city streets are funnels of flowing heat mixed with drifting smells, this 'district of Pedum' is a cool and gracious oasis.

Yes; but there is something else. There is something too quiet and secretive about this district. There is what Robert Frost calls a 'darkness, not of woods only and the shade of trees'. To celebrate a rite of spring here, with a feast of sacrificial lamb, and wine, and dancing afterwards, would no doubt be gay. It would be pleasant to see the oxen tug in the harvest, to watch the threshing (with or without Delia counting the bushels), and to help in treading out the new wine. But at other times this place might be less healthy than Horace believed. It would not always be visited by Bacchus, grape-garlanded, and Ceres, wreathed with wheat-ears. In the summer silences, the voice of Faunus, speaking unintelligible prophecies, might be heard far among the woods. In the winter, wolves would howl among the glens, or the wind would howl as cruelly as wolves.

Healthy it may be, the district of Pedum. But there is a darkness in its valleys, there are a mystery and a hint of cruelty in its air. After seeing it, we begin to understand why Tibullus preferred the fever of city life and love to these haunted shadows; why he wrote about the country only in springtime; and why, at the close of his happiest poem, there came

> silent, on wings of darkness,
> Sleep, and black Dreams on hesitating feet.

VI

OVID

THE most sensual and sophisticated of the Roman poets was born and brought up in a small town in a remote part of Italy, among simple, healthy, rather primitive people. This was Ovid. Publius Ovidius Big-nose was his name, *P. Ovidius Naso*—doubtless because of the bold features of one of his ancestors. Nor far from his home we have found the tombstone of one of his kinsmen, Lucius Ovidius Big-belly (*Ventrio*). The Mediterranean peoples often say that a man with a big nose is a sexual athlete. Nothing in Ovid's life or his poems contradicts this idea. Although it was Ovid's ancestor, not himself, who got the nickname, yet perhaps Ovid's friends agree that it was quite appropriate.

Ovid's birthplace lies in the remote and difficult province named the Abruzzi. This region lies due east of Rome, facing towards the Adriatic sea. Although it is only a few hours' drive from the capital city and the populous western provinces, it has been, until recent years, almost a medieval country, where religion is profound and primitive, where folklore and superstition fill people's minds, where custom is strong and change is resisted, where life is never easy, usually hard, and sometimes savagely cruel. The province of the Abruzzi is surrounded by mountain ranges; it contains the highest of all Italian mountains, the Big Rock (Gran Sasso, Grande Saxum), a good nine thousand feet high and seldom free from snow; it has deep forests, in which live wild boar, wolves, and bears. For centuries it was preserved as a lonely and almost roadless area, because if it were made easy of access it might become an avenue through which some power from the north could invade the kingdom of Naples and the States of the Church. All that has gone now, and new highways have been built into the Abruzzi. But change takes a long time; and in Italy spiritual change moves more slowly than material change. The villages are still very small and lonely. From time to time one sees a religious procession winding among them: banners borne by thin young men with burning black eyes; crowns and robes carried by lovely girls and watched reverently by haggard women of middle age: all very poor, and all deeply, bitterly in earnest.

Ovid describes his own home several times. Once, giving his autobiography towards the end of his life, he says:

> Listen, posterity, and learn who was the singer
>   of those delicate love-songs you enjoy.
> My native land is Sulmo, cool and rich in water,
>   a good ninety miles distant from Rome.[1]

But earlier, in one of those same love-songs, he goes affectionately into detail:

> My home is Sulmo—one-third of Paelignia:
>   a little place, but healthy, bathed in streams.
> Even when the summer sun stoops and splits the ground
>   and when the savage Dog burns in the sky,
> the liquid waters wander through Paelignian meadows
>   and green grass flourishes in the soft soil.
> The earth is rich in corn, richer still in grapes,
>   and here and there brings forth the berried olive.
> Beneath the little plants, refreshed by gliding brooks,
>   the earth is moist, and dark with shady green.[2]

[1] Ovid, *Tristia* 4.10.1–4.
[2] Ovid, *Amores*, 2.16.1–10.

And at the end of his first book of collected poems, as he says good-bye to love-elegy, he contrasts his insignificant birthplace with his own astounding success, and sets himself boldly up as a parallel to Catullus and Vergil.

> Find a new poet, Mother of the tender Cupids.
>   This is the last page of my elegies.
> I sign them as a son of the Paelignian land
>   and not ashamed of my frivolity.
> I hold (in case it matters) an ancestral knighthood
>   and no new revolutionary rank.
> Mantua boasts of Vergil, Verona of Catullus,
>   I am the pride of the Paelignians—
> who took up arms in honour for their liberty
>   when Rome trembled before Italian swords.
> Some stranger, looking at the little city walls
>   of Sulmo, rich in rivers, small in acres,
> may say, 'Diminutive you are, and yet you bore
>   a mighty poet—therefore you are great!'[1]

These few lines tell us virtually all Ovid wished us to know about his birthplace. It was a little town called Sulmo. It lay in a cool valley, with plenty of water. So much of Italy is bone-dry for half the year that both the ancient and the modern Italians have always thought a landscape without a river was little more than a desert. A spring which never dried up, even in the hottest days of the Dog-star—like Horace's Bandusian fountain or the springs of Clitumnus—had something divine about it. A valley where rivers and brooks flowed all summer long was blessed. Northerners scarcely appreciate this until they have spent a hot season in the south. Our rivers flow on and on, month in, month out, perhaps dropping a few inches in the summer and rising in the winter. But I remember walking through Juvenal's country, between Rome and Naples, and tramping across the dry bed of the Garigliano, and shuddering at it just as the Italians do. It was a

[1] Ovid, *Amores*, 3.15.1–14.

channel some fifty yards broad, obviously full of torrential water
in the winter and spring, but in July bone-dry, oven-dry, a bed of
hot stones with a few scattered meagre pools here and there,
quivering under the lash of the sun—what Eliot calls a

Dead mountain mouth of carious teeth that cannot spit.

A few days later, when I saw the Clitumnus emerging quietly and
lavishly and deathlessly from the earth and winding away through
its fertile valley, I could feel what the Romans felt as the blessing
of water.

Ovid tells us that the country was devoted to the staples of
farming: wheat, vines, and some olives. It still is. He speaks with
much pride of his fellow-countrymen: the Paelignians, tough
independent tribesmen, who fought hard in one of the most
terrible of all Rome's wars—the war in which the Italians rebelled
against the special privileges of Roman citizens. The Italians even
declared Italy a free non-Roman republic. They chose a fresh
capital and called it Italica: it was the new Paelignian city of
Corfinium, seven miles from Sulmo. Although the revolt failed,
the Italians won their point, and were admitted at last to full
citizenship.

All that happened about 90 B.C., nearly fifty years before Ovid's
birth, and was recalled only as a heroic but obsolete episode. The
grievances had disappeared. The stalwart courage of the Paelig-
nians was still remembered. Ovid himself was not a brave man.
His gallantry was confined to duelling with pretty girls. As he
said himself, he thought every lover was a soldier, and Cupid
conducted a permanent war. But, like many another sophisticated
writer, he enjoyed pointing to his own primitive origins. Sturdy
peasants, good fighters: he was proud to spring from them—
although of course his family had been local notables for several
generations. . . .

Seldom has there been a grosser contrast between a man's origin
and his writings. The Paelignians were sturdy, brave, simple;
doubtless they had their own strong moral code. Ovid, the only

Paelignian poet, was hedonistic, soft, sophisticated, and cheerfully immoral. This is not *our* judgment. It was the judgment of his own contemporaries and successors. He was punished for his immorality, more severely than any Roman poet had ever been so punished; a later Roman critic said 'he educated his entire generation, not only in the techniques of love [i.e. love outside marriage] but in its epigrams and ideas'; and again and again in his own poetry he attempts to defend himself against criticism by explaining that he himself leads a virtuous life although his poems are naughty. He convinced no one. His poems are very naughty indeed. Their chief subject, almost their sole subject, is heterosexual gratification. They explore almost every known aspect of it, from rape to incest, from impotence to abortion, from the techniques of seduction to the best positions for intercourse. He himself repeatedly said that—except for poetry—love was the only thing that absorbed his interest. His acute knowledge of women's psychology, the astonishing variety of adventures he describes (many of them such as lie quite outside ordinary experience), and the unmistakable tone of personal emotion which constantly reappears in his poems, make it quite clear that he deserved the title given him in the Middle Ages, the Teacher of Love.

Nevertheless (as Hilaire Belloc put it), 'his sins were scarlet, but his books are read.' Ovid is wicked; but he is an exquisite writer. His style is full of charm; his poetry flows on as effortlessly as a stream; its grace is as pervasive as perfume, and as delicate and intimate as the couch of silk. He perfectly expresses one aspect of the attitude of the Latin peoples towards love: not the overpowering, almost selfless passion of Romeo and Juliet, but the unscrupulous gaiety of Don Giovanni with his many hundreds of conquests. Both in the apparently pure lyricism of the song in which Mozart's hero sets out to seduce the innocent peasant girl, Zerlina, ('Là ci darem la mano') and in the cynical humour of Leporello's catalogue of his master's triumphs throughout Europe ('Madamina'), we can hear the true Ovidian notes and recognize the true Ovidian charm. With all his naughtiness he is polite. He seldom uses a shocking phrase and never a dirty word. Part of the pleasure of reading him is to appreciate the tact with which he can say wicked things in words as pure as sunlight.

The rest of his charm lies in his effrontery. When he describes
the love of a woman for a man, he is often serious, sometimes
almost tragic. When he describes the love of a man for a woman,
he is rarely serious—although he may occasionally have tears in his
eyes. In the second book of his *Loves* there are two characteristic-
ally witty poems, placed deliberately together. The first is a bold
protestation of innocence, addressed by Ovid to his mistress
Corinna.

So, must I always be accused of new offences?
   Although I win, I hate these endless fights!
If, in the marble theatre, I should glance around,
   at once you see a woman to complain of;
or if some handsome girl looks silently towards me,
   you notice secret messages in her eyes.
If I admire one, you tear out my hair by the roots:
   if not, you think I am concealing guilt.
If I don't look lovesick, you call me cold to you;
   if I do, I'm dying for another woman.
In fact, I wish I had committed some real sin,
   for guilty men accept their punishment;
but with your random charges and your vain suspicions,
   you make your anger seem pointless and cheap.
Just look—even the wretched little long-eared donkey,
   used to the whip, will never change his pace.
Now here is a new indictment! Your deft maid Cypássis
   is charged with violating her lady's bed.
God forbid that I—if I *should* think of sinning—
   should ever choose to love a wretched slave!
What gentleman would care to mingle with a servant,
   and fondle a back seamed and scarred by the whips?
And then, consider: she makes your hair elegant,
   she is your favourite maid, light-fingered, neat:
would I approach a girl who was so loyal to you—
   to be repelled, and then denounced as well?
I swear by Venus, by the air-borne archer's bow,
   that I am innocent of any guilt.[1]

[1] Ovid, *Amores* 2.7.

This sounds absolutely sincere, doesn't it? He does not even protest too much. He does not give too many proofs of his own purity; nor does he (as some lovers, when caught in a tight spot, have done) smother his mistress with affection: in fact, he does not once call her by her name, Corinna, far less use any endearments. This is the very voice of injured innocence. We may remember, for a moment, that Ovid was trained in legal oratory, and specialized in pleading difficult cases in which emotional persuasion was needed. But when we hear these simple, natural words, we forget that he is collecting types of argument; and in particular, when he refrains from quoting Greek mythology, we moderns find his speech sounds quite sincere. We would rather have a poet compare himself to an ill-used donkey than to an unjustly suspected hero. And Corinna herself?

Apparently Corinna was convinced also. The elegy ends in peace. There are no tears, no counter-accusations, no further defences: silence and a mute regret.

The next poem in Ovid's book, opening with an elaborately beautiful compliment, is addressed to Corinna's maid, Cypassis. The tone is calm. Corinna, we gather, has left; or—more probably —this interview takes place well out of her sight and hearing in a quiet little side-room. Ovid enters, with a smile of persuasive gaiety and courtesy, and begins:

> Expert in ornamenting hair in a thousand fashions,
>   but pretty enough to set a goddess' curls,
> Cypássis, my sophisticated fellow-sinner,
>   deft at serving *her*, defter for me—
> who could have betrayed the mingling of our bodies?
>   how did Corinna sense your love-affair?
> Surely I did not blush? or stumble over a word
>   that gave some evidence of our stolen love?
> Of course I said the man who loved a servant-girl
>   must be a hopeless idiot—of course!
> But the Thessalian hero loved the slave Briséis,
>   captive Cassandra fired Mycenae's king.
> Achilles and Agamemnon fell. I am no stronger:
>   so, *honi soit qui mal y pense*, say I.

Yet when she fixed those furious eyes upon your face,
    I saw the blushes covering all your cheeks:
therefore (if you recall) I shouted all the louder,
    calling Venus to witness my good faith.
Kind goddess, please absolve my mental reservations,
    and let the warm winds blow them out to sea.
And now, tan-skinned Cypássis, will you not repay me
    with sweet embraces, for my loyalty?
Do not object—I've earned it. Don't invent new dangers:
    to please *one* of your masters is enough.
If you are foolish and refuse, I shall betray us,
    and turn state's evidence for both our guilt,
and tell your lady where I was with you, Cypássis,
    how often, and in what positions, too.[1]

The best Roman elegies, like the best Greek epigrams and the best Japanese *haiku*, always suggest more than they say. So at the end of this little poem, we can see the girl Cypassis burying her dark face in her hands, and looking up with her eyes glinting through her fingers, and surrendering once again: so that Ovid is perfectly happy, with two women, both distrusting him, both loving him, and both—how shall we put it? cheated and betrayed? or dominated by him and left, beaten once again in the old game at which he was an undisputed champion?

SUCCESS AND DISASTER

Ovid was born in 43 B.C., just a year after the removal of Julius Cæsar. His father was a knight, and his family had been knights for several generations: which means that they were both rich and respected—not rich enough to take part in the government of Rome as senators, yet rich enough to be local dignitaries and to have access to the best circles in Rome. He and his brother were given a first-class education in Rome (where his brilliance in speaking was remembered after his death), and then sent on a finishing tour in Greece and Asia Minor.

[1] Ovid, *Amores* 2.8.

His first book, *The Loves* (from which the above two poems are taken), came out while he was still in his twenties. It had an enormous success—all the more because it was so frivolous. The love-poems of Catullus, published about 60 B.C., were filled with unbearably genuine passion, suffering, and conflict. The love poems of Tibullus, which appeared about 26 B.C., were melancholy though graceful, and perfectly sincere. The love poems of Propertius, the first volume of which was published about 30 B.C., were a curious mixture of genuine passion and detached cynicism. In Ovid's *Loves* (issued in 23 B.C. or so) younger readers were delighted to find that there was 'no zeal', nothing heart-breakingly sincere, only eloquence, which often lies, and charm, which is in the eye of the beholder, and the art of enjoyment, which fascinates all young men and women.

He followed *The Loves* with a much more serious and beautiful work: *Letters*, or *Ladies of the Past* (*Heroides*). This is a remarkable collection of letters in verse, each from a famous heroine of Greek mythology to her lover or husband, written at some great crisis of their love. They average less than two hundred lines each; but each holds the equivalent of a modern full-length novel, in dramatic episodes related or implied, in variety of emotional tone, in subtle exploration of the different relations between men and women, and in psychological subtlety. If Ovid could not take his own amours seriously, he could at least watch, with fascinated sympathy, the pageant of a woman's bleeding heart.

After that, about A.D. I, came his most delightful and sophisticated work, *The Art of Love*. This is a treatise on the technique of finding, winning, and enjoying a lover. In order to take full pleasure in this exquisite poem, one must either do as Charles Lamb did with the Restoration comic dramatists, laugh heartily at all the characters and the intrigues, consider them all to be as inhuman and as elegant as butterflies, and admire them for a grace utterly divorced from morality, or else transport oneself into the world of light opera, where one always takes a bottle by the neck and a woman by the waist, where everyone has enough money, no one has any ideals except good looks, good manners, and physical pleasure, where all thoughts of family duty and even of serious work are forgotten, and one is always on the way to

Maxim's to dance with Lolo, Dodo and Joujou. Perhaps the only thing wrong with *The Art of Love* is that it is a good deal too systematic, too determined. It reminds us of those elaborate treatises on other, more conventional sports—the five-hundred-page manual of trout-fishing, with statistics of water-temperature; the three weighty volumes on fox-hunting, with many illustrations and an appendix on the longest runs in the last fifty years; the complex mathematical dissertations on canasta, bridge, and poker. The chief advantage it has over them is its perennial light-heartedness and its rapidity of movement: it is something between a didactic poem and a parody of didacticism. Yet, there is something surprising, even shocking, in the spectacle of a Roman knight, one of the nation which has conquered the western world, sitting down to write twenty-three hundred lines on the techniques of making love. The energy, the determination, the systematic drive of the Romans had been diverted from great aims to little ones, and—as the elegiac poets themselves often said —the young men cared nothing for victories won in war and secured by statesmanship: their only triumphs were gained in bed.

Immoral Ovid was, but he had high standards in art. He seldom repeated himself. He made nearly everything new when he touched it. He kept aiming higher. After *The Art of Love* he started two remarkable poems. One, *The Metamorphoses* or *Transformations*, was a sort of *Golden Bough* in poetry: a collection of all the strangest myths (those containing miraculous trans-figurations) from the epoch of creation to the death of Julius Cæsar. This wonderful book has been the source of stories, poems, plays, fables, pictures, allegories, and operas ever since it was published. The other poem remained incomplete: it was a survey of the chief religious festivals of Rome, with accounts of their origins: *The Fasti* or *Calendar*.

Before either of these books was completed, Ovid was accused of high treason and sent into exile for the rest of his life. Aged fifty, he was banished to the remote frontier post of Tomis, now Constanza on the Rumanian coast of the Black Sea. He lingered there for nearly ten years, writing pathetic letters home, begging the emperor for mercy, protesting his partial innocence; then he died, still unforgiven. No one to this day knows why the most popular and distinguished poet in Rome was suddenly arrested and expelled from life. He himself knew, but did not dare to say. Still, when we observe that, at the same time, the emperor Augustus banished his own grand-daughter Julia for having an illicit love-affair with a young nobleman (who himself left Rome), that Ovid admits his *Art of Love* had something to do with his trouble, and that the rest, according to Ovid's own account, was a scandal which he *saw* but did not *share in*—then it is not hard to conjecture that the young princess did something exceptionally indiscreet, either under the inspiration of *The Art of Love* or possibly to the accompaniment of the appropriate passage from it: that Ovid was among the spectators; and that he suffered as an accessory before and during the fact. The emperor was famous for his mild temper, and for his ability to forgive, if not to forget. But he had tried hard, very hard, to clean up the moral abuses which had been wrecking his own family life and the family life of many of the best citizens of Rome, the moral abuses which Horace, in a powerful ode, denounced as a dreadful disease growing steadily worse from generation to generation, and which, a century later, Juvenal was to describe as intolerable and ineradicable. Now he saw Ovid as the spokesman and the teacher of all those who opposed him, and a man who had encouraged the corruption of his own daughter and perhaps assisted at the corruption of his grand-daughter. For such a man, banishment was a mild penalty.

In fact, Roman society, during the first century before and the first century after the birth of Jesus, was torn asunder by a number of severe conflicts. Any one of them would have been enough to destroy a weaker people. There was a conflict of economic interests—the poor, the rich, the middle class, the slaves, all competing with one another. There were bitterly contested political conflicts: conservatives against revolutionaries, Romans against Italians and provincials, powerful individuals against the sovereign State. There were financial conflicts within Italy, and all over the empire. There were grave moral conflicts, particularly in sexual matters: to some observers, it seemed as though what had started as a good movement for the emancipation of women from their chattel status was degenerating into an irresistible avalanche, destroying the very ideal of chastity, breaking up the structure of the family, and fatally altering the normal relation between the sexes. As women grew bolder and more independent (these observers said), they grew more selfish, more cruel, vain and irresponsible. Once they had been faithful to their husbands. Now they were disloyal even to their lovers. Divorce grew commonplace. The moral education of children was neglected, or else utterly perverted. Distinguished writers could publish sympathetic poems such as Ovid's Loves 2.13, 'On Corinna's successful but dangerous abortion'. Other distinguished writers openly displayed their homosexual deviations—although this was still going rather too far for ordinary sentiment. Rome had grown great (said her own thinkers) through rigid adherence to a set of moral standards which placed the welfare of the family and the nation above the inclinations of the individual, which despised wealth and comfort and praised austerity and simplicity and honesty, which thought of pleasure as a harmless relaxation rather than the single aim of life. Now that she was great, she seemed to be abandoning all those standards, and adopting a code utterly unworthy of her past and herself.

Statesmen, writers, philosophers, teachers, and private individuals did much to prevent the total collapse of morality. Cicero, for example, although extravagant, appears to have led a calm and sensible sexual life. Throughout his works, though he does express indulgence for silly young men sowing their wild oats, there is an unshaken confidence in strong ethical standards as bringing true satisfaction and spiritual health; he is openly contemptuous of the fake Epicureans who disguised their libidinousness as adhesion to a philosophical creed, and outspokenly bitter about such conscienceless voluptuaries as Mark Antony. Cæsar's heir Octavian, when he gained supreme power, made many attempts by legislative action and personal admonition to restore the venerable ideals of pure marriage and family life. Horace, one of his favourite poets, wrote several powerful negative odes on the theme, while Vergil's superb evocation of the toils and rewards of farming life, the Georgics, is a positive assertion of the nobility of unsophisticated, hard-working men and women, bound to each other, to their children, and to the land by ties of both duty and affection.

But the moral conflict went too deep to be completely removed. Augustus himself had three wives in succession. He took his third, Livia, from her husband while she was pregnant; then he hurried her through divorce and remarriage. His only daughter Julia, and her daughter Julia minor, went publicly and emphatically to the bad. (The elder princess's final offence was blatant, and appears to have been meant as an insult to her father. She used to pick up unknown men in the Forum during the day, and allow them to make love to her at night in the Forum, and hold wild parties on the Rostra. The Forum was the centre of the city's social and political life, overlooked by the noblest symbols of its religion. It was from the Rostra that her father had promulgated his laws against the spread of sexual vice.)

The same conflict appeared in the work of many of the poets. Catullus celebrated his own adultery with Clodia by describing it as a visit from a goddess; but later the goddess became a prostitute and a female devil. Propertius opened his first volume by describing himself as a slave of a bad cruel woman; yet by the end of his final volume he shook off much of her power, and set up an ideal of nobility and chastity which was greater than her careless vice. Horace wrote gravely of the moral degeneration of the family; yet he himself never married, and his gayest poems were addressed to pretty conscienceless girls and pretty soft boys. Tibullus knew that stern moral obligations existed, that other men lived powerful energetic lives, but he could not live up to such standards: he was content to be 'nothing in his home'.

Ovid, when we first read him, appears to be merely frivolous and gay. But, set in its own spiritual context, his poetry becomes more important and more dangerous. It is, as Augustus concluded that it was, a manifesto of sexual liberty and irresponsibility, created to counter the stern social measures of the emperor, and to offset the almost forced severity of Vergil's two great poems. The *Georgics* is a didactic poem about hard work, for small rewards, in the Italian countryside, its chief satisfaction being consciousness of duty done and kinship with the natural life of earth, plants, and animals. Very good. Ovid's *Art of Love* is a didactic poem about

hard work rewarded by delicious pleasure in the richest quarters
of Rome, its chief satisfaction being absolute freedom from the
ties of family, personal loyalty, or public morality, and the sense
of perpetual youth. Vergil's *Aeneid* is a heroic poem about a single
man who surmounts enormous difficulties and temptations and
perils in order to carry forward a majestic plan of destiny, of
which he himself is only a small part: it is all as carefully arranged
and developed as a game of chess or a classical symphony. Very
good. Ovid's *Transformations* is a huge poem, partly didactic and
partly heroic, in which neither men nor gods have any continu-
ous plan of life, both men and gods live by their passions alone,
and the entire course of history—viewed on an even grander scale
than in the *Aeneid*—is nothing more than a disconnected succession
of exciting, touching, and generally irrational incidents. Ovid even
takes up several of the stories told in the *Aeneid*, and retells them—
always in such a way as to make them more exciting and less
meaningful, shallower and more vivid, occasionally almost comic.
It is as though Byron had composed, in the style of *Don Juan*, a
poem which was designed to outdo and occasionally to mock
Milton's *Paradise Lost*.

If Ovid's *Art of Love* had been merely an unconventional book,
Augustus would doubtless have taken no action against it. It came
out ten years before the blow fell on its author. Many defenders
of absolute freedom in literature were ready to say (in the words
of a cheerful American immoralist), 'No girl was ever seduced by
a book.' It was only when women of the emperor's own family
proved that such a book could suggest and encourage and describe
corrupt acts, that Augustus banished the poet. Even then, Ovid
was not prohibited from writing poetry. True, his earlier works
were expelled from the public libraries, but nothing was done in
the way of collecting and destroying the copies of them which
were still in the hands of ordinary readers: that is why we still
possess them, after two thousand years. But still, Ovid himself was
never to return to Rome; and—unlike the invincible Marquis de
Sade in his prison—he wrote no more poems about his favourite
subjects, the joys of adultery and the techniques of evading and
flouting traditional morality.

Strange how quickly the tides of ethics shift. In A.D. 8, Ovid was banished for seeming to recommend moral laxity when the emperor was trying to raise moral standards. Almost eighty years later, Juvenal was banished for seeming to denounce moral laxity in a court where the emperor permitted corruption. Ovid never returned: he collapsed into a morass of unadmirable self-pity and unconvincing self-justification. Juvenal returned; and embarked on fiercer denunciations of Roman vice and crime than Rome had ever heard. This was a conflict which cleft the soul of Rome.

SULMO

Sulmo mihi patria est, says Ovid with the pride of a man who has risen from small beginnings: 'Sulmo is my birthplace.' Since he is the greatest man who has ever come out of the little town, its inhabitants are very proud of him: they use the initials of his phrase, *S M P E*, as the municipal motto. In the Middle Ages he was known throughout the European courts and universities as a subtle psychologist and a learned cosmologist; but then and thereafter the simple folk of Sulmo preferred to think of him as a formidable wizard, a memorable preacher, or a powerful knight. (So, in the folklore of Naples, Vergil became a sorcerer.)

Towards the end of last century, the stories told about Ovid were collected from old inhabitants of the district. These men could scarcely read and write, and they knew nothing of Ovid's poetry; but still, somehow, they knew he had been a great man.

Some said that he was an ancient paladin, so strong that only three other paladins were equal to him: they were Ciciarone d'Arpine, Razielle de Rome, and Arasce de Barlette—superb names, under which it is difficult to recognize Cicero of Arpinum, Horace, and (perhaps) the late emperor, Heraclius. Others faintly remembered the story of the rebellion of their distant ancestors against Roman domination and the creation of a new Italian capital: they said that there was once a city called Curfinia, very large, covering the whole valley, and that Ovid was king of this city.

Others told tales of his wisdom. The king of Naples, they said, never made a law without sending it to Ovid to have it 'verified'.

Ovid and 'Ciciarone' travelled throughout the world for seven years to increase their knowledge; but Ovid learnt more and knew more Latin than Cicero because he could read with his feet. (This delightful absurdity comes from the fact that there is a statue of Ovid in Sulmo, standing upon a book.) He wrote many wise books, but they are all lost today, not a scrap remains. Only once, when Napoleon was in Italy, one of his generals got hold of one of Ovid's books at Sulmo, and read it, and went quickly back to France. The result was that the French have made many marvellous inventions, giving them comfort and wealth: 'and who suffered? We poor Italians!'

Then there were legends of the places where Ovid had lived. He had a *huge* house in the town, which impressed 'Ciciarone' so much that he could only stand with his mouth open; and you know the statue at the Caffè San Giorgio, which they say is St. George on horseback? That is really Ovid as a cavalier. Some say he lived at the Morrone Monastery, because he was the head of all the monks there. Others are sure his house was outside the town, on the hillside at Santa Lucia, where the ruins are. There is a big spring there called the Spring of Love, Fonte d'Amore: Ovid used to meet a fairy lady there, and make love to her, and that is where he wrote his *Loves*. People find coins and bits of pottery there still. They say there is a treasure buried in the ruins, but 'Viddie will not allow it to be dug up. It is guarded by lions, tigers, wolves, bears, and three enormous snakes. Yet once a peasant went into a cave there among the ruins, and what do you think he found? He found 'Viddie himself, sitting in a room surrounded by barrels full of silver and gold. 'Viddie threatened him with a huge iron mace, so that he ran out, mad with terror. And still, on the night before the Feast of the Annunciation, 'Viddie drives through the ruins in a four-horse carriage, to frighten marauders away from his treasure, and makes such an uproar that he sounds like 'the train of the iron highway'.

One or two of these stories told of Ovid's prowess as a lover and of his unhappy end. It was 'Viddie, said the story-tellers, 'Viddie of Sulemone, who dared to make love to the daughter of the emperor. As a result, he was sent to the City of Siberia—far away, *mamma mia!* far away—and there he died of cold.

Sulmo is now the town of Sulmona, in the province of the Abruzzi. It is not far from Rome and Naples, as the eagle flies. But it feels remote. By road, we approach it over splendid passes which cross some of the highest mountains in Central Italy: the well-watered plain which Ovid loved is surrounded by a formidable wall of lofty cliffs and steep slopes. Up in those mountains the villages are miserably poor. Driving through them, we pass women in sombre clothes, with leathery faces, carrying huge bundles on their heads. Fodder for the hard winter must be cut from every inch of the hillsides, and carried home, either by tiny overburdened donkeys, or by the farmer and his family. Everything in these mountains is steep, hard, dry. The highland people are tanned, bony, prematurely aged. The mountain villages look like relics of the Middle Ages, filled with refugees from some long-remembered disaster, clinging to the peaks and the upper slopes for safety. Some of them have dramatic names: one is called The Castle of Yesterday.

But the road slopes rapidly downwards from those grim heights. Soon it reaches the flat rich moist plain that Ovid knew. It is heavily and prosperously cultivated, neatly fenced, well watered. The road runs across it straight and easily. The people of the plain are prosperous, plump, easy-going, comfortable of aspect. There are many holiday-makers from the cities cycling about; even the women at the well wear black silk stockings. It is clearly a good place to live, this countryside: safe and quiet, with long straight roads passing between cheerful cottages and well-tended vineyards.

The Roman town of Sulmo was quite tiny. It has been all destroyed by earthquakes. The modern town of Sulmona is larger and more ambitious, pleasantly laid out, with clean streets, quiet little piazzas, cool shops, a neat cathedral, and an atmosphere of provincial calm. Ovid is well remembered. A statue of him stands in the central square, with the inscription *Paelignae dicar gloria gentis ego*, 'I shall be called the pride of the Paelignian people'. A few score of yards away stands the cathedral, and the town hall is just behind it. As I photographed the statue, noon struck out from all the spires, and a flight of pigeons, the birds of Venus, rose into the air around the statue of the poet.

But we come closer to Ovid in the little museum of the town. It contains many finely carved Roman inscriptions, some of them only recently discovered; and many memories of Ovid. And it has a delightful statue of Ovid as he was conceived by the men of the Middle Ages. He wears a doctor's gown and cap and carries a book—because, being a poet, he was a highly educated man. He points to the letters *S M P E*, standing for 'Sulmo is my birthplace', and gazes outwards with medieval decorum.

(Some say that the statue really represents a Sulmonese poet of a much later time. It might be Francesco Marco Barbato, Petrarch's friend, who died in 1362; or Remigio Fiorentino, who translated Ovid's *Heroides* into Italian in 1554. But the pedestal says it is Ovid; and the curator of the museum *assured* us that it was Ovid.)

During the Middle Ages, the steep mountains near Sulmona were the abode of a saint, lonelier than St. Francis and almost as unworldly. He was Peter, who lived as a hermit high among the rocks of the Morrone, founded a new congregation of Benedictines called the Celestine monks, became Pope in 1294, and abdicated the Papacy within the same year, to return to the simple and mystical life which had made him great. Dante stigmatized him in a single line, as the man

who, through his cowardice, made the great refusal.

His hermitage lies a few miles outside Sulmona, among precipitous slopes. Just below it, overlooking the fertile valley, are the ruins of a Roman villa. Among these ruins, the old people used to say, Ovid still dwelt, watching over his treasure. It might well have belonged to Ovid's family, for it was built in his lifetime. Excavators who worked on the villa found that it was (like Horace's house in the Sabine country) a comfortable twelve-room place, with a fine view. Its most considerable relic now is a long wall, the wall of a colonnade or a terrace, which measures about seventy-five yards and is still standing.

To reach this region, we drive out of Sulmona by a road leading towards the hills. We turn off the highway, up a side-road blazing white with sunshine, and run into a small and unattractive village on the first slopes of the mountain wall that rims the valley. This village looks as though it had been dumped there by a garbage-removal squad. It is dirty. Sleepy-eyed girls lounge in the doorways, sketchily dressed. There is something indefinably disreputable about it, which does not come only from poverty. We drive on.

Just before the road begins to climb the steep hill towards the ruins of the villa, we reach a tall and massive building, faced with blank yellow and white, standing all alone. This was once the Monastery of Mount Morrone, inhabited by Celestine monks. But it has none of the tranquillity of a house of religion. It looks run down, and even on a hot bright afternoon, an air of wretchedness and gloom hangs over it. Two soldiers, carbine on shoulder, pace back and forward outside its gates. We ask one of them whether this is still the Monastery of Mount Morrone. It is not. It is now a prison.

We turn away sadly. It is too harshly appropriate that, just outside the birthplace of Ovid, and within sight of the house that may have been his home, there should be a prison. Prisons always look grim, and this, strongly built and terribly lonely, looks utterly dismal. We cannot see it without hearing the melancholy couplets of Ovid's lamentations in exile, and thinking, with useless sympathy, of the wretched genius eating his heart out among the remote Goths.

Driving back to Rome, through the Paelignian plain and up the slopes of its mountain wall, we think of Ovid, not in prison, but in his home of Sulmona. He wrote kindly of it, if not generously; but after we have seen the town, we observe how much he omitted. He knew his countryside far less well than Tibullus or Vergil. He cared very little for it. At best, he praises its rich farms and vineyards, and the cool waters that make them prosperous. He never mentions the people who work the land. (He speaks of their fighting ancestors, but not of themselves.) He says nothing of the splendid hills that embosom the plain. He never describes the dramatic landscapes, the bold passes, the high peaks, or even the little painful trails which are visible on every hill—signs (to us) of man's energy and courage. Ovid thought the hills and the passes were comfortless and dangerous. No doubt they are; yet they have a wild grandeur that other Greek and Roman poets would have felt. He had no eye for landscape, although he was born and brought up among some of the finest scenery in Italy. He liked Sulmo with its surroundings because it was fruitful and well-watered—in fact, a tidy farm, a large garden. As for the inhabitants, he does not seem ever to have noticed them.

One other eminent Italian poet came from the same province. This was Gabriele D'Annunzio, born in Pescara, some forty miles south of Sulmona. His character and his poetry are in a number of ways curiously like Ovid's: extremely, almost incredibly, sensual, devoted to the love of women but ruthlessly cruel to them; grace-ful and often amazingly eloquent in style, though rather too pro-lific; daringly revolutionary in subject-matter, eager to impose himself on the public even to the detriment of elder poets; and often blending extreme delicacy of expression with an unmis-takable coarseness and brutality of thought. However, D'An-nunzio had a strong sense of responsibility to the society in which he lived. In war and after war, he risked his own life many times as a soldier of his country; and he did have the penetration to admire (although he could scarcely share) the deep-rooted morality of the peasants. Some of his finest work deals with the violent passions and the strong ethical code of the Abruzzese people. Ovid had no such feeling for his fellow-Paelignians. They were rustics. When he lived in Rome, the words of praise which he preferred for himself and for others were words such as 'urbane', 'polished', 'city-bred'. A girl who would not yield to a seducer was guilty of—not frigidity, but worse: rusticity. She was behaving like a peasant, a coarse ridiculous peasant girl. When he called Corinna's maid his 'sophisticated fellow-sinner', his exact words were 'you whom I know, by our delightful deceit, to be no peasant girl'.

The Italians still think that there is an enormous gulf between the educated people of the towns and the ignorant, primitive, almost beast-like *contadini* who work the land. No doubt there is a gap, and no doubt there was in Ovid's time. But the intellectual of the cities is mistaken when he believes that his own moral values, his own sense of beauty, and even his own power of enjoyment are necessarily superior to those of the country folk. All Vergil's work proclaimed that the country was prior to the city, and was more real. The tender Tibullus echoed that thought. Ovid chose to be urbane and to despise simple rustic morality. He brought a bitter retribution on himself, and a talent which had not yet reached its full development was ruined by shallowness and frivolity.

JUVENAL

THE last great pagan poet of Rome was born about A.D. 60,
during the reign of Nero. He was the satirist Decimus
Iunius Iuuenalis, whom we know as Juvenal.

When he started his career he had no intention of becoming a
poet. He wanted to be something much grander: an official of the
Roman government. It was only when he failed of his first am-
bition that he turned to poetry. And even then he was a com-
parative failure—at least as judged by his own bold ambitions and
his resounding challenge to rival poets. During his lifetime, his
satires produced hardly any effect whatever. After his death, they
were forgotten for nearly two hundred years. It would have
astounded him, accustomed as he was to bitter disappointments
and to ironic twists of destiny, to learn that centuries after he died
the Romans would rediscover his poems, and re-publish them,
and edit them with explanatory notes, and imitate them; that he
would become one of the most popular of all Roman poets,
admired both for his burning moral fervour and for his sinewy
epigrams and for his magnificently vivid descriptions of imperial
Rome; and finally, that after he had been dead for more than a
thousand years, he would be read in lands which during his life-
time had been inhabited by barbarians, or even concealed beyond
the unexplored and infinite Ocean. The poet who wrote so
pessimistically of Fame and so contemptuously of Fortune was
crowned with glory when he could no longer enjoy it. Fate did
not smile upon him until his eyes were closed for ever.

The story of Juvenal's immortality is strange. The story of his
life is even stranger.

He came from a prosperous town called Aquinum, lying in a

fertile valley about eighty miles south-east of Rome. His family
was well-to-do: doubtless they owned fifty or sixty farms in the
neighbourhood and controlled a few businesses. Juvenal did not
have to work for a living. He went to school until he was sixteen
or so, and then joined the army, serving as a junior officer. There
was no universal military training in his time: Rome had no
dangerous foreign enemies, as yet. But if a young Roman with
money of his own wished to enter government service, he first
had to serve in the army for at least six months.

After his military service was over, he came back to his home in
Aquinum, and got some experience in local government. He was
elected mayor of the town—or rather, one of the two mayors.
(The Romans had an old and deeply-rooted distrust of unchecked
authority, and whenever they could they appointed, not one single
official, but two or more holding the same rank.) Juvenal and his
colleague were particularly honoured by being elected in the year
when they had to take the census of the township, which involved
a revision of the tax-rolls and assessment-plans, and could be
carried out only by reliable and impartial officials. He was also
appointed priest of the lately deceased and deified Emperor Ves-
pasian: another post which combined responsibility and honour.

Juvenal was still quite a young man. Perhaps he was in his early
twenties. To show his gratitude to his native town, he presented
it with a memorial of his mayoralty: a shrine or a temple. In
return the citizens set up a statue of him, bearing a complimentary
inscription saying how popular he was. The shrine and the statue
have both vanished, but the inscriptions which they bore actually
survived until the nineteenth century. They were seen and copied
by several historians and antiquaries. They are almost the sole
evidence for the earliest and happiest period of Juvenal's life.

Happy, proud, and ambitious, he left Aquinum and went to
Rome. He had served as an army officer; he had risen as high as
possible in local administration; he was a knight. Now he applied
for a post in the service of the imperial government. The emperor
and the Senate ruled the whole of the western world. In the service
of either, a capable man might go far—particularly in that of the
emperor, who controlled the armies, the frontier provinces, and
the rich land of Egypt. All that was needed was a step on the

ladder, and then . . . One could rise to be a powerful general; governor of a province; even (conceivably) the emperor of Rome.

But Juvenal never set his foot on the ladder. For some reason— we can never know why—he received no appointment, however insignificant. Possibly a bitter censorious nature was apparent in his manner even then. Lieutenants and assistant under-secretaries are expected to look bright and co-operative, not coldly critical; to smile and say 'Certainly, sir', not to maintain a morose and dubious silence. The months passed. The years passed. Juvenal was still unemployed. He had enough to live on, but he felt his talents were being wasted. Year after year, he stood in the corridors of the emperor's palace, and visited influential noblemen, hoping to be noticed, perhaps to be called in to fill a sudden vacancy. But he was always passed over. And gradually he saw that the posts of greatest value were allotted, not to the men who best deserved them, but to those who had the right friends at court, who knew how to flatter, who could share a dirty secret with a powerful minister, or toady to a ballet-dancer who had caught the emperor's fancy. For some time he brooded on this. He had been dabbling in literature as a pastime. Now he tried his hand at verse, and produced a short lampoon on the corruption of the court and the government. A few lines of it have survived.

Actors have far more power than gentlemen. Do you
still haunt the homes of old and noble families?
Now ballet-dancers hand out rank, and make promotions.[1]

Perhaps he thought this was too vague to be dangerous to him; perhaps he was so angry that he did not care. He was terribly, almost fatally, wrong. The cruel, suspicious, and vengeful Emperor Domitian read the little poem, interpreted it as a sneer at the vileness of his own court and his army (which it was), and sent Juvenal into banishment for the rest of his life. All his property was confiscated by the government. His wife (it is likely that he had married a proud Roman lady) divorced him. He was sent off

[1] Juvenal 7.90–92.

under military guard, penniless and homeless, to the remote frontier of southern Egypt, to live for the rest of his days in the garrison post of Assuan. He had nothing left in life, and nothing to hope for except death. He was about thirty years old.

Other men have languished for many years in prison, or in the exile which is almost as unbearable as prison. Juvenal's predecessor Ovid lingered for nearly ten years on the remote and icy shores of the Black Sea. There are today, over half the world, prison-camps where intellectuals who dared to criticize a despotism are sweating and starving and going mad and dying by inches. It was only something like a miracle that saved Juvenal. The emperor Domitian was murdered. All those whom he had imprisoned and exiled were set free and allowed to return to Rome. Their careers were broken, their livelihood was gone, but they were once again free citizens.

Juvenal had now no hope of a government career. He was too old, and too discouraged. He had no profession. He had no trade. For some years, apparently, he still 'haunted the homes of the old families': a free dinner, or a little gift of money in lieu of dinner, kept him alive day after day, while he grew older and bitterer. Hanging about the mansions of the rich, he rubbed shoulders with many a penniless writer; he heard many a poet recite enormous tragedies (on Greek themes, rehandled for the thousandth time) and world-shattering epics (*The Labours of Hercules*, *The Battle of the Centaurs*, endlessly repeated). All that he heard seemed to him to be equally tedious, and repetitive, and—what was worst— unreal. One kind of poetry remained which could both tell the truth and be original: yes, and powerful. This was verse satire. The vices and the crimes of Rome, thought Juvenal, were so atrocious that they demanded to be turned into poetry filled with satiric realism, epic grandeur, and tragic intensity. And so, at some time late in his forties, Juvenal faced a recital hall, and began, with a memorable cry of boredom and indignation:

So! Must I always be only a listener? never reply
though bored to death so often with hoarse Cordus' epics?[1]

[1] Juvenal 1.1–2.

These words, whimsical but violent, containing both a summary of his own experience in poetry and a description of his poetic aim, open the first poem of the first book of Juvenal's satires: some four thousand lines of the best satiric verse ever written, and the last truly original creation of any magnitude in Latin poetry, until the rise of Christian Latin literature.

His satires are almost all about Rome in the first century after Christ—except for one, the ferocious fifteenth, which deals with the barbarous cruelty of the Egyptian fellaheen: a subject which has not changed very much in two thousand years. He takes us into the noisy, thronged, hurrying streets of the capital of the world, and shows us the changing spectacle of their crowds. During the day the soldiers of the praetorian guard stride arrogantly forward in their hobnailed military boots, and the crowds are thrust apart by the steady advance of the Rolls-Royce of ancient Rome, the litter, cushioned and curtained, carried by four sturdy slaves. At night the great noble walks slowly home from his banquet, surrounded by friends and dependants and slaves, his purple cloak glowing in the darkness like a reverberation of the flaming torches, while the poor man lights his solitary way through the unlighted streets with a tiny taper in one hand shielded by the other, and hopes to avoid both the heavy pots which crash down from upper windows and the drunken bully waiting at a dark corner, flown with insolence and wine. Juvenal is the supreme satirist of big city life.

He never mentions his home. Or rather, he never speaks of it directly. But at the end of one of his most pungent poems, he makes his old friend Umbricius say (as he leaves the city for ever, disgusted with its corruption and its passion for money):

> Good-bye. Remember me. Whenever Rome
> returns you, eager for rest and peace, to your Aquinum,
> ask me to visit you and your Ceres and your Diana
> from Cumae. Unless your satires are ashamed of me,
> I'll stride in my heavy boots through your cool fields to
>   hear them.[1]

[1] Juvenal 3.318–322.

'Your Aquinum' is Juvenal's way of telling us that Aquinum was his birthplace and his home. The next line names the chief goddesses who were worshipped in the town. And it was near Aquinum that the inscriptions bearing the name of Juvenal were discovered, although, quite recently, they have been lost again.

AQUINUM

There is Aquinum, the old Volscian town,
  Where Juvenal was born, whose lurid light
Still hovers o'er his birthplace like the crown
Of splendour seen o'er cities in the night.
                                    —LONGFELLOW.

Aquinum was rather a distinguished town. It produced famous men. After Juvenal, it became the birthplace of a Roman emperor, Gaius Pescennius Niger, one of the hard military adventurers who cut his way to the throne by the sword. In the Middle Ages, at the castle of Roccasecca a few miles away, was born the greatest philosopher of the medieval church, the successor of Aristotle, the angelic doctor, St. Thomas Aquinas. Not far to the east stands the huge precipitous hill of Monte Cassino, once crowned by the ancient Benedictine monastery which preserved so many priceless books through the Dark and Middle Ages, and which was taken with fire and slaughter after the German army converted it into a fortress in 1944. Now it has been rebuilt, and stands as austere and white as one of its own monks, on the summit above the cemeteries of the soldiers who fought to keep it and to take it.

Aquino, the modern successor of Aquinum, suffered sorely in the same campaign. It is now being rebuilt. The central square has been laid out, spacious and sunny, with trees and one or two quiet little caffès. But facing the new buildings there are dismal ruins, uninhabitable and hopeless. It is a poor little town at present. Its people wear dark clothes. They look as though they had not recovered from their sufferings, but were trying to be cheerful.

On one side of the square there are open fields: perhaps, later, they may become a park. On one side there are ruins. From the other two sides, narrow streets curve away, climbing and descending little slopes as though clinging to them for safety. There is a Juvenal Cinema—closed at present; there is a Juvenal Inn—which the guide-book tactfully describes as 'extremely unpretentious', *modestissimo*; there is little else.

As we pick our way along the cobbled streets, it becomes more and more evident that this is a medieval town. It was not the Roman town at all. Juvenal's home was a flourishing township with twenty thousand inhabitants, lying in the plain near the river Melfe. This is a cowering village of two thousand people at most, crusted along rocky slopes, comfortless and sad. Juvenal's Aquinum was destroyed in the Dark Ages by the German invaders—the tough Lombards who pushed down the Italian peninsula from the Alps, dominated some of the country for a time, and gave their name to the northern province of Lombardy. The survivors of that catastrophe built a new Aquinum some miles to the east, near a castle where they could take refuge in any later invasion; and this is now Aquino. Again and again in Italy, we see how the peaceful prosperity of the Roman empire was followed by the dangers and disasters of the Dark and Middle Ages. In a peaceful valley, among fertile fields, lie the ruins of a Roman town, often traceable only by the faint lines of its market-place or a few pillars built into a farmhouse. High above it, on the peak of a hill, wedged into the topmost crags and slipping nervously down the gentler slopes, like a cat that has run up a tree and clings there spitting at the savage dogs, is its medieval successor. The snarling face of the cat is usually a castle, on the loftiest peak of all. Rome fought many wars, but during the five centuries when she had no foreign enemies to threaten her heartland, the towns and cities of Rome grew and prospered in the rich Italian plains, unfortified and happy and secure.

Facing westward on the outskirts of medieval Aquino stands a tall church, built in the twelfth century. It is the largest building in the whole place: dark, cool, quiet. Much of it was made with the stones from Roman Aquinum. The marble steps leading up to its entrance are good Roman work; in the porch stands an

elegant Graeco-Roman stone coffin; inside there are capitals from
Roman pillars, a relief showing a Roman funeral, and other
classical decorations. A quiet little priest makes us welcome, and
shows us the beauties of the lonely sanctuary; but he tells us that
the place contains no inscriptions with the name of Juvenal.

Leaving the church behind us, we walk off into the country-
side. At first, nothing is to be seen except farmland, on each side
of the narrow road. It is hot. Why did Juvenal boast of his 'cool
fields'? Then we realize that the air circulating between the trees
and beneath the vines which are trained from one tree to another
is in fact gentler and more gracious; surely, also, the Romans
irrigated this land more generously than the modern Italians do.

Vineyards; fields; little lanes; quiet countryside. No sign of
Roman remains—until we look down, and discover that we are
walking on one of the least picturesque, oftenest forgotten, and
most useful of all Roman works: a road. This is in fact the Latin
Highway, a narrow but well-drained and stoutly-paved pike
which runs all the way from Rome to Capua. Juvenal himself
names it in the last word of his first satire; and he travelled along
it whenever the greedy city returned him

eager for rest and peace, to his Aquinum.

A few steps further on, and we find ourselves walking beneath a
solid Roman arch, now (like so many old things in Italy) renamed
with a Christian overtone: St. Lawrence Gate. This was the old
gate of the Roman township. The remains of the town wall on
each side still join on to it, in powerful blocks of pale limestone.
It is a very early gate, built perhaps under the late Roman republic;
and when we stand under it, we see that it is not only a gate, but
a vault. Therefore it has been called the only surviving example of
a Janus Gate: one of the strange gates which were both passages
and doors, and therefore, like the two-faced god himself, could be
said to look both ways. Certainly, with its heavy walls and its
stout vaults, this gate may give us the model on which we can
reconstruct the gates of the republican city of Rome.

Near the Gate, round a curve of the Highway, suddenly appears a graceful little building, roofless, and overgrown with ivy. It is an abandoned church. But into its framework are built relics of Roman Aquinum and of Roman paganism. Outside the building there is an inscription commemorating some local dignitaries. Around the entrance are decorations in stone, graceful and vivacious: the winged spirit called a 'genius' which was to become the Christian idea of an angel; flowers and leaves twining upwards; branches with birds perching among their twigs. At the corner of the old church a fig-tree looks into what was once the sanctuary, with its roots plunging deep beneath the walls. Juvenal of Aquinum once asked 'What is fame?' and answered:

An inscription
bitten into the stones that shelter our ashes, the stones
which can be broken apart by the rough strength of a fig-tree.[1]

Weeds and grass grow where once there was the floor of the church. Dragonflies dart and hover above them. Around the door wild mint and wild chestnut flourish happily—together with that strange American invader of Italy, the spiky cactus. It looks like a cruel Mayan deity, but in these regions it is only a sign of the fertility of sun and soil.

Leaving the lonely little church and walking onwards among the vineyards, with the Latin Highway still firm beneath our feet, we begin to feel that we shall never find any more traces of Juvenal's Aquinum. Every inch of the land is cultivated. Generations of spades have turned it over. The soil is humming gently as it drinks in the sun. No one appears ever to have lived here, still less to have built the massive buildings which are the expression of the Roman will to power and permanence.

Down the highway glides a solitary cyclist. He is a brown man of about thirty-five, wearing a white shirt and work pants. We halt him.

[1] Juvenal 10. 143–145.

'Good day, sir. Excuse me. We are looking for Roman remains, Roman ruins. Can you be kind enough to direct us?'

'Ah, you speak Italian! It will be a pleasure.' (Dismounting.) 'Roman remains?'

'Yes, sir. I understand that the Roman city of Aquinum lay in this beautiful plain. There should be some Roman buildings, or relics of buildings.'

Pause. Meditation.

'Fortunate that you asked me, sir. They are near where I work. Please come with me.'

'But you were going in the other direction?'

'No importance, sir. It is a pleasure. This way, please.'

We never learned his name. As he walked his bicycle back up the hot road in the late afternoon, he told us he had been a sergeant in the Italian army. 'The captain told me to lead the unit at maximum speed towards the front. We had no maps!' Later, he was picked up by the Germans and sent into Bavaria as a slave-labourer. He escaped during an Allied air-raid, made his way south over the Brenner Pass ('seventeen days sleeping on the ground'), and so home to his wife. 'But look, over there, sir, there is the Roman building.'

The Roman building is a couple of masses of masonry, solid walls of stone and concrete, about ten and fifteen feet high. They stand alone, apparently unconnected, at the edges of a field. The field is full of what the Italians call 'Turkish grain'—maize with only one ear to each stalk. Nothing beside remains, of what was once a powerful building. It was seen and drawn in a much fuller state of repair, by several visitors to Aquinum during the seventeenth and eighteenth centuries. 'The old people,' said our friend, 'thought that no human beings could have built such walls. The work of devils, they called them.'

These, it seems, are the last relics of the Capitol of Aquinum, the central temple where the trinity was worshipped, the trinity of Jupiter, Juno, and Minerva. The remains of fine statues were found among its ruins. The best opinion is that it was built in the time of Augustus himself, and so was old and venerable when Juvenal was an official of Aquinum.

When the empire became Christian, this building was converted into the first cathedral of Aquinum, and dedicated to St. Peter. It was called Old St. Peter's, and is still remembered under that name. It is known to have existed as late as A.D. 1137, but it was destroyed at some indefinite time after that, and now it is practically gone.

Early in the nineteenth century several scholars saw the cathedral (converted from a temple), took measurements of it, and drew its remains. Its value was recognized. But it continued to lapse into ruins. The mayor of a small neighbouring village, Castrocielo, was entrusted with the plans of the Roman town, and was directed to preserve the Roman relics. Shortly afterwards a great quantity of Roman sculpture and architecture was sent away as useless rubble, to be employed as foundation stuff for the new bridge over the river Melfe, on the highway from Rome to Naples. I am glad to say that the official who permitted this outrage was discharged, but by that time the damage had been done.

At an earlier stage, a marble statue of a woman, found in Aquinum, was exported and sold in Rome; it is now in the Berlin State Museum. It is thought to be a Demeter, changed (by the alteration of the head) into a memorial statue.

There are a few more relics of Roman Aquinum, but very few: a circular depression with remains of seats, which was 'the grass-grown theatre' at which Juvenal once smiled; traces of walls; an arch which was built in the age of Augustus and is now half sunk into a paper-mill. The rest has been ploughed under, and forgotten. Soon it will all be absorbed by the fertile Italian fields and the industrious Italian farmers.

Our guide escorts us back towards medieval-modern Aquino, a mile or more—although he has been working in the fields since early morning, and although his dinner is waiting for him. He is unwilling to quit us until we assure him that we now know the rest of the way into the town. We thank him. He wishes us a good journey. With some difficulty, we push a little gift into his shirt-pocket 'for the new baby'. With embarrassed eloquence, he thanks us, mounts his bicycle, kisses his hand to the lady, and rides off, a soft-hearted, hard-working, optimistic, likeable Italian.

In this fertile plain, then, lay the town that Juvenal knew. He speaks of it only once, but then warmly; and even when he had become a disappointed Roman parasite, he looked back on towns of its type with affection. In one of his best satires he wrote of a man leaving the capital, to settle in just such a town and to escape the corruptions and dangers of the great city.

> If you can tear yourself away from the circus, a fine
> house at Sora or Frosinone can be bought
> for no more than a year's rent of your super-slum in Rome.
> You'll have a garden, and a shallow well which needs
> no bucket to help irrigate the tender plants.
> Live with spade in hand, the boss of a neat garden
> which could provide a lavish vegetarian banquet.
> After all, it is something, even in a lonely corner,
> to make yourself the landlord of a single lizard.[1]

And in the same poem he gave a delightful description of the informal manners of the small Italian towns, where no one ever wore the irksome Roman toga except to be buried, and public entertainments, instead of being rich and complex like the games of the Roman amphitheatre, were rare and simple.

> To tell the truth, there is a lot of Italy where
> no one puts on the toga till he dies. And even
> when in the grass-grown theatre they celebrate
> a civic holiday, with the long-expected return
> of a well-known farce, when the gape of the actor's pallid mask
> scares the country children into the laps of their mothers,
> there you will see the same dress for one and all,
> both in front seats and behind: the costume for high officials,
> the mayors of the town, is a plain clean white shirt.[2]

---

[1] Juvenal 3.223–231.
[2] Juvenal 3.171–179.

In these vignettes and a few others, we can see Juvenal remembering the community where he once admired the small peaceful gardens, and was himself one of the 'high officials, the mayors of the town'. He thinks of it with a kindly indulgence, an only slightly satiric nostalgia.

But there is hardly anything left of Juvenal's Aquinum: only a wall of a temple here and there, and the outline of a 'grass-grown theatre'. The thriving town which he knew was wrecked by barbarian invaders, then abandoned, then ploughed under. In some other lands, the ruined cities of the past are left to moulder alone. They become haunted places. The wild beasts of the desert dwell there, and the owls dwell therein, and they shall no more be inhabited for ever. But in fertile Italy, the ploughs and the people come back, generation after generation, and sink their predecessors under new fertility. The present, in Italy, constantly buries the past.

THE LOST INSCRIPTION

Yet once, not so long ago, there was a tangible relic of Juvenal near this place: a stone inscribed with his name, or at least the name of one of his family. (We cannot certainly tell, because the forename was missing when the inscription was seen and copied, but the place and date are right.) It said:

THIS OFFERING TO CERES

IVNIVS IVVENALIS

CAPTAIN OF THE (?th) DALMATIAN BATTALION

MAYOR IN THE CENSUS YEAR, PRIEST

OF THE DEIFIED VESPASIAN

VOWED AND DEDICATED

AT HIS OWN EXPENSE

The stone is lost now. No doubt it was misused by the same vandal officials who destroyed or shipped away other relics of old Aquinum. But we know where it was.

The scholars who saw and copied it said it came from the neighbourhood of Roccasecca, a village near Aquino; and, to be exact, from an old church called St. Peter in the Country, S. Pietro a Campea. So we leave Aquino, and drive up a steep hillside to the village of Dryrock, Roccasecca—about four miles away, but clearly part of the same community, and administered from Aquinum in Roman times. It was in the castle above this village that St. Thomas Aquinas was born.

Our arrival creates some surprise. The winding streets see no traffic except patient donkeys, powerful women with bundles on their heads (the inspiration for the architect who first made them hold up the lintel of a temple), and an occasional local bus. No one here has ever heard of the church of St. Peter in the Country, but lots of little boys and girls and caryatid women peer into our car with a wild surmise. At last we are lucky enough to find the local postman, who does know about the church of St. Peter in the Country; and he finds a youth who says he can guide us to it. The youth, Pasquale, is about twenty, five foot six, and a hundred and twenty pounds: he wears a T-shirt and an old pair of army trousers; unemployed but cheerful, and a remarkably good walker. He neither pants nor sweats—nor pauses.

Pasquale does not really know where St. Peter's is; but he has a good general idea. Under his guidance we drive out of Roccasecca to a point where a footpath leaves the main road. There the cross-country uphill walk begins, and (as the Sibyl told Aeneas) 'this is the work, and this the labour'. Down a long pebbly track past farmhouses; across the bed of the river Garigliano, dry, parched, and blinding, full of hot white pebbles rounded by past winter floods; up hillside after hillside between rows of olives and thickly terraced vines, all basking in the noonday sun. It is as arduous to live and work in a hot country like this as in a cold land like Scotland. We overtake a solid matron wearing a dark blue dress, rope-soled shoes, and not much else: she has been in Roccasecca selling eggs and chickens, and on her head she is now carrying back a basket full of vegetables. She lives beside St. Peter

in the Country, and will show us the way. Off she strides, over
the rough gravel—she must make this trip many times a year,
sometimes over wet and slippery glair, sometimes, as now, over
the burning marl; up and up, with Pasquale after her, and myself
panting in the rear. After half an hour we reach a little hilltop,
fertile and green, with a spring of blessed water: she says a curt
adieu and vanishes.

There is the church of St. Peter in the Country. It stands on an
eminence, overlooking a hundred square miles of fruitful plain.
This is a splendid site, and if it only had plentiful water, it would
be a delightful place for a home. Around the church are some low
greyish-brown farm buildings. No sign of life, except for the
confidential cluck of hens.

St. Peter's is an oblong church which has lost its roof. It con-
tains a fresco painting behind the altar, showing St. Peter himself
landing in Italy—a symbol, meant for the early congregation, of
the triumph of Christianity over the heathen gods. Paganism
lingered for a long time in the remote country districts. The very
word 'pagan' means 'from the back country'. But now the church
is empty and deserted, with no trace of anything in it older, or
newer, than the sixteenth or seventeenth century.

But beside it, within a few yards, on the brow of the hill, is a
Roman wall about six feet high, with the remnants of an arch,
and traces of a terrace, now almost absorbed into the olive planta-
tions. The experts say the masonry belongs to the first century
A.D. This then could have been the site where Juvenal's family, the
rich landowners, had their mansion. Beside it Juvenal dedicated
the shrine of a goddess during his term as mayor, and the grateful
townsfolk erected a statue of him here. The shrine has been
demolished, rebuilt perhaps into a Christian church, now deserted
too. The mansion has almost vanished. The bronze statue was
converted into weapons for some Lombard warrior. The inscrip-
tion was sent away to be turned into concrete—but fortunately not
before it had been copied and perpetuated. There remain the
spacious view which Juvenal saw as a young man; the quiet he
longed for amid the noise and stress of Rome; and the inex-
haustible cheerfulness and fertility of the Italians who have in-
herited and reclaimed his land. No wonder the Romans built an

empire. They began by colonizing one of the most difficult and rewarding lands in Europe. The personal disaster of Juvenal was simply that he felt in himself this power of colonizing and administering, and wished to use it on a far greater scale; but—as in all despotisms—he found no worthy career open to his talents.

ROME

THE GATE

BIG cities are both hateful and enticing. Men are often miserable while living in them, and yet they cannot leave them. Better the vigour and the violence, the corruption and the charm, the conflicts, agonies, and adventures, than the moribund calm of a village or the petty concerns of a little town. So they feel. They are constantly pulled by that magnet which, year by year, draws more and more men and women towards the populous centre, where the millions struggle and shout and live eagerly and die without regarding one another. And yet they constantly think of pretexts for leaving the city, and make plans for their escape.

Few men have ever felt this ambivalent emotion so keenly as Juvenal. Although we believe he had a home in the country town of Aquinum, and know he later acquired a farm in Tivoli, yet in all his poems from the first to the last he remains attached, with loathing and loyalty, to the city of Rome.

In one of his finest satires—often copied by later poets—he sums up nearly all the arguments which a man might use when finally deciding to leave the metropolis. Since he himself cannot utter them without seeming to be insincere, he puts them in the mouth of his friend Umbricius—a man of about his own age, with a similar education and the same disappointed ambition. Embittered and ageing, Umbricius is taking his slender capital and investing it in a small house in the lonely old decaying village of Cumae (at one corner of the bay of Naples), where nothing much lives but the memory of the thousand-year-old prophetess, the Sibyl. Juvenal cannot go with him, but he approves his friend's decision.

To journey from Rome to Cumae, it was necessary to leave the city at the south-eastern corner, by a gate leading through the antique walls. The main road was the Appian Highway, laid by the formidable statesman Appius Claudius nearly four hundred years before Juvenal was born. It held on to Cumae, then pushed further south. A few miles out of Rome, the Latin Highway split off from it. This was the road which would take Juvenal to Aquinum. It is easy to see that the departure of his friend Umbricius from that very gate along that road was a symbolic fulfilment of his wish to leave the city and return to his boyhood home.

Umbricius is a poor man. He will have to walk all the way to Cumae. To carry his furniture and books and clothes, he has hired a wagon drawn by mules. Since no wheeled traffic is allowed within Rome during the daytime (except government transport), his slaves have carried his property to the city gate to meet the wagon. While they are loading up, Umbricius and Juvenal walk away from the busy gateway and the noisy highroad, to bid each other goodbye; and Umbricius delivers a long and powerful denunciation of city life.

While his whole house was loaded on a single waggon,
he stopped at the old arch, the wet Capena Gate.
Here once king Numa used to meet his midnight mistress;
but now the sacred spring, with grove and shrine, is rented
to Jews, whose furniture is a bundle of straw and a basket:
for every tree must now bring in a regular income
to the state; the nymphs are evicted; the wood goes begging.
We turned down to Egeria's Glen, towards the grotto
now spoilt and artificial. The waters would surely possess
a deeper sanctity, if they were closed in a green verge
of grass, and the native stone were not polluted by marble.[1]

This is an admirable setting for the satire. Umbricius hates the huge cruel city so bitterly that he will not linger within its walls. Together with his friend Juvenal, he passes the gate. (It was 'wet'

[1] Juvenal 3.10–20.

because one of the great aqueducts, the Marcian Waterway, crossed its arch, so that water dripped down between its stones; but no one knows why it was called Capena.) Outside the gate, the two friends turn into a little park, once sacred for its memories of an ancient sanctity. This is Egeria's Glen.

Egeria was a mysterious goddess, a spirit of springs and running water. She was a friend of the Italian muses, the 'Ladies of Song', the *Camenae*. She was the lover of the second king of Rome, Numa Pompilius, who was the Moses of his people and laid down most of their religious laws. It was here, in this tiny glen, in the cave beside her own spring, that Numa met her. Even when Rome had grown to be a mighty city, this was a venerable spot, surrounded by ancient shrines. But now (says Juvenal) a group of vagrants has been allowed to rent the grove and settle in it. For him, the Jews are not merchants and financiers, but something much less powerful, more like gypsies, fortune-tellers and poor pedlars. (Their furniture is a basket and a bundle of hay, he says— either because he has noticed them keeping food warm in a hay-basket during the sabbath, when cooking is forbidden, or because he means they have literally nothing but a bundle of hay for a bed and a few dishes and clothes in an easily portable basket.) He does not hate the Jews. He merely thinks it is miserable that a place once sacred in Roman tradition should now have lost all its religious aspect and be rented out to a group of foreign squatters; and that it should be so desecrated in order to bring in a little more revenue to the city.

Then his eye turns to the cave and the spring of the goddess. They have not been rented out or neglected. On the contrary, they have been too carefully and too elaborately decorated. The cave has been encrusted with choice marble, and the spring enclosed in a sumptuous marble basin. It is beautiful. But it is artificial. The spirit, the divinity which once dwelt there when the water moved through its natural path, was a deity of nature; and she has been put to flight.

So, even before Umbricius has opened his mouth to denounce Rome, we are made aware of his chief charges against it. First is the exaggerated importance of money—as shown in the poverty with which he himself is afflicted, in the meanness of renting a sacred place to a tribe of nomads, and in the lavish extravagance which has ruined the rest of the sanctuary. And second is the destruction of old Roman traditions by the irruption of new religions and of foreigners who do not wish to be assimilated. Covered with inappropriate marble and swarming with beggarly strangers, Rome has ceased to be itself. It is unrecognizable. It is uninhabitable. Although Umbricius does not explicitly foretell it, the fall of Rome has begun.

Even today we may find the place where Juvenal said goodbye to his friend.

The road running south and east out of Rome follows the route of the ancient Appian Highway. It is busy with traffic. Yet it is strange to notice that its surroundings are quieter and emptier than they were in Juvenal's time. On the way out of the city, it led behind the Palatine hill, rich and heavy with the palaces of the emperors, and past the magnificent Circus. Now there is nothing of the Circus Maximus but a huge empty football field, with a few relics of the thousands of stone seats; and the Palatine is a lonely heap of ruins, half choked by trees and undergrowth, curved and rounded under the accumulated earth and humus of many centuries. Palaces still lie there, deep underground; and the grandeur of the Hill can be felt only when we gaze up at the vast outworks of the imperial citadel, the towering buttresses and broken arches which, like the escarpments of a cliff, disappear into the hillside with its descending waves of green.

In this region the ancient wall of Rome has vanished; and so has the Capena Gate. Traffic now streams out of the metropolis along several different avenues, divided by grassy tree-planted strips. Walking along one of these, we reach a huge shapeless block of masonry inscribed

THE BEGINNING OF THE APPIAN HIGHWAY.

This is a mediaeval ruin, the last thing above ground to show where the Roman wall crossed the highway at this point. It was not far from here, and in surroundings not very dissimilar—a quiet little park just within earshot of the traffic—that Juvenal walked with his friend. Three or four men lie about, with heads pillowed on their arms, enjoying the siesta; couples sit whispering on the benches. It is peaceful. In such a spot Umbricius uttered his farewell to Rome.

Today, the spring of Egeria is lost. It is buried, and the ruins of the shrine which enclosed it probably lie within the grounds of one of the religious houses which stand to the left of the Appian Highway, on the slopes of the Caelian hill. Lord Byron looked for it, with Juvenal in his mind, and was misdirected to a ruined 'nymphs' grotto' a mile or two outside the walls of old Rome. He recalled Juvenal's complaint about the artificiality of the earlier decorations and was glad to find this spring surrounded by flowers. 'Egeria!' he cried,

> The mosses of thy Fountain still are sprinkled
> With thine Elysian water-drops; the face
> Of thy cave-guarded Spring, with years unwrinkled,
> Reflects the meek-eyed Genius of the place,
> Whose green, wild margin now no more erase
> Art's works; nor must the delicate waters sleep
> Prisoned in marble—bubbling from the base
> Of the cleft statue, with a gentle leap
> The rill runs o'er—and, round—fern, flowers, and ivy, creep
> Fantastically tangled.[1]

Byron's punctuation is as capricious as his emotions. Still, it is delightful to see him, admiring Juvenal so deeply, now trying to revisit a spot immortalized in Juvenal's poetry and (even although mistaken) recreating it by his imagination.

Rome has never quite forgotten her traditions. Today, beside the park, runs a shady, uncrowded street. It is called the Avenue of the Valley of the Camenae. On its left rises one of the Hills, the Caelian—studded with large villas, occasional embassies, and

[1] Byron, *Childe Harold's Pilgrimage*, 4.116-117.

religious institutions. At its end lies a square named after the venerable king Numa Pompilius himself.

Just before the square, there stands a decrepit building, which was evidently once a Christian sanctuary and is now derelict. It is called the Church of St. Mary in Tempulo. It is all that is left of a monastery founded early in the Christian era, which was deserted and decaying six hundred years ago. Clearly it was made of materials taken from a pagan building; it contains Roman columns and arches; slabs of Roman marble have been built into its walls. Perhaps in this way the shrine of the kindly instructress Egeria was reconsecrated in the name of the Virgin Mary. Now her shrine also has been abandoned. Yet still the Appian Highway bears the ceaseless flow of traffic from Rome to the south; still the pines and beeches make a sanctuary of coolness and calm between the road and the city; and over the place there broods, quiet-breathing, a gracious female presence.

THE BOILING STREETS

Where did Juvenal live in Rome? We do not know, but we can make a fairly good guess.

His friend Martial, the Spaniard who came to Rome and became a famous epigrammatist, returned to Spain after collecting just enough money to retire on. From his farm among the woods of Calatayud, he wrote a poetic letter to Juvenal, describing his happy, lazy country life, and contrasting it (a little maliciously) with the existence he had shared with Juvenal, wandering among the crowded streets of Rome and laboriously climbing the steep sloping avenues of the capital, to pay dutiful morning calls on the rich and the powerful.

> While you, Juvenal, feverish and restless,
> may be drifting through the clamorous Subura,
> or footslogging it up Diana's hillside
> while you visit the mansions of the mighty,
> costumed formally, sweating in your toga,
> up one Caelian hill and down the other . . .

—I (Martial goes on) have come home to my farm, where I never wear the stuffy gown of ceremony any more, where I need not rise from bed until nine or later, and my walks are not through roaring city streets but among the whispering oak woods.[1]

The hills which Martial mentions were occupied by the mansions of Roman noblemen and millionaires—as they still are. But the Subura—that was something different. Anyone might wish to have a big house on the Caelian hill, among cypresses and fountains; no one wanted to live in the Subura. Juvenal himself began his satire on the city by saying:

> Although sadly distressed at my old friend's departure,
> still I approve his choice, to live in empty Cumae
> and be the Sibyl's only fellow-citizen.
> It is next door to Baiae: pleasant sands, and charming
> seclusion. Rather a barren rock than the Subura![2]

(Juvenal actually names the 'barren rock'—it is the hot volcanic offshore island of Prócida near Naples.) This is emphatic enough. The Subura is evidently the most crowded, noisy, and unpleasant part of Rome. Juvenal mentions the quarter again and again, always with distaste and contempt. He calls it 'the boiling Subura', he speaks of its noisy clatter (apparently it contained schools for waiters, where servants were taught how to carve, using wooden models—it is a strange coincidence that one of its New York counterparts, the Bowery, is full of shops selling cook-knives and restaurant equipment); he contrasts the Subura with the cool and airy Esquiline hill; and once, in a peculiarly loathsome description of a horrible dinner-party, he says that the poorer guests, instead of sharing the best of the fish course, a moray from the deep waters of Sicily, get an eel that looks like a snake, or a pike fed on sewage—

> born on the banks of Tiber, fat with the gush of the drain,
> and well accustomed to scavenge the pipes of central Subura.[3]

[1] Martial 12.18.
[2] Juvenal 3.1-5.
[3] Juvenal 5.105-106.

Yet the Subura was not exactly what we should call a slum. It was not so low as the Bowery. It was noisy, and busy, and common, and full of naughty ladies; but it was quite near the rich and fashionable quarters of Rome. It lay between the Esquiline hill and the Viminal. You could walk from it into the centre, the Forum, by passing through the smart shopping street—the Argiletum, which was the Bond Street of Rome. Formerly, towards the end of the Roman republic, the Subura seems to have been fairly chic. Julius Cæsar had a house there, no doubt because it would enable him to combine the enjoyment of wealth and distinction with the appearance of friendliness towards the working class and the poor. It was there that Cynthia lived, apparently with a rich and suspicious lover, when Propertius first made her his mistress. Long afterwards, her ghost recalled their clandestine meetings.

'Can you forget those wakeful nights in the Subura?—
    the well-known window, open for my escape,
  through which I dropped the rope, night after night, and
        dangled,
    climbing down hand by hand into your arms?'[1]

But by Juvenal's time it had apparently deteriorated, as many quarters once rich and fashionable have deteriorated in modern cities.

Juvenal's friend Martial pictures him wandering through the Subura. Juvenal himself mentions it often, as though obsessed by it. It is a legitimate guess (although it is no more than a guess) that he lived in that district, or near it. We know from inscriptions found there that there was a Jewish community, with a synagogue, in the Subura: that may well have been where Juvenal derived his strong interest in the Jews of Rome, and his knowledge (very unusual for a Roman born) of their manners and beliefs. There is something about the surge and energy of a busy street which both attracts and repels a contemplative man. It is easy to imagine

[1] Prop. 4.7.15–18.

Juvenal wandering restlessly among the boiling crowds, like Dickens through the roaring, filthy streets of Victorian London, at once appalled, repelled, amused, and fascinated. He himself has described his experiences in one of the finest passages of his satires.

> Most sick men here die from insomnia (of course
> their illness starts with food undigested, clogging
> the burning stomach)—for in any rented room
> rest is impossible. It costs money to sleep in Rome.
> There is the root of the sickness. The movement of heavy
>   waggons
> through narrow streets, the oaths of stalled cattle-drovers
> would break the sleep of a deaf man or a lazy walrus.
> On a morning call the crowd gives way before the passage
> of a millionaire carried above their heads in a litter,
> reading the while he goes, or writing, or sleeping unseen:
> for a man becomes sleepy with closed windows and comfort.
> Yet he'll arrive before us. We have to fight our way
> through a wave in front, and behind we are pressed by a
>   huge mob
> shoving our hips; an elbow hits us here and a pole
> there, now we are smashed by a beam, now biffed by a barrel.
> Our legs are thick with mud, our feet are crushed by large
> ubiquitous shoes, a soldier's hobnail rests on our toe. . . .
> Newly mended shirts are torn again. A fir-tree
> flickers from the advancing dray, a following waggon
> carries a long pine: they swing and threaten the public.
> Suppose the axle should collapse, that axle carrying
> Ligurian stone, and pour a mountain out over the people—
> what would be left of the bodies? the arms and legs, the
>   bones,
> where are they? The ordinary man's simple corpse
> perishes like his soul.[1]

So we have thought, many of us, as we fight our way through

[1] Juvenal 3.232–248, 254–261.

crowds at the rush-hour, battle for a foot of standing-room on a bus, or twitch back from an onrushing stream of ruthless, mindless, ceaseless traffic. So thought Juvenal as he struggled with the whirlpools of the boiling Subura.

Centuries passed. The great city fell. The population diminished, in wealth, in numbers, in vigour. The streets of the city were partly deserted. Thousands of tons of drifting dirt and silt from periodical floods and débris from earthquakes gradually filled them up. The great houses, the rickety tenements, the busy shops fell into ruin. Squatters built hovels here and there: these too fell into ruin. Sometimes an entire region of the city would lie derelict for many years after its inhabitants had been cut off by a pestilence. During these periods of darkness, the Subura gradually disappeared—although its name survived. The little old church now named St. Agatha of the Goths was known in the Middle Ages as St. Agatha above the Subura, and is still sometimes called St. Agatha by Subura. In more modern times, as the city was re-occupied, repopulated, and rebuilt, the buildings above the Subura region were laid out in a largely new pattern. Yet fragments of the very pavement which Juvenal trod, and inscriptions which he may have read, have been unearthed beneath certain modern streets, in a quarter almost as cheap, as busy, and as noisy as the old Subura.

Some of these fragments were found below St. Vitus Street, the Via di San Vito. This is a narrow road about fifteen feet wide, in which a neglected Roman archway stands above a smelly open-air lavatory. Others again were excavated in the old Via Santa Lucia in Selci. This street follows the same slope as the old Subura Hill, the *cliuus Suburanus*. Today it starts from another lavatory, and runs downhill past a tall lonely medieval tower—a relic of the Middle Ages, when the city was broken up into the armed camps and fortifications of rival noble families. It goes on past several very ancient churches. (Very close is St. Praxed's, where the Renaissance bishop of Browning's witty poem wished to lie in eternal peace, to 'feel the steady candle-flame, and taste Good thick strong stupefying incense-smoke'). Finally, it tapers

off into squalor. A beggar asks the visitor for ten lire. Loafers
stand about the corners, examining each stranger with bold and
hostile eyes. Smells circle faintly around in the warm air. At a
crossroads near by, a huge sign advertises the competence of a
doctor who claims to cure venereal diseases. A few hundred yards
away we come upon the remains of the mighty public baths built
by the emperor Trajan during Juvenal's lifetime. (The 'axle carry-
ing Ligurian stone' was the axle of a heavy truck carrying in
building material for this enormous structure.) Now a cheap fair
has been set up among the ruins. Electric bulbs are strung across
the avenues; there is an irregular clack-clang from shooting-
galleries, and shouts and whirrs from booths offering games of
chance. In the other direction, we soon come upon a big modern
square, the Piazza Vittorio Emanuele. Around it there is a noisy
market, with fruit-stalls, meat-stalls, and stalls full of cheap cloth-
ing standing flimsily on the footpath. In its centre is one of those
contrasts which Rome loves and protects. Among the grass and
flower-beds rises a powerful amorphous mass of brickwork, with
all its decorative marble facing long since torn away, and yet with
some trace of antique power and beauty still haunting it. This
building is surrounded, day and night, by a group of roaming
animals, which crawls and stretches, fights and parades and begs,
hides and dozes and strolls and lounges like a mass of slowly
moving parasites. The brickwork is all that remains of a huge
monumental fountain, once decorated with statues and flowers.
It may once have stood in the gardens of the rich and noble
family called the Lamiae. The animals are homeless cats, who live
there in the park, and are fed by casual patrons as well as receiving
an official dole from the city of Rome.

Could Juvenal now return to the city which repelled and
fascinated him, it would give him a grim delight to see the
elegant fountain of the proud Lamiae, now dry, stripped, and
shapeless, surrounded by 'clients' and freedmen reincarnated as
a host of starveling cats; and there, close to his own Subura, a
urinal exhaling its acid fœtor beside a crumbling triumphal
archway.

CITY OF THE SOUL

Few of the Latin poets were Roman born. Most of them came from the country towns and cities of Italy, some from the provinces both near and far. The comedian Terence was a North African, and saw the city first as a slave. Horace came from the far south-east of Italy, Catullus and Vergil and others from the north; there were good writers from Gaul, from Spain, and later from Africa and Egypt. It is possible with sympathetic imagination to trace in each of them something of his origins; and few indeed are those Roman poets who never speak with affection or indulgence of their homes.

But, as artists for these last centuries have turned always towards Paris, as Jews throughout their long wanderings over the globe have turned towards Jerusalem, so all the Roman writers, be they poets or orators, historians or philosophers, turned towards Rome. Some of them loved it unequivocally: such was Propertius. Some hated it and satirized it, yet could scarcely leave it: such was Juvenal. Some enjoyed its liveliness when young, but grew into country-loving recluses when old: such was Horace. All found it a perennial spring of aesthetic and intellectual energy, in which the power of ancient traditions blended with the activity of new authors, new artists, new critics and patrons, and a never-satisfied public, to make an intoxicating drink for any imaginative soul. And all found it a beautiful city—although, at first, it had rather a rude and archaic dignity, and only under the emperor Augustus (who changed it 'from brick to marble') began to grow into a superb multitude of mighty buildings which appeared, like certain statues, to be inhabited by a superhuman life of its own, and to deserve the phrase in which Vergil described it, 'the fairest thing on earth'.

And so it has remained for many centuries. Each century has destroyed something of its early grandeur. Each century has added some new beauty, if it is only the beauty of ruins; some new sanctity, if it is only the sanctity of a tomb. Rome is a city of conflicts. It grew great through warfare. It was always torn by internal dissensions—parties massacred each other, families exhausted themselves in bitter rivalry, monarchs (beginning with the first) were murdered, the armies of republic and empire fought to the death within and without its walls. It is still instinct with conflict: rich and poor and middle-class, Christians and pagans, Romans and provincials, Italians and foreigners, innovators and traditionalists, communists, democrats, fascists, royalists, and anarchists, voluptuaries and ascetics, they all mingle in its streets, dispute in its caffès, loathe and wound one another in wartime, and revere their mother-city, in peace and war, for ever. The very name, Roma—what does it mean? We do not know; but the Greeks turned it into their own tongue, Romé, and said it meant Strength. Strength is nourished by struggle; and although the Italians are not now a militant nation, this one city is and will remain a centre of the invaluable spiritual energies which are fed by frustration and competition. Even its ruins have a massive power, like the face of an old general. Its baroque palaces and churches, insolently grand or contemptuously austere, challenge the onlooker to rival them in pride or outdo them in self-dedica-tion. The appalling monument to the first king of united Italy, a collection of purposeless pillars and pediments which is unfor-tunately visible from all over the city, has all the arrogance of a newly regenerated nation. The supercolossal structures left by fascism, some of them disconcertingly convenient, are like much Italian opera, vulgar but energetic. And across the Tiber, the biggest building in the world, symbol of the Church Militant, raises an enormous Roman helmet toward heaven and stretches two long arms outwards to enfold the City and the World.

It is because Rome contains so much activity, because, like the men who built it, it embodies so many conflicting spirits, that it has always attracted poets and thinkers.

Outwardly, Edward Gibbon was quiet, controlled, and con-temporary. But, as he sat 'among the ruins of the Capitol and listened to the barefooted fryars singing vespers in the temple of Jupiter', he conceived the idea that grew into *The Decline and Fall of the Roman Empire*. Calm and balanced as his phrasing is, it still contains the conflict which he was to deploy throughout six massive volumes, the contrast between the temple of Jupiter, sanctuary of 'a polite and powerful empire', and the barefooted monks, representatives of 'Barbarism and Religion'.

Only a generation later, in 1786, a young German poet visited Rome, filled not with baroque melancholy and tranquillity, but with powerful romantic excitement. Goethe had 'stolen away' from Germany into another world in which he found so much superb art, passionate love, vivid popular life, and still living history that, even with his tremendous powers of assimilation, he could not take it all in. Still, something of Rome—its most immediate and sensual aspects—emerged in his *Roman Elegies*; and his brief and deliberately incomplete sojourn in the city is symbolized in one of his strangest fantasies: the union of the Germanic Faust and the classical Helen, who gives Faust a son and then vanishes, a sculptured divinity dissolving into a cloud.

Many other poets and artists have come to Rome, and all have found it greater than their visions. Byron, who detested tradition and pretended to loathe some of the best in Latin literature, lived for some time in the city during 1817, and translated his impressions into a long passage of finely romantic poetry, which begins with the unforgettable paradox:

Oh, Rome! my Country! City of the Soul!

and moves on to eighteen pages of sombre and moving rhetoric. Next year Shelley was there—looking, as always, into the ideal future, and building visionary heavens upon the débris of past empires. In the preface to the magnificent drama in which he described the overthrow of a cruel god, *Prometheus Unbound*, he paid a noble tribute to the city even in its decay.

This Poem was chiefly written upon the mountainous ruins of the Baths of Caracalla, among the flowery glades, and thickets of odoriferous blossoming trees, which are extended in ever winding labyrinths upon its immense platforms and dizzy arches suspended in the air. The bright blue sky of Rome, and the effect of the vigorous awakening spring in that divinest climate, and the new life with which it drenches the spirits even to intoxication, were the inspiration of this drama.

In those days, Rome was a place of grassy ruins and elegant palaces and whispering melancholy churches, little changed from the strange half-visionary city immortalized in the engravings of Piranesi: tall pillars standing among rocks and mounds which prove to be the fallen walls and earthquake-shattered arches of some vast mansion; huge fields in which a few peasants stand gossiping while their goats scramble among carved pilasters, and which are at a great distance revealed as being, not fields, but the overgrown floors of temples and baths; lonely obelisks once designed to perpetuate some Roman glory, and now purposeless, incomprehensible, haunted by stray dogs and crazy legends; mighty circular tombs converted during the Middle Ages into fortresses; hills which covered buried palaces.

Much of that Rome still remains, in spite of the tremendous clearances undertaken by Mussolini and the smaller but more persistent excavations of the archæologists, both Italian and foreign. The main streets and avenues of the capital are bright, noisy, and busy. Yet the city still seems bigger than all its population and all its visitors. Within a few hundred yards of a highway filled with modern traffic, it is easy to walk into the millennial past: to sit for a few minutes in a quiet hall, where, it may be, Maecenas chatted with his friends Horace and Vergil; to stand in a little church that was once a Roman temple, and admire the exquisite classical sculptures around the altar; or, among the pine trees in a solitary park, to watch the lizards run and the birds perch among the colonnades where emperors strolled, plotted, and died.

There is no one Rome. There are many Romes—pagan, Christian, ancient, modern, baroque, medieval, even prehistoric, commercial, tripperish, aesthetic, republican, imperial—they are all there, and many more; they are all visible, though few eyes and minds can take them all in. There is not even one single ancient Rome: there are many. The old city grew continuously for more than a thousand years.

THE HILL OF PALACES

The beginnings of Rome were unbelievably humble: a few tiny villages clinging to the hilltops—more like American Indian pueblos than anything else in the western world today. Still, the later Romans loved to look back on those origins, so poor and so remote. They felt that the primitive virtues which were rooted there ought never to be forgotten; they remembered that the early inhabitants of Rome had deep religious faith before they had either wealth or power; continuing to practise many of their prehistoric rites, they looked back with admiration to those first days when gods moved among men to teach them good conduct and pure worship; and, in the incredible growth of the little village-settlements into an unequalled empire, they saw the manifestation of an irresistible, a divine destiny.

Exiled from Asia Minor after the ruin of Troy, Aeneas roamed the Mediterranean with a few ships and a few hundred survivors, searching for a new home. At last he landed in central Italy and established himself on the coast—somewhere near the modern seaport of Ostia. He was made welcome, because of his noble descent and culture, by some of the Italians, but attacked by others as a greedy interloper. Elementary strategy suggested that he should look for allies to strengthen his own small forces. He found them in another settlement of 'displaced persons'. These, says the legend, were Greeks, who had been driven into exile some time before the Trojan war, and had settled in a lonely Italian river valley. The valley was the valley of the Tiber. Their little fortress and their grazing lands lay on what later became the site of Rome. Vergil enjoyed evoking those early idyllic days, when the Tiber was as primitive as the Upper Amazon today, when the sacred hill of Jupiter, the Capitol, bore no rich temples and yet was still possessed by a powerful divinity, and when Arcadian cattle pastured where, in Vergil's own time, nothing could be seen but crowds, temples, statues, mighty mansions, and marble pavements. As Aeneas and his men travelled up the Tiber from the coast, Vergil says they were like explorers of an undiscovered country:

Now they wore out the night and the day with steady rowing,
passed the long river windings, crept beneath the shadows
of varied trees, cut the green forests on calm waters.
Then, when the fiery sun had climbed the middle arch,
far off they sighted walls, a fort, and roofs of dwellings,
a scattered few: what Roman power has raised as high
as heaven, then Evander ruled, humble and poor.[1]

Vergil seems to have thought of the tiny settlement as being placed, with Arcadian simplicity, in the valley where later the Forum was to be built. On this side rose the Palatine hill, the home of a fire-breathing ogre killed by Hercules; on that, Evander pointed to another eminence.

He showed him the Tarpeian height, the Capitol
now bright with gold, then rough with trees grown into
   jungle.
'This wood,' he said, 'this hill, with its peak crowned by
   leaves,
some god—we know not who—inhabits. Our Arcadians
believe they have seen Jove himself, shaking his dark
thunder-shield on his arm, mustering clouds of storm.
And here, these two old settlements with shattered walls
are ruins left by heroes of antiquity.
This stronghold father Janus built, the other, Saturn:
this was Janiculum, and that Saturnia.'
And so, exchanging talk, they moved towards the home
of poor Evander: all around they saw his cattle
bellowing in the Forum of Rome.[2]

[1] Vergil, *Aeneid*, 8.94–100.
[2] Vergil, *Aeneid*, 8.347–348, 351–361.

Vergil looked back to that dim past, a thousand years before his time, with indulgent and sympathetic wonder. Around him the power of Rome seemed immense and unshakeable. Yet, a thousand years and more after his time, the populous Forum once again became a rural solitude. Filled up with silt, dust, blown earth, humus, débris, and then overgrown with grass and bushes until only the tops of its pillars could be seen, it was called the Cattle Pasture, *Campo Vaccino*. Thus, for centuries, until the time of the French revolution at least, the little valley reverted to its primitive state, with a few Arcadian herdsmen driving their bellowing cattle among half-obliterated relics of antiquity.

Vergil's imagination showed him much of the truth. The earliest settlements in what is now Rome were just such primitive communities as he describes: except that they were not Greek by origin, were apparently democratic rather than paternal and monarchical, being ruled by a council of elders, a 'senate', and were built not in the valley but on the hills. The first of all these settlements seems to have been on the Palatine hill, the big steep-sided plateau that overlooks the Forum from the south. Its very name symbolizes the changing destiny of Rome, for it means (originally) 'pasture-place'; but with the growth in Rome's power it became first the Latin, and then the European word for a princely mansion, *Palatium*, 'palace'.

Here were the relics of primitive Roman religion, magic, and history. Here was the cave of that mysterious wolf-spirit, Faunus Lupercal, in whose honour men wearing girdles of goatskin ran around the Palatine, whipping every woman whom they met to cure her of barrenness. The festival appears in the second scene of Shakespeare's *Julius Cæsar*, with Mark Antony as one of the runners: he at least had the qualifications, for he was part goat and part wolf.

> Forget not, in your speed, Antonius,
> To touch Calphurnia; for our elders say,
> The barren, touched in this holy chase,
> Shake off their sterile curse.

Even then, in Julius' time, it was very old, and yet it was more than five hundred years later before the Pope succeeded in abolishing it.

On this hill also can still be seen the stone walls of the earliest city, Foursquare Rome, *Roma Quadrata*. Here careful excavators have discovered the foundations of a very ancient, very simple little house. In shape it is like the round straw cabins which the Italian peasants still build. But it is probably the relic of the original, the sacred, the long-preserved Cottage of Romulus, where the twin founders of the city, after being found on this same hillside (in the cave of Faunus Lupercal) being suckled by a she-wolf, were brought up by a shepherd and his wife.

But the Palatine hill as we see it now is covered with the ambitions and the ruins of a later age. The great revolutionary, Augustus, succeeded because he was *apparently* a great conservative and traditionalist. Therefore he bought a house on the sacred hill, lived there all his life after gaining power, restored the ancient sanctuaries, rebuilt the decaying temples, and added a new and magnificent temple, dedicated to his patron Apollo. (It contained the second public library ever opened in Rome.) His descendants and his successors, the later emperors, gradually growing into superhuman power and arrogance, treated the ancient holy place both as a Sinai for the worship of a deified ruler and as a lofty citadel guarding the power of a wary tyrant. Below them lay the Forum, where, for centuries, the Roman people had gathered to discuss their own affairs and appoint their representatives to manage them. Now, from the Palace, the emperors dominated the Forum. Indeed, from the Palace, one of the maddest emperors, Caligula, built a 'bridge' across the Forum—so that he could cross over to the Capitoline Hill and visit his rival the supreme god Jove, without soiling his feet with the base earth trodden by his subjects. The Palace grew loftier and more powerful century by century, until at last, not with a bang but a whimper, the western empire drained away into a morass of barbarian kingdoms.

When we look among the many living Romes for the old but powerful Rome of the emperors, we see, first of all, not their harems nor their Berchtesgadens, but the remains of the huge public buildings they erected. Baths, these vast structures are called; and they did keep the populace cleaner than they ever were for fifteen centuries during later dispensations. But they were also enormous homes-from-home, combining clubs, cafés, concert-halls, parks, favourite strolling-streets, sports-grounds, libraries, and a dozen other amusements for a dilettante city crowd.

So, though it is far from the Palace, the biggest group of buildings left from ancient Rome is still a projection of the imperial power. This is the Baths of Caracalla. Son of an African-born emperor by a Syrian empress, Caracalla murdered his brother and twenty thousand of his brother's supporters, gave Roman citizenship to almost every human being living within the frontiers of the empire, and built enormous baths in which everyone could feel 'the attractions of civilization'. Thus he combined the arts of a late empire, to destroy rivals and to bribe subjects.

His very name, or nickname, is late and foreign. Caracalla—you can hear it—is a Celtic word: it means a sleeveless cloak with a hood, a garment which this man adopted and wore publicly, to replace the toga. And yet, there is a Roman grandeur about his greatest act, by which he made all the western world into a single citizenry. And there is something of the same splendour about his mighty buildings. Too far from the centre of Rome to be used as medieval forts, they were gradually neglected after the fall of the city. They have been slowly rediscovered. Architects have recognized the genius of their builders, and have imitated their boldest features. One of the biggest rooms in any building in the United States, the main hall of Pennsylvania Station in New York, is modelled on one room of the Baths. In Rome, operas are performed in one single corner of that titanic convenience. Art survives political power. Although Caracalla himself was almost a barbarian, the architects and decorators whom he employed drew from a long tradition, and possessed almost Michelangelesque talents.

One of Caracalla's most eccentric predecessors, the emperor Nero, built a palace for himself which did not, like so many insubstantial pageants, dissolve. Some of it was demolished by his successors; some burnt; and much of it buried. Like Aladdin's cave, its relics are concealed within a green hill, and it is still incompletely explored. Nero called it his Golden House.

After the great fire of Rome which the Christians were accused of setting, he took over vast areas in the centre of the city. There, like Kubla Khan, he girdled round many miles of fertile ground, and constructed a huge mansion surrounded by private landscapes, vistas, and solitudes. The result was more like the dwelling of a fabulous oriental potentate than the home of any western man, whether ruler or subject. With its grounds, it covered a slope of the Esquiline hill, stretched across to the Palatine, took in the region where the Colosseum now stands (Nero created an artificial lake there), and all but encroached on the Forum. He was a lover of the incredible. Most of his grandiose plans—such as cutting a canal through the isthmus of Corinth—remained unfinished; and the Golden House was never completed. We can still see a hall in the west wing with the walls roughly plastered and the floor unlaid. Perhaps Nero could never have completed it, for it was part of the mania for the superhuman that possessed him. At the most modest estimate, the Golden House and its grounds covered 125 acres. The whole of the Vatican, including the garden and St. Peter's, is no more than 75 acres. We can see why an anonymous Roman wit circulated an epigram about it, referring to an ancient proposal that the population of Rome should migrate to a near-by Etruscan town.

> Rome is becoming a single House. Move to Veii,
> Romans!—unless that too is part of the House.

Here is a description of the Golden House as given by Suetonius, the biographer of the emperors.

Its entrance hall was large enough to contain a gigantic statue of Nero himself, one hundred and twenty feet high; and the grounds were so spacious that they contained three colonnades each a mile in length. There was also a lake resembling a sea, surrounded with buildings made to look like cities; and, in addition, imitation country estates set out with fields, vine-yards, meadows, and woods, inhabited by all sorts of animals, both tame and wild. In the other parts of the house everything was inlaid with gold and decorated with jewels and mother-of-pearl. The dining-rooms were roofed with plates of ivory made to turn on hinges so that flowers could be scattered from them, and piped so as to sprinkle perfume from above. The main banquet-hall was round, and built so that its ceiling revolved night and day, like the firmament. The baths were supplied with running sea-water and sulphur-spring-water. When he was dedicating this mansion after it was ready, he said no more in approval than simply, 'Now at last I can live like a human being.'[1]

This, and the rest of his monumental follies, soon brought Nero to his destruction. The tough ex-soldier Vespasian, who succeeded him after a civil war, destroyed much of the Golden House or put it to better uses. Soon it was built over, and reconverted. A fire some forty years after its first construction destroyed its most important vestiges. The Golden House sank into darkness.

But in the time of the Renaissance, when all through Italy men were rediscovering the relics of their ancestors, someone dug into a hillside in central Rome, and found a palace. It was the Golden House, buried for nearly fifteen centuries beneath a mass of earth covered with grass and trees.

At first no one recognized it. Artists were called in to examine the beautifully proportioned rooms, the long corridors, the sculptures and the elaborate decorations on the walls. Treasures were discovered in it and carried off—the most famous being the Laocoon group. The Italian painters copied all the painted designs they could see, and hastened to imitate and adapt them above ground, in the new palaces of the Roman prelates and nobles. But they could not understand the fact—which every archæologist

[1] Suet. Nero, 31.1–2.

now assumes as a starting point—that what *they* saw as a labyrinth of rooms within a mound of earth, with tunnels and cells buried deep in darkness and trees growing high above its topmost storey, had originally been a large and sumptuous mansion on the street-level, open to the air and sky all around, and that it had simply been buried by age, disaster, neglect, and oblivion. They looked at the richly decorated halls, far beneath the level of what they knew as Rome; they saw the elegant and comparatively fresh decorations, complex patterns combining the impossible and the geometrical, satyrs and garlands and wreathed columns, sacrificial emblems and trumpeting tritons; they decided that such fantasies were appropriate for the subterranean orgies of a bad emperor, and that, just as Tiberius had gone to the topmost summit of Capri to indulge his nameless vices, so Nero, to hide his delights from the eye of heaven, must have buried himself in a subterranean cave, a grotto, secret but brightly lit and brightly decorated. It was all nonsense, of course; but the legend of Nero's 'grottoes' remained. The artists who copied the newly discovered decorations from the buried walls called them 'grotto-style', *grottesco*; and to this day fanciful decorations which combine the real and the impossible in a carefully-controlled dream are called *grotesques*.

Nero's Golden House melted away so rapidly that it became an obliterated ruin within Rome long before Rome itself became a half-obliterated ruin. Experts find traces of it at the north-east end of the Forum. Much else has vanished. But many of its rooms still remain, buried under one corner of a hill not far from the Colosseum. Children play above it in a little park, and old men sun themselves. A few quiet, poorly dressed guards sit at the entrance, where the hill opens. We pay a little admission fee, and plunge in. Room after room, corridor after corridor, now empty and clean and economically lit, stretch out into the darkness. The ornaments have all been carried away to enrich museums and collectors. The marble facings were evidently ripped off soon after the discovery; and now the Golden House is something between a pagan catacomb and a bombed-out mansion. The subterranean rooms are damp, gloomy, and dismal. Here and there only, where the roof has been broken in, we can see the solid masonry of the walls, touch fragments of the marble which still clings to them, and enjoy the paradox that, so many centuries after Nero shocked his contemporaries by insisting on making a private landscape in the midst of a crowded metropolis, the ruins of his palace have gone back to nature. Bees hum through the roofless corridors; flowering weeds flourish among the imperial brickwork; from the sunlight above we hear the voices of children running and laughing on the grassy slopes.

The official residence of all the other early emperors was on the Palatine hill, a few hundred yards away. Here Vergil and Horace visited Augustus, in his scrupulously modest but exquisitely decorated home. Part of it still exists. From the Forum we walk up the Sacred Road, reach the crest of the hill, and after a few steps enter the reception halls. The walls are delicately painted, to give the small rooms the illusion of greater size. There are two scenes from Greek myth, an idealized landscape, a Roman street-scene, festoons of leaves, flowers, and fruit, and even painted *trompe-l'oeil* branches and colonnades. The rest of the house has the same restrained charm and good taste, the same soft elegance and love of imaginative variety, that we see in the best poetry of the early empire. Augustus ruled the western world for over forty years; but, in spite of the earnest assurances of Vergil, in spite of the altars to the Saviour and the Peacemaker which were rising here and there throughout the empire, he never thought of himself as superhuman. That folly was reserved for some of his successors. His quiet, elegant, and essentially humane house proves that he was always sane.

The hill is covered with the palaces, the monuments, and the extravagances of later Cæsars. In fact, much of the hill is composed of their ruins. When you visit Rome for the first time, one of the strangest discoveries you make is that much of the past still remains buried. So it is on the Palatine. Byron, seeing it in 1817, was astounded by the confused mass of wreckage which had once been the proudest buildings in the world. He called it

> This mountain, whose obliterated plan
> The pyramid of Empires pinnacled.[1]

[1] Byron, *Childe Harold's Pilgrimage*, 4.109.

And he evoked its sombre chaos in a finely chaotic stanza:

> Cypress and ivy, weed and wallflower grown
> Matted and massed together—hillocks heaped
> On what were chambers—arch crushed, column strown
> In fragments—choked up vaults, and frescos steeped
> In subterranean damps, where the owl peeped,
> Deeming it midnight:—Temples—Baths—or Halls?
> Pronounce who can: for all that Learning reaped
> From her research hath been, that these are walls—
> Behold the Imperial Mount! 'tis thus the Mighty falls.[1]

Since Byron wrote, archæologists have cleared away some of the confusion. They have opened up the house of Augustus. They have penetrated the palaces of his successors Tiberius and Caligula, which still lie beneath the beautiful Farnese Gardens on the summit of the hill. They have revealed the school of the imperial page-boys, with its walls scribbled over in childish hands. One group of these scribbles is particularly interesting and touching. It shows a little boy standing in an attitude of reverence, with one hand upraised. He is gazing at a cross, on which is hanging the figure of a man with an ass's head. Beneath is written, in large awkward letters, with one misspelling, ALEXAMENOS WURSHIP-PING GOD. Evidently Alexamenos was the only Christian in the school, and one of his classmates drew a spiteful caricature of him, representing Jesus in the most degrading of all situations, being executed as a common criminal, and wearing the head of a donkey. (For some reason not entirely clear, the Jews were supposed to worship a donkey, or a figure half-man and half-donkey; and the Christians were at first associated with the Jews in the popular imagination.) But even more touching is another inscription in a different hand. It says simply ALEXAMENOS IS FAITHFUL! Evidently the boy wrote this on the wall of his own cell, to strengthen himself against those who derided him. One of the hardest things for us to realize about the early Christians is that

[1] Byron, *Childe Harold's Pilgrimage*, 4.107.

they were not believed to be pure and noble, but rather mean and vicious: a schismatic Jewish sect worshipping a criminal who died on the gallows. Poor Alexamenos suffered from 'the scandal of the cross' and did his best to resist it.

Scholars are still working on the Palatine, in the face of tremendous difficulties and complexities. They have rediscovered the sanctuary of Apollo; they have restored the area where the emperor Domitian watched athletic contests and chariot races; they have dug out many of the arches which supported the titanic palaces of later monarchs—arches which now look not so much like relics of human architecture as fragments of mountain-ranges into which dwellings have been built, as in the canyons of the cliff-dwelling tribes in the American South-West. Now we may wander along the steep eminences on the north of the Palatine hill, and gaze down hundreds of feet into the ruins of the Forum. We pick our way among the broken arcades of the southern slope. Below us, on the level of the valley, lies the great Circus, a soundless echo. Far in the distance floats the dome of St. Peter's. On each side rise towering arches, mass upon mass of brick and concrete, long stripped of the marble that made the palaces glitter like the sun. But still, beneath our feet, most of the imperial past remains undiscovered and obliterated.

It is moving to sit in the gardens laid out above the Palatine by the Farnese family, to feel the ephemeral happiness of summer flowers and summer birds all around, to enjoy the fresh warm air and the genial quietness, and to reflect that below, buried beneath the very roots of the trees, clogged with hundreds of tons of earth and fallen masonry, shrouded in the darkness of many disastrous centuries, there lie some of the foundations of our world. There may still be the imperial archives; portraits of rulers great for evil or for good; beauties of art; lost secrets of policy and of religion. There are buried the fortress of Romulus, and the council room of Constantine. Frail and scanty is our knowledge of the past. Many of the mightiest problems can never now be solved. Many of the supreme beauties are gone for ever. All that we can surely say is that we know the main outlines, and many of the greatest things; that more may yet be discovered, if we have faith and energy. The statue of Athene the Guardian has vanished, yet we have the Parthenon. The Palatine is a heap of ruins, yet, by patient effort, we have reconstructed the administrative system of the mighty and long-lived empire which centred upon it. We still possess the poem of Vergil, which proclaimed the virtues of that empire, and the poem of Lucan, which denounced it as a crime against humanity. And even among these ruins, earth-choked, mutilated, silent, we can still feel the ideals which they expressed and symbolize: order, symmetry, intellectual control, together with artistic sensibility, a strong taste for the luxuries of this world, and an indomitable will.

THE HEART OF THE CITY

The heart of the city of Rome, the vital centre of a republic that lived for nearly five centuries and the ceremonial nucleus of the empire which succeeded it, was an oblong area of land called the Forum. The word means only 'the place outside'. Originally it was the cemetery outside the walls of the small hilltop citadel which was the earliest Rome; the market-place for the citizens and neighbours; and the meeting-place where the inhabitants could debate their own affairs at ease, celebrate religious and official ceremonies, and hold athletic contests. As Rome rose into a large city, then into a strong nation, and at last into a world power, the Forum grew more grand, more formal, more crowded with people, and more surrounded and cluttered with shops and monuments and important buildings. Something of this profuse confusion is still to be seen in it.

Centuries later, as Rome fell into decay—after it was abandoned for the new imperial capitals at Milan and Constantinople, after it was sacked by barbarians and suffered depopulation and earth-quake and other natural disasters—the Forum was gradually deserted, emptied of its fine statues and stones, filled with earth and ruins, until its level rose above its original pavement. By the twelfth century of the Christian era, it had become a majestic desolation. The solemn processions led through Rome by the Popes avoided it entirely.

During the Renaissance, when other parts of Rome were being

excavated and re-explored, the Roman Forum was still further forgotten. The Farnese Pope, Paul III, constructed a special road across it between the triumphal arches of Titus and Severus, to welcome the Holy Roman Emperor Charles V after his conquest of Tunis. Many buildings were torn down, and the level of the Forum was raised even more. It became merely a halting-place for cattle, and remained so until the beginning of the nineteenth century, when excavation of the magnificent old square really began.

During the last century or so, the Forum has been largely cleared. It is not all clear yet. The task is hard—not because any great mass of material still remains to be moved, but because here, more than anywhere else, many ancient Romes lie close together. It is difficult, often impossible, to reveal one Rome without destroying others. Christian churches are constructed inside pagan temples. Official buildings of the early empire are restored and enlarged by later emperors. A late inscription commemorating a victory over the Goths (erected only seven years before they sacked the city) stands just beside an inscription written in Latin so ancient that no modern scholar can interpret it. Near one entrance to the Forum lie the faint and mysterious relics of the grave of the founder of Rome, Romulus. A short walk away there is a Christian church which was originally a pagan temple dedicated to another Romulus, an imperial prince who died in boyhood a thousand years and more after the city was founded. The proudest monument in the entire Forum is a pillar set up in gratitude for the gift of the Pantheon to the Church by the eastern emperor. Within a few dozen yards of it, excavations are now disclosing prehistoric tombs.

The result is that when we first walk through the Forum, or stand above it on the Palatine hill, looking down, we are confused and a little disappointed. It looks too small, too crowded, too disorderly, to have been a worthy centre for so much reverence, a focus for so much ambition. It is scarcely as large as Trafalgar Square, and has no fountains. It is far smaller than the Place de la Concorde, is less regular, and has no such vista of long streets and green trees. It is far less imposing than the Piazza della Signoria in Florence, with its majestic battlemented palace and tower. The vast Piazza of St. Peter's, and indeed other piazzas in modern Rome, make it look tiny, old-fashioned, and haphazard. And we reflect that, when it was filled with all the buildings whose foundations and broken columns we now see, it may have looked like an outdoor art exhibition.

This is true. The Romans themselves felt it, because they were constantly renewing and improving the Forum, clearing spaces and building colonnades in which citizens could walk without discomfort; diverting business and traffic into other new forums; and finally, under the empire, building larger and less cluttered squares elsewhere, for those great official ceremonies in which the emperors and their subjects delighted.

But it tells us two things about Rome. First, it shows us how human the ancient Romans were. Reading their hard monumental prose and their lofty, controlled poetry, studying the records of their vast political schemes, their military and engineering feats, their wise legislation and their humane provincial administration, we are apt to think of them as distant marble figures, statues rather than people. One of the chief difficulties which teachers of classical literature meet is the problem of convincing young readers that, behind the smooth artistic surface of Vergil's poetry or Cicero's prose, there are conflicts as violent and painful as those which agitated the souls of Shakespeare or Goethe; and the historian, who sees 'forces' and 'movements' everywhere, can be misled into forgetting the humanity of the Romans. However, it is not possible to pass an hour in the Roman Forum without re-living the events of Roman history, and seeing them as vivid, comprehensible, close to our own lives. On this spot the body of Julius Cæsar was burnt after his assassination. Here is the base of the platform called the Rostra: Cicero spoke to the people from it, and his head and hands were nailed to it after his murder, by the order of Cæsar's heir, Mark Antony. Here are the pedestals on which the statues of great dignitaries once stood. In the train of his patron, Juvenal lounged among them, and observed with loathing that they were not even Roman by birth, these men.

First, morning calls; and then the Forum—lawyer Apollo,
and the triumphal statues: some Egyptian
Pasha or Bey has dared to set his dignities there![1]

Within these few hundred square yards, Horace walked, quizzic-
ally observing the crowds; Catullus and his friends strolled, deep
in gossip about love and poetry; and Ovid stopped beside the
perfumed palanquin of a white-skinned dark-eyed beauty. On
the slabs of marble left from the floors of great public buildings
here and there, we can see the gaming-boards scratched out by
idlers; and sometimes, as we look at the fine sculptured reliefs of
sacrificial processions, we can almost hear the grave voice of the
officiating priest calling for silence.

The Forum also shows us one of the essential strengths of the
Roman people: their reverence for tradition. That is why it was
so crowded. That is why it is now so wonderfully confused—
because they preserved everything which had ever been valuable
for them. Emperors ruling a vast and complex empire would still,
with complete solemnity and with no trace of hypocrisy, take part
in rites which were largely incomprehensible, repeat religious
formulæ which went back before the beginnings of the written
Latin language. Ancient customs were maintained long after
their origin and meaning had been forgotten. Venerable relics
were carefully preserved, repaired, restored; buildings of remote
antiquity were rebuilt, but never quite abolished. So the crowded
and untidy Forum is a living monument to the crowded and
intricate history of Rome.

Thus, the most sacred thing in Rome was simply a burning fire.
It lived in the sanctuary of Vesta, whose name means Hearth. It
was tended by sacred and unpolluted maidens. It burned for a
thousand years and more, until a Christian emperor had it ex-
tinguished. We can still see the precinct of Vesta, with the muti-
lated statues of the priestesses, in the Forum. This was not the
worship of fire as an element, nothing so complex. It was the cult
of hearth and home. Closely connected with it was another
simple cult: the worship of the spirits protecting the food-store—

[1] Juvenal 1.128–130.

the Penates. Hearth and food-store, these were the origins of the
oldest cult of Rome. The worship of Vesta and the Penates was
symbolic of the idea that Rome was itself a single home, sacred as
all homes should be, which grew outwards into a city containing
several groups of citizens (who all were, or ought to be, members
of the same family); then into an ever-broadening empire always
centred on Rome and its hearth-fire; and finally into an entire
world of fellow-citizens. Like many other Roman ideas, that has
passed into the conception of the Catholic church, which places in
Rome the focus, or hearth-fire, of universal Christianity.

Here too, along the eastern side of the Forum, is the oldest
street in Rome, the Sacred Road. It slopes down from a ridge of
the Palatine hill into the valley of the Forum, runs past the ruins
of great porticoes and temples, and finally turns into the ascent
towards the Capitol. Although it was occasionally realigned and
although the buildings around it kept changing, the street itself
followed essentially the same line as it does today. This old road
was most important when it was the scene of that peculiarly
Roman ceremony, the triumphal procession of a victorious
general: a fantastic blend of ancient ritual, modern power-politics,
sacral formality, and truly Italian informality—unless the obscenity
too was religious. The general, reaching the pinnacle of earthly
felicity, wore a magnificent robe of crimson and gold, a sump-
tuous tunic embroidered with figures of victory, and a golden
crown. The crown was held above his head, partly because it was
too heavy for him to wear, and partly so that he should remember
it was not his to own for ever. It symbolized the fact that he had
almost crossed the line between humanity and divinity: he was
nearly a god. His face was painted red. The Romans themselves
did not know why, or did not say; but we believe it was a symbol
of blood, his own strength and the strength of the defeated
enemy. The custom surely went back to a remote epoch, when the
victorious general was felt to have taken the blood from the
enemies of his state and given new blood to his own countrymen.

Behind the general marched, or lurched, his soldiers, usually
singing disrespectful songs about their leader. Yet they were not
arrested, or even discouraged. They were felt to be doing the
right thing. Cæsar himself scarcely dared to object when his faith-

ful troops marched into Rome behind him, singing (in the fine old metre of most Roman folk-songs):

Watch your wives, you poor civilians, here comes
Baldhead Lover-Boy!

Such behaviour took the curse off the triumphant general's good luck. It diverted the energy of any enemy who might put the evil eye on him. It was like the deprecatory words of a primitive mother whose child has been praised for its beauty. A Roman triumph was a combination of grave political and military thanksgiving with jolly care-free human irreverence. The general was almost divine. The soldiers were human, all too human. Such was the ancient tradition.

Then came the symbols of the general's victories: his booty—gold dishes, rich clothes and tapestries, jewels, works of art—and models of his battles and sieges, in the form of floats showing the cities he had captured, the rivers he had crossed, the tribes he had subdued. There were the prisoners he had taken, headed by their princes and their captains, such as had not been wise enough to commit suicide before their capture. And there were priests and musicians and dancers and jesters, and the relatives of the general and his friends and dependants, and the friends of the returned soldiers, and Roman prisoners set free by their victories, and hundreds of grateful people. They all marched along the Sacred Road, singing and rejoicing. At this corner, on the north-west of the Forum, where we can stand today, the procession broke up. The soldiers went off to mingle with the crowd, to spend their back pay and their share of the plunder on jollification. The chief prisoners went down to the cells hidden below the spurs of the Capitol hill, there to be executed. This was a rare and cruel ceremony. It took place after a triumph because a triumph was an ancient ritual, going back to the era when every war was a holy war and had to be concluded by a sacrifice to the gods who had granted victory. Meanwhile, the general with his suite and with attendant priests climbed the Capitol hill, to offer, with white bulls from the banks of the Clitumnus, gratitude to supreme Jupiter. That was Rome: power, efficiency, cruelty, frank humanity, frequent gaiety, and grave reverence for the gods.

Above the Forum on one side towers the Palatine. Diagonally opposite it, there rises the Capitoline hill. On both these hills, there were ancient relics and potent sanctuaries. But the Capitol held the temple of the supreme deity Jupiter. As the disease of absolutism ate deeper and deeper into the spirit of the Romans, the two hills became competitors. We have seen how the mad emperor, Caligula, after deciding that he himself was a god, built a passage-way high in the air across the Forum, between the two hills, so that he could visit Jupiter. A later emperor called himself the Thunderer and his palace Sacred, as though he had out-stripped the sky-god. And yet the sanctity of the shrine of Jupiter and the ancient citadel of Rome remained. It was always the greatest and most august temple in the city, until the early Christian emperors closed all the pagan sanctuaries.

For centuries afterwards, the Capitol was a lonely place of ruins. A few convents and churches were built on its slopes. But its meaning was forgotten. In the Renaissance, the grandeur if not the sanctity of the place was recaptured by Michelangelo. The central place on top of the hill was cleared and levelled. The statue of Marcus Aurelius which had been preserved for so many hundred years—under the belief that it represented the first Christian emperor Constantine, instead of a determined persecutor of the True Faith—was set in the middle of the newly built square. Michelangelo designed splendid palaces in the classical style to occupy three sides of the new square, and a noble staircase to approach it on the fourth. The city councillors of Rome now meet in one of the palaces. The others are filled with strange relics of the past: portraits of emperors and philosophers, the statue of the she-wolf herself, an exquisite Venus, fantastic figures created by the oriental cults that insinuated themselves into imperial Rome, a model of the city, a copy of the law validating the power of the emperor, vases, mosaics, reliefs, magnificent junk, beautiful débris. In the courtyard and along the corridors there stand colossal fragments, from the monuments of the later empire: an enormous head of the emperor Constantine, a giant foot with large marble veins, titanic square-nailed hands, their forefingers pointing to heaven.

On one side of the hill, difficult of access from above and impossible from below, is a steep cliff. A hundred feet or so beneath its rim, there are boulders, and then the roadway leading down to the corner of the Forum. This is the famous Tarpeian Rock. Convicted traitors to the republic were not stoned, nor burned, nor hanged. They were thrown off this cliff, as though the protecting divinities of the state rejected them.

Capitol; Forum; Palatine. The three names were once merely local names in an insignificant village settlement: the Head place (because of its abrupt contours, or because a huge skull was found in it when the foundations of the temple were laid?); the Outside place, for marketing and meeting the neighbours; and the Grazing place. But now they have entered the languages of many peoples, and have brought with them the meanings given them by the history of our ancestors the Romans. The Palace is the home of a powerful ruler whose acts may not lightly be questioned, and whose person is sacrosanct. The Forum is the meeting-place of free men who want to exchange goods and services, ideas and diversions. The Capitol is the centre of civil government, and stands for the administration of law above all individuals or parties. It was the Greeks, in their city-states, who first conceived and practised democracy. It was the Romans who worked out most of its harder implications, and who most spectacularly failed to cure its most dangerous weaknesses.

This is the centre of Rome. It was once the centre of the world. It is still one of the roots of our life. Within this small mile dwelt many of the men whose names have become permanent ideals; were born many of the institutions which we now accept without question, as natural to our lives. The Roman poets and thinkers proved, in the end, to be builders and civilizers as great as the Roman generals, engineers, and statesmen. For them, too, this was the centre of the world.

Catullus said this was his home, far more than his northern birthplace. Vergil shunned it because he shunned crowds and hated pomp; yet he loved to dwell on the city in his imagination, and in his greatest poem he portrayed it both as a simple pre-historic settlement and (in anticipation) as the imperial home of Augustus the peacemaker. Propertius and Tibullus both loved its adventurous gaiety, and Ovid's *Art of Love* is an amorist's guide to the metropolis. Horace formed his talent as a satirist and philosopher while walking through its busy streets, and still, even when withdrawn in his country seclusion, thought of his friends in the city with pleasure. Juvenal described its mansions, its temples, and its slums with fascinated repulsion. These and many other Roman poets communicate to us the deathless nobility not only of Italy but of its captain city, Rome. Here the history and poetry of antiquity become tangible. The tomb of Romulus; the Sacred Road; the precinct of Vesta; the Senate House; the towering arches of the imperial palaces: here are three thousand years of history. The stones are dead. The history is alive, running through our hearts and through our minds. Walking among the stupendous ruins, we still feel the power of the Romans and the tragedy of their failure; and we remember that it was one of their greatest poets who gave them the counsel which, to their sorrow, they abandoned:

Bow down to God, you Romans, and rule the world.

NOTES

INTRODUCTION

p. 13. conclude the Why. Pope, *Moral Essays, Epistle* 1.99.100.

p. 13. speak in vain. Catullus 101.1–4. The entire poem is translated on pp. 21–2.

p. 14. a metre of Catullus. Tennyson, *Hendecasyllabics*.

p. 16. of a single lizard. Juvenal 3.230–1: see p. 209.

CHAPTER ONE: CATULLUS

p. 17. Scholars have made different reconstructions of Catullus's life story, and in particular of his love affair with Clodia. (M. Rothstein, 'Catull und Lesbia', *Phil.* n.F.32 (1923) 1–32, goes so far as to suggest that the intrigue took place after Catullus returned from Bithynia, and that the woman was not the famous Clodia, wife of Metellus, but her younger sister, wife of Lucullus. But this is highly improbable, for many reasons.) The version given in the text of this book is largely the same as those of Münzer in *RE* 3.1266f. and 4.105f., Schuster on Valerius (123) in *RE* 2nd series 7.2.2353f., and Wilamowitz-Moellendorff in *Reden und Vorträge* (Berlin 1913³) 261–70 and *Hellenistische Dichtung* II (Berlin, 1924) c.8. The following table shows the landmarks in Catullus's life as nearly as we can establish them.

87 B.C. Catullus born

70 B.C. Catullus sent to Rome

61 B.C. Catullus falls in love with Clodia

60 B.C. His brother dies and he is called back to Verona, where he writes the long poems 61–8

59 B.C. Clodia's husband Metellus dies. She becomes Caelius's mistress

57 B.C. Catullus goes to Bithynia

56 B.C. (spring) Clodia inspires the prosecution of Caelius; Catullus on his way home from Asia

55–54 B.C. Catullus's last poems: his enmity with Cæsar and his
   reconciliation

Soon after 54 B.C.: Catullus dies.

p. 19. Verona became a colony by the Lex Pompeia, passed in 89
B.C. through the efforts of Pompey's father, Cn. Pompeius Strabo. (See
Panegyrici 12.8 and Asconius on the Lex Pompeia, with discussions in
J. Marquardt, *Staatsverwaltung* 1.2 (1881) 13–14, E. Kornemann in
RE 4.517, and H. Rudolph, *Stadt und Staat im römischen Italien* (Leipzig,
1938) 89.) Many tombstones of Catullus's family, the Valerii, have
been found in and near Verona.

p. 19. J. Whatmough, *Prae-Italic Dialects of Italy* II (Cambridge,
1933) 206, admits the possibility that *basium* may be Celtic in origin,
and refers to A. Holder, *Alt-Celtischer Sprachschatz* (Leipzig, 1896),
who is quite sure of it. A. Ernout and E. Meillet, *Dictionnaire étymo-
logique de la langue latine* (Paris, 1951³) 120, are also inclined to accept
the word as a borrowing from Celtic. Holder on 1.853 says that the
name Catullus itself is Celtic. He derives it from the word *catu*, 'battle',
which is found in known Celtic names such as Catuvellaunus. Catullus
is also accepted as Celtic by W. Schulze, *Zur Geschichte lateinischer
Eigennamen* (in *Abhandlungen der königlichen Gesellschaft der Wissen-
schaften zu Göttingen*, phil.-hist. Kl., n.F. V, No. 5, 1904), p. 23, n.2.
He cites similar names: Catalus, Catulla, Cintullus.

p. 20. On the shape of Catullus's book, Kroll in his edition (Berlin,
1929²) pref. ix, says we know of no other ancient book arranged in
such a way. Clearly it is a posthumous collection, and the cheerful little
preface with the dedication to Cornelius Nepos (1) must have led off a
slighter book published in Catullus's happier days.

p. 20. 54 B.C. at least. Poems 29, 55, and 113 show that Catullus was
still alive in 55. But there is no mention in his poetry of any event
later than 54 B.C.—although there was a great deal of lively political
activity going on, which would surely have interested him and elicited
his comments, if he had lived to see it.

p. 23. accomplices in mutual vice. Catullus 29 and 57.

the two were reconciled. Suetonius, *Diuus Iulius* 73.

'achievements of great Cæsar.' Catullus 11.10.

p. 24. Cicero's letter to Memmius is *Ad fam.* 13.1.

got the best of all his staff. Catullus 10 and 28.

cities of Asia Minor. Catullus 46.

palanquin and eight slaves. Important personages in Bithynia
were carried in litters borne by eight men: Cicero, *Verr.* 5.27.

p. 25. Clodia's burning eyes: Cicero, *Har. Resp.* 38. The word 'ox-eyed', *boöpis*, was thought to be particularly neat for Clodia, since it was the epithet of Hera, who, in addition to having large beautiful eyes, was married to her *brother* Zeus. It occurs in Cicero, *Att.* 2.9.1, 2.12.2, 2.14.1, 2.22.5, 2.23.3, and elsewhere.

p. 26. Hortensius. Catullus 65 is a tribute to him.

p. 26. Why does the other man 'equal the gods'? Because he is *strong* enough to endure Lesbia's beauty and the charm of her voice without flinching, whereas Catullus, a mere human being, almost faints? Or because he is supremely *happy*, so that he seems to be in heaven, while Catullus, frightened and envious, is miserable? Commenting on this poem and on its model in Sappho, many modern scholars seem to think that Catullus and Sappho are envying the *strength* of the fortunate lover or husband. But there is something very forced and mawkish in saying to a beloved woman that any man who can endure being near her must have superhuman strength to keep from becoming weak and ill. It is not even effective love-making, since it makes the favoured man into a hero while it reduces the poet to a weakling, and thus implies that the other has a better right to go on possessing her. And it is very doubtful whether any ancient poet, even in the ecstasies of hyperbole, could say that a man seemed to be stronger than the gods, although he could say that someone he envied was happier than the gods. Again, to envy the assured *happiness* of a familiar lover or husband, is natural for a new aspirant, as Catullus was; and to say so is a delicate way of wooing, for it implies 'I wish I were in his place, possessing the happiness which he enjoys through constant intimacy with you'; or, putting it in another way, 'I was overwhelmed by your beauty at first sight, but now I wish to be near you constantly, supplanting that other man whose happiness I envy.' Wilamowitz, Kroll, and others hold to the former interpretation (strength), but the latter (happiness) is accepted with sound common sense by D. L. Page, *Sappho and Alcaeus* (Oxford, 1955), 21, 26–33: see his notes for the most recent discussions of the problem. In the manuscripts this poem is followed by a quatrain in the same metre, in which Catullus reproaches himself for wasting his time in idleness and warns himself against it. Many scholars have tried to interpret this stanza as being part of the Sapphic paraphrase addressed to Lesbia, but this can scarcely be accepted. The four lines are in quite a different emotional mood, sober self-reproach as opposed to passionate excitement; they are not parallel to anything in Sappho, on whose work the first three stanzas are closely modelled; and they represent Catullus talking to himself, while the first three stanzas are Catullus talking to Lesbia—an improbable change within a short poem. The structure of Catullus 8 is not parallel, for there Catullus is talking to Lesbia in her absence. In fact these four lines are a poem, or part of a poem, written in an earlier stage of the dis-illusionment evidenced in Catullus 8, and they have been attached to the Sapphic paraphrase because of the similarity of metre in the same way as the fragment *tam gratum . . . ligatam* has been attached to Catullus 2. See a discussion by E. Bickel in *RhM* 89 (1940) 194f.

pp. 28–9. Clodia's patron goddess: Cicero, *Cael.* 52: *Venerem illam tuam . . . spoliatricem.*

p. 31. On the words for 'kiss', see M. Haupt, *Opuscula* 2 (Leipzig, 1876), 106–10, and R. Pichon, *De sermone amatorio apud latinos elegi-arum scriptores* (Paris, 1902). Haupt shows that *basium* cannot be an old Latin word, since it never appears in Plautus (although there is plenty of room for it in his works), and that it is rather 'low', since no other Roman love-poet uses it. After Catullus it appears in colloquial writers such as the fabulist Phaedrus, the satirist Petronius, and the epigram-matist Martial (who took it to mean very special kisses, *basia Catulliana*, 11.6.14). *Sauium* also is rather low. It is not uncommon in Plautus and Catullus, but appears only once in Propertius and never in Tibullus or Ovid, and never in Vergil's unquestioned works—only in *Catalepton* 13.32. Horace has it only in the *Epodes*, which are often coarse. On the other hand, Catullus uses *osculum* only once (in 68.127, of birds billing) and *osculatio* once (as a conveniently metrical synonym for *basiatio* in 48.6).

p. 31. On the counting of kisses, H. L. Levy, 'Catullus 5, 7–11 and the Abacus', *AJP* 62 (1941) 222–4, shows that Catullus alternates thousands and hundreds, not capriciously, but because his image of rapid counting involves an abacus with separate columns for hundreds and thousands. On such an instrument it is easy to sweep one hand over the counters and 'destroy the accounting', *conturbare rationem.*

p. 33. Apart from Catullus 68.136, the word *era* is never applied to a beloved woman in Latin love-poetry, except once, when it describes Omphale—who was both the slave-owner and the lover of Hercules (Ovid, *Her.* 9.78). Catullus calls Lesbia his *domina* only twice (68.68 and 156), both times in close connection with the word *domus*; it is far more common in other poets. He uses the word *mulier* now and then with no possessive adjective (63.27, 63.63, 68.128, 70.3, 87.1), but then it means merely 'the woman'. It occurs in the other love-poets also without the possessive: e.g. in Prop. 2.29.9, 3.8.11, 3.24.1; Ov. *Am.* 1.10.29, *A.A.* 3.95, 3.421, 3.523, 3.765, etc.; but there is a world of difference between these usages and the intimate *mulier mea*. Pichon (see note on p. 31).

records no other example of *nubo* in the love-poets with any meaning except that of legal marriage.

p. 33. The three long poems about marriage are Catullus 64, 62, and 61.

p. 34. 'the limper'. This metre, invented by the bitter Hipponax, is the ugliest in all Greek or Latin literature. It is composed of six feet. The first five are iambic; but the last is inverted, and can be either a spondee or a trochee. I have tried to reproduce its effect: 'You póor Catúllus, dón't be súch a cráss-braíned fóol!'—but it is very difficult in English.

p. 34. Kroll's edition shows some of the colloquial expressions which fill Catullus 8, and adds parallels from comedy: *quod uides perisse perditum ducas*∼Plautus, *Trin.* 1026; *rogaberis nulla*∼Plautus, *Trin.* 606; *scelesta, uae te*∼Plautus, *Asin.* 149 and *Most.* 563.

p. 36. Caelius Rufus: see Catullus 69 and 77 to Rufus, and compare 73.

filthy back alley. Catullus 37, with an echo of 8.5; and 58, to Caelius.

p. 38. Catullus's poem on the Attis myth is 63. Wilamowitz, 'Die Galliamben des Kallimachus und Catullus', *Hermes* 14 (1879) 194–201, shows that Catullus is adapting a poem by Callimachus. He also points out that the work cannot be taken as a document for the religious sentiment of Catullus's own time. By implication he shows that it is a personal poem, since it omits such important points as the fate of the young man's companions, who appear in 11 and fall asleep in 35–6 but are never heard of again. On the resemblance between Clodia and Cybele, note that Catullus uses *era* of Clodia in 68.136 (a very rare word for a woman in the speech of a lover) and uses *era* of Cybele in 63.92.

p. 40. Cybele and her temple on the Palatine: Livy 29.14.12; C. Huelsen, *The Forum and the Palatine* (tr. H. H. Tanzer, New York, 1928), 61–3; Tenney Frank, *Catullus and Horace* (New York, 1928), 72–3; G. Lugli, *The Roman Forum and the Palatine* (Rome, 1952), 101–2. It was Tenney Frank who pointed out the proximity of the temple to Clodia's house.

p. 40. a little yacht. See Catullus 4 and 46. There is a good section on the yacht in A. L. Wheeler's *Catullus and the Tradition of Ancient Poetry* (Berkeley, 1943), 97–104.

p. 40. truly happy. Catullus did have another country place: a farm in the Sabine country near Tivoli; but he speaks of it with far less enthusiasm than of Sirmio. He says merely that it was peaceful and healthy—it cured him of a bad cold which he caught from reading a frigid speech (Catullus 44).

p. 41. laugh! laugh! The last line is pretty colloquial: its structure is like 3.2, and *cachinnus* (although Catullus himself used it for waves in 64.273) is mainly a prose word, sometimes pejorative—used by Lucr. 5.1397 and 1403; Catullus 13.5 and 56.2; Cic. *Brut.* 216; Ovid *A.A.* 3.287; and Persius 3.87. The last three lines make a neat tricolon: Sirmio, the lake, and Catullus's little house.

p. 42. CLODIVS. The inscription is *CIL* 5.4026. It is a part of a marble tombstone, nearly three feet square. It says simply P. CLODIO P.L., beneath a design showing two hares, ivy leaves, and a bird—no doubt emblems of immortality. See Conte G. G. Orti Manara, *La Penisola di Sirmione* (Verona, 1856), 77.

p. 42. old deserted country church. The church of St. Peter is believed to go back to the time of the Lombards, and was rebuilt in 1320.

p. 43. On the 'grottoes', see N. Degrassi, *Le Grotte di Catullo* (Sirmione, n.d.), with plans and photographs.

p. 44. 'O venusta Sirmio!' comes from Catullus 31.12; 'Frater Ave atque Vale' from 101.10; 'Lydian laughter' from 31.13-14; and 'all-but-island' from 31.1.

p. 44. Tennyson's description of his visit to Sirmio: Hallam Tennyson, *Alfred Lord Tennyson, a memoir by his son* (New York, 1898) II 247-8.

p. 45. The mortgage was for 15,200 sesterces, just about right for a small farm. A man in Horace bought one, which he worked himself, for 14,000 (*Ep.* 1.7.80-1). There is no way of proving whether the poem is about his place in Sirmio or the other near Tivoli (see note on p. 40), but it is slightly more probable that Furius would ask information about the situation and outlook of the farm further away from Rome. Professor Gilbert Bagnani suggests the equation of one sesterce to about 1s. 9d. 1956.

p. 46. Dante and the suicides, *Inf.* 13; the lustful, *Inf.* 5.

p. 46. a grinning Spaniard: this was Egnatius, who is pilloried in Catullus 37.17-20 and 39.

p. 47. the cheapest coppers: he meant that she was what the Greek comedian called a χαλκιδῖτις.

p. 47. The story about Cicero's wife and Clodia is in Plutarch, *Cicero* 29.2; Caelius's jokes about Clodia are in Quintilian 8.6.53, and Cicero alludes to them in *Cael.* 62 and 69.

p. 47. Cicero's speech for Caelius has been edited by R. G. Austin (Oxford, 1952²).

p. 51. There are many different explanations of the curious little poem to Cicero. They are discussed by D. Romano, 'Il significato del

C.49 di Catullo,' *Aevum* 28 (1954) 222–9, who suggests that the poem is a sincere expression of Catullus's gratitude to Cicero for delivering the speech *Pro Cornelio*—in which he saved Catullus's friend Cornelius (praised in his 102nd poem) from an attack by his enemy Cominius (reviled in his 108th poem). 'Best of lawyers': not that Cicero was an expert in jurisprudence, but that he was a skilful counsel.

p. 52. The name of Verona is Celtic. On the city, see H. Nissen, *Italische Landeskunde* 2 (Berlin, 1902) 1.204–8; A. L. Frothingham, *Roman Cities in Italy and Dalmatia* (New York, 1910) 244–63; I. A. Richmond and W. G. Holford, 'Roman Verona: the archæology of its town plan', *Papers of the British School at Rome* 13 (1935) 69f.; and P. Marconi, *Verona Romana* (Bergamo, 1937).

p. 53. The invitation to the young poet is Catullus 35. Poems 17, 67, and 100 deal with local Veronese scandals.

pp. 53–4. On the Gate of the Bursars see Marconi (cited in note on p. 52) c. 4,A, who places it in the latter half of the 1st century A.D. However, Frothingham (cited in the same note) 254–6 credits Augustus with the lower tier of the gate. In another article he says it was the western, or decuman, gate of the city. See his 'Discovery of the Capitolium and Forum of Verona' in *AJA* 18 (1914) 129–45, in which he records how, far below the cellars of the existing houses, he divined the existence of the capitol of Roman Verona and its other (judicial) forum—the Piazza delle Erbe being above the purely commercial forum.

CHAPTER TWO: VERGIL

p. 57. 'smooth-sliding Mincius'. Milton, *Lycidas* 86.

p. 62. too near (alas) to poor Cremona. This line was used by Dean Swift in one of the finest puns ever made. He was at a party where a fashionably dressed lady, with a sweep of her gown, knocked a violin to the floor, where it broke. Swift put Cremona violin and silk mantua together, and observed 'Mantua uae miserae nimium uicina Cremonae!' (Vergil, *Bucolics* 9.28).

p. 64. 'his town-bred audience.' So T. E. Page in his introduction to *Vergil's Bucolics and Georgics* (London, 1898) xii.

p. 74. 'noble lie.' This is Plato's phrase for the story to be told to the citizens of his Republic about their racial origins: *Rep.* 414b.

p. 77. 'live in secret.' This is one of the mottoes of Epicurus: see

Epicuri Ethica, ed. C. Diano (Florence, 1946), p. 61, No. 130, and note on p. 148.

p. 77. his Roman follower Lucretius. See pp. 67–8.

p. 78. 'should be removed.' So the life attributed to Servius (ed. C. G. Hardie, *Vitae Vergilianae Antiquae*, in *Appendix Vergiliana*, Oxford, 1954) 31.

p. 79. He was fifty years old. Born in October 70, he would have been fifty-one on 19 October, 19 B.C.; therefore he was only fifty. So says the *Vita Probiana* (ed. Hardie: see note on p. 78) 17, although the *Vita Donati* 125 says he died *anno aetatis quinquagesimo secundo*.

p. 80. phenomenal revenge. The legends are collected in D. Comparetti, *Virgilio nel medioevo* (Florence, 1896²) and J. W. Spargo, *Vergil the Necromancer* (Cambridge, Mass., 1934).

p. 80. not a vestige of it now remains. Details in A. Maiuri, *I campi flegrei* (Itinerari dei Musei e Monumenti d'Italia 32, Rome, E.F.XII) 7–11.

p. 81. 'vanity of everything.' Leopardi, 'A se stesso' 16. On the poet's burial see Iris Origo, *Leopardi* (London, 1953²) 261.

p. 82. exalts the place. The couplet is by an anonymous scholar of the sixteenth century:

Quod scissus tumulus, quod fracta sit urna, quid inde?
sat celebris locus nomine uatis erat.

E. Cocchia, 'La tomba di Virgilio', *Mouseion* 4 (1927–8) 67–81 and 129–40, and F. S. Dunn, 'Vergil's vanishing tomb', *Art and Archæology* 29 (1930) 23–31, describe the place before it was as well cared for as it now is. Cocchia mentions a period when it was owned by a private landlord: he planted laurels to succeed the laurel of Petrarch, but they were always stolen before they could grow very big.

CHAPTER THREE: PROPERTIUS

p. 86. It was at Spello that St. Francis and St. Clare were mocked with such ill-natured jokes that they were driven away (E. Hutton, *Assisi and Umbria revisited*, New York, 1953, 58–9). The gate pictured is the 'Porta Consolare', half-buried by the raising of the road level: the holes are still visible where its marble facing was torn away. (A. L. Frothingham, *Roman Cities in Italy and Dalmatia*, New York, 1910, 190–1.)

p. 92. 'Odious endeavours!' This is from Congreve's *Way of the World*, 4.5.

> Mirabell: '*Item*, when you shall be breeding——' Millamant: 'Ah! name it not.'
>
> Mirabell: 'Which may be presumed, with a blessing on our endeavours——'
>
> Millamant: 'Odious endeavours!'

p. 93. The Mighty Mite, *Magnus*, was evidently a dwarf kept as a clown.

p. 95. Orlando and Rosalind: Shakespeare, *As You Like It*, 3.2.136.

p. 97. Byron devotes three stanzas to the springs of Clitumnus in *Childe Harold's Pilgrimage*, 4.66–8: in a characteristic phrase he says that their beauty brought him a 'suspension of disgust'. Carducci's poem is *Alle fonti del Clitunno*. And see U. von Wilamowitz-Moellendorff, 'An den Quellen des Clitumnus' in *Reden und Vorträge* (Berlin, 1913³), 370–90.

p. 102. his beginning and his end: Propertius 1.12.20.

p. 104. charmed the bull: Pasiphae, wife of Minos king of Crete, had an evil passion for a bull, and had a wooden cow constructed in which she placed herself to receive her beloved.

p. 104. Hypermnestra was one of fifty sisters who were forced to marry fifty brothers and agreed to kill their husbands on the wedding night: she alone spared her bridegroom.

p. 106. a moment's surrender. T. S. Eliot, *The Waste Land*, 403.

p. 107. inheritors of unfulfilled renown. Shelley, *Adonais*, 397.

p. 107. late espousèd saint. Milton, Sonnet 19.

p. 111. purposeless and wanton life. Propertius, 1.1.5–6, translated on p. 86.

p. 111. beneath the suffocating night. A. E. Housman, *A Shropshire Lad*, 30.

p. 111. something greater than the Iliad. Propertius, 2.34.66, of the nascent Aeneid.

CHAPTER FOUR: HORACE

p. 114. private secretary to the emperor Augustus. Suetonius, ed. C. L. Roth (Leipzig, 1924), 2. p. 297.

p. 114. Byron. *Childe Harold's Pilgrimage*, 4.77.

p. 115. Venusia. On the town see H. Nissen, *Italische Landeskunde* 2 (Berlin, 1902), 2.826–32, and Walter Wili, *Horaz* (Basel, 1948), 11–18.

p. 115. slave of the township of Venusia. See Wili (cited in previous note), 11.

p. 116. 'poor on a meagre farm': Hor. *Serm.* 1.6.71.

p. 116. a dealer in general merchandise. There are other examples of this kind of career. When Horace was 17, a man who had been on the wrong side in the civil wars came back to Italy and became a dealer, very much in the same way as Horace's father. He prospered. His son became a tax-collector, and prospered. His grandson became emperor of Rome. See Suetonius, *D.Vesp.*, 1.2–3.

p. 117. to his table and his confidence. Suetonius, *D.Aug.* 74.

p. 117. high moral conduct. Horace, *Serm.* 1.6.

p. 118. 'poor dishonoured shield.' Horace, *Carm.* 2.7.10.

p. 118. stopped my tongue from saying more. By repeating the *s*, as in a hesitating stammer, I have tried to produce something of the same effect as that of Horace's alliteration:

> infans namque *pudor* prohibebat *plura profari.*

p. 123. 'snow-white foam.' Macaulay, 'The Battle of Lake Regillus', 10.

p. 124. The house believed to be Horace's. See C. H. Hallam and T. Ashby, 'Horace's villa at Tivoli', *Journal of Roman Studies* 4 (1914), 121–38; C. H. Hallam, *Horace at Tibur and the Sabine Farm* (Harrow, 1927); C. H. Hallam, 'Horace's Tiburtine villa', *Classical Review* 42 (1928), 125–7; and a strongly negative criticism by R. L. Dunbabin, 'Horace's villa at Tivoli', *Classical Review* 47 (1933), 55–61. But Walter Wili (cited in note on p. 115) makes it quite clear on his p. 257, n.1, that Horace says explicitly that he lived and wrote poetry in Tibur: see *Carm.* 4.2.27–32 and 3.10–12. He suggests that Augustus gave him a villa there towards the end of his life (p. 372–3).

p. 125. sweetness and light. Swift, *The Battle of the Books*. On Horace as a bee there is a good chapter in Walter Wili's book (cited in note on p. 115): *Apis Matina*, c. 21.

p. 127. wet chalk and crocodile dung. Horace, *Epod.* 12.10–11.

p. 128. more durable than bronze. Horace, *Carm.* 3.30.1.

p. 128. only one group which can be read together. These are the 'Roman odes', 3.1–6.

p. 129. A. Y. Campbell. See his stimulating book, *Horace, a new interpretation* (London, 1924).

p. 130. jewels five-words-long. Tennyson, *The Princess*, 2.355–7.

p. 130. The rest is silence. *Hamlet*, 5.2.372.

p. 130. Magnificently false, *splendide mendax*, Horace, *Carm.*, 3.11.35.

p. 130. Before Agamemnon, *uixere fortes ante Agamemnona*, Horace, *Carm.*, 4.9.25.

p. 130. Dust and shadow, *puluis et umbra sumus*, *Carm.*, 4.7.16.

p. 130. Pluck today, *carpe diem*, *Carm.*, 1.11.8.

p. 130. Cruel to strangers, *Britannos, hospitibus feros*, *Carm.*, 3.4.33.

p. 131. o'er vales and hills. Wordsworth, 'I wandered lonely as a cloud.'

p. 134. smoothing your yellow hair. Of course *cui flauam religas comam?* means 'for whose benefit are you binding back your yellow hair?' but that in turn implies an expected caress.

p. 136. in praise of Augustus. Horace, *Carm.*, 4.2.

p. 136. in praise of Agrippa. Horace, *Carm.*, 1.6.

p. 137. the coquettish whore Lydé. Horace, *Carm.*, 2.11.

p. 138. move stones, shift clods. Horace, *Ep.*, 1.14.39.

p. 140. like his own father. Horace, *Serm.*, 1.4. 105–14.

p. 143. greedy Cinara. Horace, *Carm.*, 4.1.4. This is the woman who haunted Ernest Dowson: 'I have been faithful to thee, Cynara, in my fashion.'

p. 143–5. Horace's farm. G. Lugli, *Horace's Sabine Farm* (translated by Gilbert Bagnani, Rome, 1930), gives the essential facts, with photographs and maps. There is much of interest also in G. Boissier, *Nouvelles Promenades Archéologiques: Horace et Virgile* (Paris, 1899²) c.1; R. S. Conway, 'The country haunts of Horace,' *Bulletin of the John Rylands Library* 12 (1928), 22–30; A. Geikie, 'Horace at his Sabine Farm,' *Quarterly Review* 225 (1916), 483–99; E. H. Haight, *Horace and his art of enjoyment* (New York, 1926); C. Jullian, 'La villa d'Horace et le territoire de Tibur,' *Mélanges d'Archéologie et d'Histoire* 3 (1883), 82–9; A. Noyes, *Horace: a Portrait* (New York, 1947), c.11; T. D. Price, 'A restoration of Horace's Sabine villa,' *Memoirs of the American Academy in Rome* 10 (1932), 135–42 and plates 34–42; and L. P. Wilkinson, *Horace and his lyric poetry* (Cambridge, 1945), 54–8.

p. 146. lost so many of their trees. In Horace's time the valley was thick with trees, while now it is bare and parched: *Ep.* 1.16.5–6. His other references to the neighbourhood make it appear thickly wooded and cool.

p. 146. a Roman inscription: *CIL* 14.3485.

p. 155. Horace's letters from the Sabine farm: *Ep.* 1.7, 10, 14, 16.

p. 155. The satire on the journey to the diplomatic conference is *Serm.* 1.5, one of the first satires on official boredom.

p. 157. smoke and wealth and noise of Rome. Horace, *Carm.* 3.29.12.

p. 157. Aristius Fuscus is the friend who played a little joke on

Horace by leaving him with an importunate social climber: *Serm.* 1.9.

p. 159. pleased the greatest Romans. Details in Suetonius's life of Horace.

CHAPTER FIVE: TIBULLUS

p. 163. flowering in a lonely word. Tennyson, *To Virgil* 3.

p. 164. basically rather sad letter. There is a good analysis of it in Walter Wili's *Horaz* (see note, p. 115), 295–7.

pp. 165–6. one of Horace's lyrics. On its structure Wili (quoted on p. 115) 179–80, has some good things to say: he points out that the theme of the trio of lovers and beloved occurs in no less than one-third of all Horace's love poems.

p. 174. Pedum. On its disappearance, see H. Nissen, *Italische Landeskunde* (Berlin, 1902), 2.2.619: he identifies it with Gallicano. F. Gregorovius, *Wanderjahre in Italien* II (Berlin, 1878⁴) 47, thinks it is Zagarolo, and so does T. Ashby, 'Classical Topography of the Roman Campagna', in *Papers of the British School at Rome* 1 (1902), 205–8; but he admits that the site is impossible to fix, and that Gallicano does probably occupy the site of some ancient city. H. Philipp in *RE* 19.1.54–5 also identifies Pedum with Gallicano.

p. 176. shade of trees. Robert Frost, 'Mending Wall.'

CHAPTER SIX: OVID

p. 177. *Ventrio*. The inscription is *CIL* 9.3082.

p. 177. Gran Sasso. It was at Campo Imperatore on Gran Sasso that Mussolini was held prisoner for some months in 1943: appropriately enough.

p. 180. cannot spit. Eliot, *The Waste Land* 339.

p. 180. permanent war. Ovid, *Amores* 1.9.

p. 181. epigrams and ideas. L. Cestius Pius, quoted in Seneca, *Controu.* 3.7.

p. 181. books are read. Hilaire Belloc, 'On his Books,' from *Epigrams.*

p. 183. trained in legal oratory. L. P. Wilkinson, *Ovid Recalled* (Cambridge, 1955) 8–12, explains what a good speaker he was.

p. 185. 'no zeal.' Talleyrand, quoted by Sainte-Beuve, in 'Madame de Staël', from *Portraits de Femmes*.

p. 189. sexual vice. There are many documents on the vicious life of these two women: Suet. *D.Aug.* 65, Dio 55.10.12–13, Vell. Pat. 2.100.3, Schol. Juv. 6.158, and Sen. *Ben.* 6.32.1.

p. 189. 'nothing in his home.' Tibullus 1.5.30 (see p. 168 of the chapter on that poet).

p. 190. 'seduced by a book.' The epigram is attributed to James Walker, Mayor of New York in the gay twenties.

p. 191. *Sulmo mihi patria est.* Ovid, *Tristia* 4.10.3; see p. 178.

p. 191. old inhabitants of the district. These stories are reported in A. de Nino, *Ovidio nella tradizione popolare di Sulmona* (Casalbordino, 1886) and G. Pansa, *Ovidio nel medioevo e nella tradizione popolare* (Sulmona, 1924).

p. 194. statue of Ovid as he was conceived by the men of the Middle Ages. Pansa (cited in the note above) says it is a fourteenth-century work, and that it used to be decorated with flowers and branches every year on the 24th of June.

p. 194. the great refusal. Dante, *Inf.* 3.60.

p. 194. ruins of a Roman villa. Notice that Ovid does not say he lived in the town, or city, of Sulmona. He says *natalem, rura paterna, locum* (*Am.* 2.16.38) and *amissos . . . agros, ruraque Paeligno conspicienda solo,* (*Pont.* 1.8.41–2), phrases which imply a considerable estate outside the town, though not one of senatorial magnificence (*Am.* 1.3.7–10). The people used to call the ruins of the villa *le potèche d'Ovidio,* 'the shops of Ovid,' but that may have been a reminiscence of their early purpose and of the early meaning of the dialect word: *apothecae,* 'storehouses'. So Pansa, cited in note on p. 191.

p. 195. now a prison. See V. Bindi, *Monumenti degli Abruzzi* (Naples, 1889), 760–4, who explains that the Abbey of S. Spirito was founded in 1268–85, became the seat of the head of the Order of the Celestines, then was converted to a college in 1807 after the suppression of the Order, eleven years later became an Ospizio, then in 1840 a home for the very poor, and finally a prison.

p. 196. rusticity. See, for instance, *Amores* 1.8.44, 2.4.13, 3.4.37; *Ars Am.* 1.672 and 2.566; *Ep.* 16.186.

CHAPTER SEVEN: JUVENAL

p. 203. cities in the night. Longfellow, 'Monte Cassino', from *Birds of Passage*, dated 30th October, 1874, but written on his visit to Italy in 1868–9.

p. 204. not the Roman town at all. Essential details in H. Nissen, *Italische Landeskunde* (Berlin, 1902), 2.2.676, and in an excellent new study by Count Michelangelo Cagiano de Azevedo, *Aquinum* (*Italia Romana: Municipi e Colonie*, ser. 1, vol. 9, Rome, 1949). On the size of the Roman township see G. Beloch, 'Le città dell' Italia antica,' *Atene e Roma* 1 (1898), 269–70, who explains that Roman Aquinum was the second largest city between Rome and Capua, quoting Strabo 5.237 and Silius Italicus 8.405. He adds that Eliseo Grossi has measured the walls and finds that they enclosed a total area of over two hundred acres.

p. 205. to his Aquinum. Juvenal 3.319.

p. 205. St. Lawrence Gate. On the Porta di San Lorenzo see A. L. Frothingham, *Roman Cities in Italy and Dalmatia* (New York, 1910), 197–9 (the plates are mistitled Arpinum); and Cagiano de Azevedo (cited in note above), 34–7, who however thinks the peculiar vaulting of the gate dates it to the third century A.D.

p. 206. of Roman paganism. See Cagiano de Azevedo (cited in note on p. 204) 57–8, 67–8, and plates IX and X, on the church of S. Maria della Libera.

p. 207. 'the Roman building.' See Cagiano de Azevedo (cited in note on p. 204), 18, 19, 38–42, and plate III on the Capitol of Aquinum.

p. 208. the damage had been done. The story appears in a note by Cagiano de Azevedo (cited in note on p. 204), note 22 on pages 39–40.

p. 208. memorial statue. See Cagiano de Azevedo (cited in note on p. 204), 68.

p. 210. inhabited for ever. Jeremiah L, 39.

p. 210. AT HIS OWN EXPENSE. This and the other inscription about Juvenal are *CIL* 10.5382 and 5426.

p. 211. 'this the labour.' Virgil, *Aeneid* 6.129.

p. 212. The mansion has almost vanished. See Cagiano de Azevedo (cited in note on p. 204), 60–1, who places the villa in Augustan times.

CHAPTER EIGHT: ROME

p. 214. In one of his finest satires. This is the third—imitated by Johnson in his *London* and Boileau in his first and sixth satires.

p. 217. THE BEGINNING OF THE APPIAN HIGHWAY. On the wall of Rome and the Porta Capena, see G. Säflund, *Le Mura di Roma Reppublicana (Svenska Institutet i Roma, Skrifter* 1, Upsala, 1932), 34–9.

p. 218. the spring of Egeria is lost. A. M. Colini, *Storia e topografia del Celio nell' antichità (Atti della pontificia accademia romana d'archeologia, Serie III: Memorie vol. VII*, Rome, 1944), 13–14, places the Valley of Egeria in the little valley which starts near S. Tommaso *in Formis* and goes up below the casino of the Villa Mattei, but says it is now impossible to find the spring itself. Lugli, *Monumenti Antichi di Roma e Suburbio* 1 (Rome, 1930-VIII), 408, says that the Renaissance scholar Pirro Ligorio discovered the ruins of the sanctuary of Egeria in 1560, and that they now appear to lie below the north-west side of the little house belonging to the monks of Panisperma on the slopes of the Caelian; and with this suggestion Colini appears to agree on pp. 46–7. H. Jordan and C. M. Huelsen, *Topographie der Stadt Rom im Alterthum* 1.3 (Berlin, 1907), 202, say that the sanctuary must be in the Villa Mattei, and suggest that the Porta Capena will be found in the Orto di S. Gregorio.

p. 218. Fantastically tangled. Byron saw the *nymphaeum* belonging to the Triopus of Herodes Atticus, in the valley of the Caffarella, some distance outside the Porta Capena. It is still known popularly as the Grotto di Egeria.

p. 219. the Church of St. Mary in Tempulo. The monastery was founded by a holy man called Tempulus; the church was built in its grounds; after he was forgotten, it was sometimes called S. Maria in Tempore. See C. Huelsen, *Le chiese di Roma nel medio evo* (Florence, 1927), 367–8.

p. 220. to live in the Subura. See S. B. Platner and T. Ashby, *A Topographical Dictionary of Ancient Rome* (Oxford, 1929), 500–1, for the facts on this interesting district; there is more in R. Burn, *Rome and the Campagna* (Cambridge, 1876), 79–80, and Jordan and Huelsen (cited in note on p. 218), 1.3.331–2.

p. 224. decorated with statues and flowers. It is now labelled *The Trophy of Marius*, but has nothing to do with the great general. It may have been originally a private *nymphaeum*, taken over by the emperor later. See Platner and Ashby (cited in note above) 363–4, and G. Lugli (cited in note on p. 218), 2.362–4, who says it is not a building of the time of Alexander Severus, but is much earlier. There is a marvellous evocation of the surrounding cats in Eleanor Clark's *Rome and a Villa* (New York, 1952), 128–36.

p. 225. 'the fairest thing on earth.' Vergil, *Georgics* 2.534: p. 69 of this book.

p. 227. 'Barbarism and Religion' comes from the closing chapter of Gibbon's *Decline and Fall* (Everyman edition, vol. 6, p. 553), and the sentence about the barefooted fryars from his autobiography. It is odd, by the way, that he did not note that the day on which he conceived his great plan was 15 October, the anniversary of Vergil's birth.

p. 228. Maecenas chatted. This hall, the so-called Auditorium of Maecenas, stands in or near the famous gardens of Maecenas, and was once floored with white mosaic and beautifully decorated with wall-paintings of landscapes and garden scenes. The floor was more than twenty feet below the level of the ground in ancient times: perhaps it was an auditorium, where poets could recite to small audiences; perhaps a conservatory for growing exotic plants. See Platner & Ashby (cited in note on p. 220), 60–1, and L. Curtius, *Das antike Rom* (Vienna, 1944), p. 60 and plate 163.

p. 232. *Roma Quadrata.* It is fairly well established now that this does not simply mean that the little fortified city formed a square, but that it was laid out in four quarters, as a holy region in primitive religion should be. So, among many other writers, F. Dornseiff, 'Roma Quadrata', *Rheinisches Museum* 88 (1939), 192.

p. 232. Cottage of Romulus. See Lugli (cited in note on p. 218), 1.260–2.

p. 233. Caracalla. On this garment, see P.-M. Duval, *La vie quotidienne en Gaule* (Paris, 1952), 101.

p. 234. Golden House. See Platner & Ashby (cited in note on p. 220), 166–72, and D. M. Robathan, *The Monuments of Ancient Rome* (Rome, 1950), 119–22, and a splendid article by F. Weege, 'Das goldene Haus des Nero', in *Jahrbuch* 28 (1913) of the Deutsches archäologisches Institut, pp. 127–244.

p. 234. part of the House. Suetonius, *Nero*, 39.2.

p. 236. *grotesques.* Weege (cited in note on p. 234) says on p. 141 that the word *grottesco* is first used in 1502 by Pinturicchio, in a contract he made for decorating the Piccolomini Library in Siena. On its derivation from the 'grottoes' of Rome, see the *Vocabolario degli Academici della Crusca* (Naples, 1746), vol. 2, s.v. *grottesco.*

p. 238. ALEXAMENOS WURSHIPPING GOD. For a reproduction and bibliography, see G. Lugli, *Roma antica* (Rome, 1946), 522–3. The scratched picture and inscription are now (1956) in the little museum on the Palatine Hill.

p. 238. ALEXAMENOS IS FAITHFUL! The two Alexamenos inscriptions are in E. Diehl, *Inscriptiones Latinae Christianae veteres* I (Berlin, 1925) p. 259, No. 1352 C. However, the second one, 'Alexamenos is faithful!', has been lost for more than fifty years; and C. Huelsen, 'Das sogenannte Paedagogium auf dem Palatin,' *Mélanges Boissier* (Paris, 1903) 303–6, suggests, following De Rossi, that it was never more than a modern forgery.

p. 240. the Forum. The area was originally a lake surrounded by woods. Dionysius of Halicarnassus says that Romulus and Tatius cleared the wood and filled up most of the lake (2.50.2).

p. 242. the Rostra. It should be emphasized that there are still great difficulties about interpreting the remains of the Republican Rostra: see Platner & Ashby (cited on p. 220), 450–1.

p. 245. Baldhead Lover-Boy. The slang is necessary to render the effect of the vulgar Greek word *moechum* and the ridiculous *caluom* (which implied 'clown' for the Romans). The line appears in Suetonius, *D.Iul.* 51.

p. 248. Bow down to God. Horace, *Carm.* 3.6.5: *dis te minorem quod geris, imperas.* Horace makes it a statement rather than a command; but the context shows that it is in fact an exhortation.

INDEX

*(A page number in bold characters, thus—**52**—indicates a reference of special interest. A page number in parentheses, thus—(72)—indicates that the subject is discussed on that page but not explicitly named.)*

Abruzzi, 177–8, 193, 195–6

Achilles, 33, 109, 183

Adige, **52**, 53, 60

Aemilius Paullus, L., 107–10

Aeneas, (72), 73, 81, (89), 121, 122, (190), 211, 229, 230

Africa, 32, 69, 108, 225; South Africa, 69

Agamemnon, 130, 183

Agrippa, M. Vipsanius, 76, 136

Alba Longa, 121

Albunea, 121, 123, 124

Alcaic metre, 14, 130

Alexamenos, 238–9, 265

Alexandrian poetry, 91

allegory, 186

Alps, 37, 40, 45, 52, 59, 204

Ambarvalia, 170–3, (176)

America: Central and South, 75, 206; North, 75; *see also* U.S.A.

American Academy in Rome, 15, 144

amica, 49

amphitheatres: 209; Flavian, (234, 236); in Verona, 53

Andes, 56, **65**

angels, 206

Anio, 105, 121, 123

Anthony of Padua, St., 124

Antony, Mark, 62, 85, 111, 188, 231, 242

Apennines, (59), 83, (193)

Apollo, 232, 239

Appian Highway, 215, 217–9

Aquinum (Aquino), 16, 198–9, 202, **203–10**, 211, (212), 214–5, **262**

Arcadia, 61, 64, 87, 229–30

arches: 205, 208, 212, 215–6, 217, 219, 223, 224, 228, 239, 248, 262; in Sirmione, 42, 43, 45; in Spello, 86; in Verona, 53, 54; of Severus, 241; of Titus, 241

architecture, 121; Greek, 53, 75, (211); Roman, 42, 53, 86, 112, 121, **124–5**, 204–5, 206–8, 212, 225, **233**, 234, 239, 246

Argentina, 69

Argiletum, 221

Aristius Fuscus, M., 157–9, 259–60

Aristotle, 203

Ascanius, (121)

Ashby, Thomas, 124, 258, 260

Asia Minor, 21, 22, 24, 39, 40, 41, 46, 51, (70), 76, 78, 83, 118, 184, 229

Asinius Pollio, Gaius, 63, 76

Asisium (Assisi), 62, 84, 85, 86, 91, 95, 97, 99, 112–3

Atalanta, (87), 88–9

Athene, 239

Athens, 24, 76, 78, 118, 140

Attis or Atys, 38–9

Auden, W. H., 131, 153

"auditorium of Maecenas, the", 228, **264**

Augustus (Gaius Octavius, Gaius Julius Cæsar Octavianus): as Julius Cæsar's heir, 62, 63, 85, 111, 118, 188; as emperor, 71, 72, 76, 78, 111, 114, (120), 136, 232, 237, 248; attitude to culture, 63, 98, (120), 207, 225, 232, 237–8, 258; attitude to morality, (92), (136), **186–91**; personal character, 107, 109, 117, 136, 187, (192), 237–8; and Horace, 118, 136, 149, 159, 237, 257, 258; and Vergil, 62, 63, 78, 118, 237, 248

Aurelius, 18, (36)

Aurelius, Marcus, 246

Australia, 69

Aventine Hill, 92, (219)

Avernus, 71, 73

Bacchus, 69, 71, 148, 170, 172, 176

Bach, 126, 129, 132, 153
Bandusian spring, **150–1**, 152
Bardella-Cantalupo, 145
basium, (17), **31**, 36, **252**
baths, 124–5, 147, 149, 224, 227–8, **232–3**, 238
Baudelaire, Charles-Pierre, 18, 34, 102, 174
Beethoven, 127, 161
Belgium, 59
Belloc, Hilaire, 181
Benacus, Lacus (Lake Garda), 40–1, 57, 71
Berenson, Bernard, 161
Bernardone, Francisco, 112–3; *see also* Francis, St.
Bevagna (Mevania), 85
Bithynia, 24, 25, 40, 249, 250
Botticelli, 11, 161
Brahms, 132
Britain and the British, 23, 37, (89), 130
British School at Rome, 124
Broch, Hermann, 78
Browning, Robert: *Bishop orders his Tomb at St. Praxed's Church, The*, 223; *Love among the Ruins*, 175; *Soliloquy of the Spanish Cloister*, 35; *Up at a Villa—Down in the City*, 141–2
Bruegel, Pieter, 61
Brundisium, 73, 76, 78
Brutus, M. Junius, 62, 118
Byron, character, 40, 75, 114, 126, 190, 227, 263; love of Italy, 75, 99, 218, 227; *Childe Harold's Pilgrimage*, 99, 114, 218, 227, 237–8, 263; *Don Juan*, 190

Caelian Hill, 218, 219, 220
Caelius Rufus, M., 36, **46–51**, 249, 253, 254
Cæsar, Gaius Julius: personal ife and character, **22–3**, 231–2; as politician, **22–3**, 62, 115, 188, 221, 242; as soldier, **22–3**, 37, 115, 244–5; killed by lovers of liberty, 62, 64, 84, 85, 91, 115, 118, 184, 186, 242; and Catullus, 20, **23**, 250
Cæsar, young, *see* Augustus
Caligula (the emperor Gaius), 232, 238, 246
Callimachus, 22, 91, 253
Camenae, 216
Campbell, A. Y., 129, 258
Campo Vaccino, 231, (241)
Can Grande Della Scala, 55

Canada, (69)
Capena Gate, 215–7
Capitol: of Aquinum, 207–8; of Asisium, 112; of Rome, 226–7, 229, 232, 244, 245, 246, 247
Capri, 43, 236
Caracalla, 227, 233
Carducci, Giosuè, 14, 99
Carthage, 89
Cassius Longinus, Gaius, 62, (118)
Castel dell' Ovo, 80
Castel Gandolfo (Alba Longa), 121
Castor, 41, 88–9
Castrocielo, 208
Catullus, Gaius Valerius: name, **250**; character, **17–46**, 50–2, 52–4, 76, 112, 167, 168, 189, 243, 248; life, 17, 19–36, 40–1, 43, 44–6, 50–1, 52–4, 76, 112, 167, 225, 243, 248, **249–51**, **252–5**; manuscripts, 17, 54; poetry generally, 14, 17–20, 23, 30–6, 44, 46, 52, 53, 55, 128, 179, 185, 189, 243, **250**; separate poems:
1: 250;
2: **27–8**, (29), (31), (36), (51), **252**;
3: **28–30**, (31), (36), 254;
4: 253;
5: (18), **31–2**, 252
7: (18), 32
8: **34–6**, 252, **253**
10: **24–5**, 250
11: 18, **23**, **36–8**, **39**, (52), (189), 250
13: **44**
16: 18
17: (53), 255
26: **45**, 254
28: (24), 250
29: (23), 250
31: **41**, **44**, **46**, 254
35: (53), 255
37: (46), 254
39: (46), 254
44: 253
46: 250, 253
48: 252
49: **51**, **254–5**
51: **26–7**, 37–8, **251–2**
52: (20), **23**
55: 250
57: (20), (23), 250
58: 253
61: **33**, 249, 253
62: 33, 249, 253
63: **38–40**, (189), 249, **253**

Catullus (*continued*)
  separate poems,
    64: 33, 249, 253
    65: 249, 251
    66: 249
    67: 249, 255
    68: **21**, **30–1**, **32**, 249, 252, 253
    69: 253
    70: **32–3**, **252–3**
    73: 253
    75: **34**
    77: 253
    85: **34**
    87: 252
    93: (20), **23**
    100: (22), 255
    101: **13**, **21–2**, **44**, 254
    102: 255
    108: 255
    113: 250
Celestine monks, 194, 195, 261
Celts: generally, 20, 23, 116; in Italy,
  19–20, 52, 60, 116, 255; their lan-
  guage, 19, 31, 233, **250**, 255
Ceres, 69, 170, (172), 176, 202; as
  Demeter, 208, 210, (212)
Cestius Pius, L., (181), 260
Chateaubriand, 75
Chénier, 18
Chile, 69
Chopin, 132, 162, (169)
Christians, 178, 212, 226, 228, 234,
  238–9, 244, 246; art, 206, 212;
  literature, Latin, 202; *and see* Church,
  Roman Catholic, churches and
  sanctuaries
Church, Roman Catholic, 177–8, 194,
  203, 226, 241, **244**
churches and sanctuaries, Christian, 15,
  81, 113, 122, 124, 125, 149, 192, 193,
  194–5, 203–5, 208, 211–2, 219, 223,
  226, 228, 241, 246, 254
Cicero, M. Tullius, 12, 24, 47, 48, 51,
  75, 76, 188, 242; letters, 24, 250, 251;
  speeches, **46–52**, 76, 242, 250, 251,
  254–5
Cinara, 143, 156, 259
Cinna, Gaius Helvius ("Cinna the
  poet"), 25
Circe and Circeii, 73
circus, 119, 209, 217, 239
Civitella di Licenza, 146, (147)
Claudia the Vestal, 40, (49), 104
Claudii, the family, 25, 48, 49
Claudius, Appius, 49, 215

Cleopatra, 111
clientship, *see* patronage
Clitumnus, 71, **95–101**, 102, 179–80,
  246, 257
cliuus Suburanus, 223
Clodia ('Lesbia'): and Catullus, (17),
  (18), 21, 25–40, 50–2, 91, 167, 168,
  189, **249**, 251–2; other relationships,
  25, 26, 28, 29, 32–40, 45, 46–52,
  249, 251, 254
Clodius, P., 25, 42, (47), (49)
Clytemnestra, 47, 104
Colchis, 70
colloquialism and slang in poetry,
  14–15, 27, 28, 29, 31, 33, 34, 36, 41,
  66, 95, 252, 253, 254
'Colosseum', 234, 236
columbarium, 81
comedy, 50, 55, 185
Como: town, 53; Lake, 71
consolation, 107, 164
Constantine, emperor, 12, 239, 246, 247
Constantinople, 240
Corfinium, 180, (191)
'Corinna', 182, 183, (184), 188, 196
Cornelia wife of Paullus, 106–12
Crassus Diues, M. Licinius, 47
Cremona, 57, 59, 60, 62, 73
Cumae, 73, 81, 122, 202, 214, 220
Cupid, 29, 172, 173, 179, 180, (182)
Cybele, 38–40, 104, 109, 253
'Cynthia' (Hostia): character, 90, 91,
  92, 111–2; and Propertius, 86–8,
  (89), 90–7, 102–6, 111–2, (189), 221
Cypassis, 182, 183, (196)

Daedalus, 73
dancing, 25, 96, 130, 135, 137, 148, 172,
  176, 200
D'Annunzio, Gabriele, 47, 196
Dante, 46, 54–5, 65, 73, 113, 194, 254
Dark Ages, 43, 54, 79, 203, 204, (232)
Degrassi, Nevio, 44, 254
'Delia' (Plania), 167, 168–9, 176
Della Scala family, 11, 42, 53, 54–5
Demeter, 208
democracy, 47, 226, 231, 247
Diana, 96, 202, 219
Dickens, 120, 222
didactic poetry, 14, (24), 66, 185–6,
  189–90
Digentia, 144, 145
Diocletian, 53
Dolomites, 59
domina, 53, 252

Domitian, (191), 200, 201, 239, (246)
Don Giovanni, 181
Donne, 153
Doric dialect, 75
drama, 159, 173, 185, 227

Egeria, 215-6, 218, 219
Egypt, 46, 74, (93), 199, 201, 202, 225, 243
elegiac poetry, 13, 20, 33, 88-90, 102, 105, 163, 164, 165, 173, 174, 179, 184, 185, 186, 227; *and see* Catullus, Ovid, Propertius, Tibullus
Eliot, T. S.: poetic techniques, 89, 90, 131, 153; *The Waste Land*, 89, 90, 106, 180
emperors, Roman, 36, 44, 54, 199, 232-3, 237, 239, 241, 243, 246, 258; *and see* names of individual rulers
engineering, Roman, 80, 242, 247
England and the English, (24), 25, 44, 59, 70, 120; English poetry, 34, 130, 132, 162
epic poetry, 14, 77, 89, 91, 190, 201, 240
Epicurus and Epicureanism, 24, (73), **77-8**, 137, 164-5, 173, 188, 255-6
epigrams, Roman, 14, 20, 23, 32, 47, 130, 181, 198, 219-20, 234
era, 33, **252**
Esquiline Hill, 220, 234
essays, 115, 155, 159
Este, Ippolito d', 121
Etna, 12, 53
Etruria and the Etruscans, 12, 19, 41n., 69, 83, 84, 85, 234
Evander, 230
excavations: in Rome, 223, 228, 232, 235-6, 238-9, 241; at the Sabine farm of Horace, 144-5, 146, 147-8; at Sirmione, 42, 43-4; at Sulmona, 194
exiles, 54, 56, 60, 61-2, 72, 74, 186, 190-1, 192, 200-1, 229

fables, 140, (157), (158), 186, 252
farces, 50, 209
farming, **57-69**, 72, 76, 116, 135, 138-45, 147, 150, 168, 169, 170-3, 189, **195-7**, 206-10
Farnese family: gardens, 238, 239; Pope, 241
fascism, 226, (228)
Faunus, 176; Lupercal, 231-2
Fauré, Gabriel, 163
Faust, 227

Florence, 54, 241
Forum: of Asisium, 112; of Rome, 119, 189, 221, 230-1, 232, 234, 236, 237, 239, **240-7**, 265; of Verona, 54, 255
France and the French, 17, 33, 59, 69, 70, 162, 192; French poetry, 130, 132
Francis of Assisi, St., 11, 85, **112-3**, 194, 256
freedmen, 114, 116, 117, (142-3)
fresco painting, 148, 212, 236, 237
Frost, Robert, 176
Furius, 18, (36), 45, 254
Fuscus, M. Aristius, 157-9, 259-60

galliambic metre, (38)
Gallicano, 174, 260
Garda, Lake (Benacus), 40-5, 57, 71
Garigliano, 179-80, 211
Gaul and the Gauls, 22, 23, 37, 225, *and see* Celts
'genius', 206
Germany and the Germans: ancient, 23, 240; modern, 52, 59, 69, 70, 203, 207, (208), 227; German poetry, 130, 227
Gibbon, Edward, 226-7, 264
Giulio Romano, 72
Goddess, Good, 25
Godley, A. D., 127
Goethe, 18, 75, 227, 242
Goito, 58
Golden House of Nero, **233-7**, 264
Gonzaga family, 65, 72
Goths, 195, 241
Gran Sasso, 177, 260
Gray, Thomas, 174
Greece: the country, 24, (38), 61, 64, **73-6**, 78, 118, 184, 247; the people, 19, 39, 63, 74-7, 116, 229-31, 247; the language, 63, 73-5, 116, 118, (133), 162-3, 226, 265; the literature, 22, 26, 33, 75-6, 91, (133), 153, 162-3; influence on Rome, 11-12, 22, 26, 36, 38, 64, **73-6**, 78, 91, 118, (133)
grotesque, **235-6**, **264**
grottoes: of Catullus, **42-4**, 254; of Nero, **235-6**, 266

Hadrian, 12, 121
Haedilia, 146
haiku, 184
Hallam, C. H., 124-5
Hebrews, 74, 122, *and see* Jews

Helen of Troy, 227
hendecasyllable, 14, (27), (31)
Hera, 25, 251
Hercules, 105, 121, 201, 230, 252
hexameter, 12–13
Hispellum (Spello), 86, 90
Holland, 59, 70
Homer, 136; *Iliad*, 111; *Odyssey*, 154
homosexuality, (18), 128, 188, (189)
Hopkins, Gerard Manley, 129, 131
Horace (Quintus Horatius Flaccus):
  character, 114, 115–20, 122, **134–7**,
  159–60, 164–6, 169, 174, 225, 248;
  life, 15, 62, 75–6, 111, 114–20, 122,
  137, 159, 225, 228, 237, 243; relation
  to his father, 114, **116–7**, 118, 136,
  140, 143, 159; Sabine farm, 123,
  137–52, 155–9, 179, 194, (248),
  259; poetry generally, 102, 111,
  114–5, 125; separate poems:
Art of Poetry, 159
Carmen Saeculare, (159)
Carmina generally, 114, 115, 117,
  (122), **126–37**, 140, **153–4**
Carmina 1.5: **131–4**
  1.6: 136
  1.9: 129
  1.11: **130**
  1.22: (148)
  1.33: **165–6**, 260
  1.38: **150**
Carmina 2.7: **118**
  2.11: (137)
Carmina 3.1–6: **135–7**, (188), 258
  3.4: **130**
  3.6: **135–6**, (187), **248**, 265
  3.11: **130**
  3.13: **150–2**, 179
  3.29: (157)
  3.30: **153**
Carmina 4 generally: 115, 128n., 154,
  159
  4.1: 143, **154**, 259
  4.2: **125**, (126), 136
  4.7: 130
  4.9: 130
Epistulae generally, 115, **153–60**
Epistulae I generally, 140, 159
  1.4: **164–5**, (167), 169, 174, 176,
  260
  1.7: **155–7**, 253
  1.8: 123
  1.10: 144, 146, **157–9**, 259
  1.14: 138, **142–4**, 259
  1.16: **141**, 144, 259

Horace (*continued*)
  separate poems, *Epistulae*,
    1.18: **144**
    1.19: **153**
    1.20: **159**
  Epistulae 2 generally, 159
    2.2: **122**
  Epodoe generally, 114–5, 117, 118,
    127, 252
    12: **127**
    14: **152**
  Sermones generally, 114–5, 117, 118
  Sermones I generally, 118, 127
    1.4: (140)
    1.5: 155, 259
    1.6: **116–7, 118–9**
    1.9: **120**, 259–60
  Sermones 2.6: **138–40**
Hortensius Hortalus, Q., 26, 251
Hostia, *see* 'Cynthia'
Housman, Alfred Edward, (110), 118,
  158
Hugo, Victor, 18, 63
Hypermnestra, 104, (130), 257

identidem, 36, 38
images in poetry, 30, 66, 87, 90, 129
Indians, American, 57, 176, 229, 239;
  East, 24, 37, 40, (71), 72
inscriptions: Christian, 238–9; Jewish,
  221; modern, 193, 217; Renaissance,
  81–2; Roman, 42, 44, 65, 85, 98–9,
  112, 146, 177, 194, 199, 203, 205,
  206, 210–2, 223, 239–40, 250, 254,
  265; literary, 73, 79, 81–2, 105
Italy and the Italians: the land, 11–12,
  40, 42, 43, 44, 55, 56, 57–64, 65–6,
  69–72, 73, 74, 75, 78, 83, 97, 114,
  115, 121, 145–6, 177, **179–80**, 191,
  195–6, 204, 206, 210, 21–23, 229–48;
  the people, 11, 15–16, 19, 62, 65–6,
  74–5, 83–4, 120, 132, 136, 138, 141–2,
  143, 145, 148–9, 177–8, 179–80, 187,
  191, 196–7, 207, 208, 210, 226, 228,
  229, 232, 244; the languages, 17,
  33, 75, 83, 116, 121, 130, 145, 194,
  207; the literature, 33, 48, 54, 99;
  the state, 180, 191, 226
Iulus (Ascanius), (121)

Janiculum, 230
Janus, 205, 230
Japanese poetry, 184
Jason, 70
Jerome, St., 20

Jerusalem, 225
Jesus, 113, 238–9
Jews, 57, 74, 116, 122, 215–6, (217), 221, 225, 239
Joyce, James, 78
Julia major, 36, (187), 189, (190), 261; minor, 187, 189, (190), (192), 261
Juliet, 28, (55), 181
Julius, *see* Cæsar
Juno, 32, 112, 207; Hera, 251
Jupiter, 32, 112, 207, 226–7, 229, 230, 232, 246; Zeus, 251
Juvenal (D. Iunius Iuuenalis): character, 16, 120, **198–202**, 205, 206, 209, 212–3, 214–7, 219–24, 248; life, 16, 179, 196, 198–203, 204, 209–10, 212–3; poetry generally, 187, 198, 200, 201–2; satires individually,
   1: **201–2**, 205, **243**
   3: **202–3**, 205, **208**, **209–10**, 214, **215–7**, **220**, **222**
   5: **220**
   7: **200**, **201**
   10: **206**

Keats, 18, 86, 107, **152**
Kipling, 126–7
knights, 179, (180), 184, 186, 191, 199

Lamb, Charles, 185
Lamiae family, 224
lampoons, 200
Landor, Walter Savage, 129
Laocoon, the, 235
Latin Highway (Via Latina), 205–6, 215
Latin language, 17, 19, 31, 33, 75, 83, 121, **130**, 131, 148, 154, 192, 241, 243
Latin poetry, 33, 64, 74, 75, 84, 131, 153–4, **162–3**, 225, 227, 237, 242, 247–8
Leopardi, Giacomo, 81, 256
Lepidus, M. Aemilius, 62
Leporello, 181
'Lesbia', *see* Clodia
libraries, (53), 190, 203, 232, 233
Licenza: river, 145, 146, 147, 150; village, 146, (147)
'limping' metre (*scazon*), 34, 36, 41
Livia, 189
Livius Andronicus, 154
Lombards, 204, 212, 254
London, (120), (221), 222, (241)
Lucan, 240
Lucretilis, Mons, 147, 150

Lucretius, T., 24, 77, 79
Lucrine Lake, 71
Lugli, Giuseppe, 144, 253, 259
Lygdamus, 92, 93, 94, 103, 105

Macaulay quoted, 88, 123
Madonna, 54, 90, 219
Maecenas: career and character, 76, 119, 122, 123, 149, 264; and Augustus, 119, 159; and Horace, 15, 119, 122–3, 128, 137–40, 149, 155–7, 159, 228; and Propertius, 91; and Vergil, 76, 118, 155, 228
Mandela, 144, 145
Mantegna, Andrea, 72
Mantua, 56–8, 59–62, (63), 64–5, 72–3, 179
manuscripts, 17, 54, 78, 190, 203
'Marius, Trophy of', 224, 263–4
marriage, 32–3, 91–2, 94, 111, **135–7**, 181, **187–9**, 252–3
Martial (Gaius Valerius Martialis), 219–20, 221, 252
materfamilias, 49
Maxim's, where all the girls are dreams, 186
Melfe, 204, 208
Memmius, Gaius, 24
Mendelssohn, 163, 173
meretrix, 50
Messalina, 36
Messalla Corvinus, M. Valerius, 171
Metellus Celer, Q., 25, 26, (47), 249
metre and rhythm, **12–14**, 26, 27, 43, 87, 126, 128, **130–1**, 133, 134, 143, 162, 163
metre, Greek and Latin, general: **12–14**, 114, 128, **130–1**, 143, 162, 163, 245; Alcaic, 14, 130; elegiac, 13–14; galliambic, (38); hendecasyllable, 14, (27), (31); hexameter, 12–13; Sapphic, 14, 26, 36, 38, 128, (130), 252; scazon, **34**, 36, 41, **253**
Mevania, 85, *and see* Bevagna
Michelangelo, 11, 233, 246
Middle Ages, 42, 43, 52, 53, 54–5, 72, 79, 83, (88), 121–2, 145, 181, 191, 193, 194, 203, 204, 223, 228, (233), (240)
Milan, 42, 73, 120, 240
Milton, 57, (107), **133–4**, 137, 190, (202)
mime, 50
Mincius (Mincio), 57–8, 60, 73
Minerva, 112, 207

Mondriaan, Piet, 148
monologues, 34–6
Monte Cassino, 203
Monte Gennaro, 147
morality, Roman, 49–50, 102, 111, 115, 117, 128, **134–7**, 155, 163, 168–70, 180–1, **185–91**, 196–7, 229
Morrone monastery, 192, 194, 195, 261
mosaic, 45, 145, 148, 246, 265
Mozart, 181
mulier, 33, **252**
Muses, 67, 163, 216
music and poetry, 38–40, 48, 126, 127, **130**, 132–3, 148, 151–2, 153–4, **161–2**, 163, 172, 173, 190; music alone, 70, 226
Musset, Alfred de, 47
Mussolini, 73, 228, 260
mythology, Greco-Roman, 31, 33, 38–40, 73–4, 87–90, 104, 112, 183, 185, 186, 201, 237

Naples: city and kingdom, 47, 72, 73, 74, 76, 77, 79, 80, 81, 82, 148, 177, 179, 191, 193; bay, 43, 76, 80, 214, 220; district, 43, 73, 74, 76, 77, **79–82**
'Nemesis', 167, 168
Nero, **233–7**
Numa Pompilius, 215–6, 219
nymphs, 68, 90, 215; 'nymphs' room', *nymphaeum*, 124, 218, 263

obscenity, 17, 18, 23, 24, 33, 38, 115, 127, 181, 244–5
Octavian and Octavius, *see* Augustus
Odysseus, 73
Ohioenses, 81
opera, 181, 185, 186, 226, 233
orators and oratory, 22, 26, 46–52, 76, 107, 183, 184, 225, 242
Oscan language or dialect, 83
osculum, 31, 252
Ostia, 229
Ovid (P. Ovidius Naso): character, **177–91**, **195–7**, 243; life, 177–81, 183, **184–7**, **190–1**, 194–6, 201, 243; poetry generally, 90, 177–91, 252; separate poems:
    Amores generally, 179, 185, 192
    Amores 1.3: 261
    2.7: **182–3**
    2.8: **183–4**
    2.13: 188
    2.16: **178**, 261

Ovid (*continued*)
    separate poems, *Amores*,
      3.15: **179**, **193**
    Ars Amatoria: 185–7, 189–90, 248
    Epistulae, see *Heroides*
    Ex Ponto: 261
    Fasti: 186
    Heroides: 185, 194, 252
    Metamorphoses: 186, 190
    Tristia, **178**, 191, 194, 195

Paelignia and the Paelignians, (177), 178, 179, 180–1, 193, 195, 196
pagans and paganism, 107, 206, **212**, 226, 228, 246
painting, generally, 30, 186, 225; Chinese, 58; Greco-Roman, 75, 148, 176, **235–7**, 264; medieval, Renaissance, and baroque, 54, 60, 89–90, 121–2, 161–2, 212, 236–7, 264; modern, 148
'palace', 231, 247
Palatine Hill (Palatium), 40, 217, 231–2, **237–40**, 241, 244, 246, 247, 253, 265
Palestrina (Praeneste), 174
Parthenon, 240
particles, 162
Pater, Walter, 173
patronage, 118, 137–9, 155–60, 201, 209, 219, 224
Paul III, Pope, 241
Pedum and district, 164, 165, 174, 176
Penates, 243–4
Perusia (Perugia), 84–5
Pescennius Niger, Gaius, 203
Peter, St., 208, 211–2, 239; Peter Celestine, St., 194
Petrarch, 54, 80, 194, 256
Petronius, 252
Phaedrus, 252
philosophy, generally, 120, 203; Greco-Roman, 66, 73, (75), 77–8, 118, 128, 139–40, 165, 188, 225, 246; *and see* Epicureanism
Phocas, pillar of, (242)
Piazza: of St. Peter's, 242; Vittorio Emmanuele, 224
Pietole, 65
Pindar, 125, 136
Piranesi, Giovanni Battista, 228
Plania ('Delia'), 167–8, 176
Plato, 75, 162, 255
Plautus, 31, 50, 252
Pliny the younger, 44, 97–9

Po river, 57, 60
Poe, Edgar Allan, 102
Pollio, Gaius Asinius, 63, 76
Pollux, 41, 88–9
Pompeii, 149
Pope, the, 121, 194, 232, 241
Porta Capena, 215, 216, 217, 263
Portuguese language, 17
Posillipo, 80
Pound, Ezra, 89, 90, 162
Poussin, Nicolas, 99
Pozzuoli (Puteoli), 79
Praeneste (Palestrina), 174
prison, 116, 190, 195, 201, 261
Prócida, 220
Propertius, character, **83–97**, **111–3**, 189, 225, 248: life, 62, **82–6**, **91–5**, 102, 105–6, **111–2**, 154; poetry generally, **84–91**, 95–7, 102, 105–6, 107, 111–2, 185, 252; separate elegies:
  1 generally, **86–9**, 91
  1.1: **86–7**, 189
  1.2: **87–9**
  1.12: (102)
  1.22: **84**
  2 generally, 91
  2.7: 92
  2.19: **95–7**
  2.34: 111
  3 generally, 91
  4 generally, 91, 112
  4.1: 85
  4.7: **102–6**, 112, **221**
  4.8: **92–4**
  4.11: **106–12**
proscriptions, 62, 117
Proust, 94
pseudonyms, generally, 165; *and see* 'Corinna', 'Cynthia', 'Delia', 'Lesbia', 'Nemesis'
puella, 33
Puteoli (Pozzuoli), 79
Pyrrha, **131–4**

religion, generally, 66, 70; Greek and Roman, (21), 25, 28–9, **38–40**, 66, 92, 97, 98–9, 128, 151, **170–4**, 176, 186, 189, 229, 243–6, 247–8, 251, 253, 265; *see also* Christians
Renaissance: art, 11, 72, 235–6; buildings, 53, 65, 72, 121–2, 241–2, 246; scholarship, 81–2, 235–6
Respighi, Ottorino, 152
Rilke, Rainer Maria, 18, 153
Rimbaud, Arthur, 18, (129)

roads, Roman, **205**, 206, **215**, 217, 219
Robert, king of Naples, 80
Roccagiovine, 146
Roccasecca, 203, 211
Roma, the word, 226; *Roma Quadrata*, 232, 264
Romance languages, (17), 33
Rome: the city generally, **214–48**; buildings, 40, 47, 69, 79, 123, 205; character and society, 46, 52–3, 73, 77, 95, **120**, **122**, 141–2, 147, 157, 184, 198, **201–2**, 208, 212–3, **247–8**; situation, 121, 137–8, 177, 178, 193, 195, 199, 204; the empire (as a dominion), 19, (21–5), 37, 52, 62, 68, 69, 71, 72, 75, 76, 83, 115, 174, 186, 198–200, 204, 212–3, 227, 229, 233, 237, 240, 242, 243–4; the empire (as a monarchical regime), 23, 76–7, 92, 115, 225; the republic, 22–3, 49, 62, 118, 221, 226, 240
Romeo, 28, (55), 181
Romulus, 12, 51, (69), 232, 239, 241, 248, 264, 265
  Romulus son of Maxentius, 241
Rostra, 189, 242
Rufus, M. Caelius, 36, **46–51**, 244, 253, 254
Russia, 70, 137
Ruysdael, Jacob van, 70

Sabine people and country, 69, 72, 137–52, 254
Sacred Road, 120, 237, 244–5, 248
Sade, Marquis de, 190
St. Agatha of the Goths, 223
S. Antonio, 15, **123–6**
St. Lawrence Gate, 205–6
St. Mary in Tempulo, 219, 263
St. Peter's, 11, 234, 239, 242
  Old St. Peter's, 208; St. Peter in the Country, (16), 211–2
St. Praxed's, 223
St. Vitus Street, 223
Sapphic metre, 14, 26, 27, 36, 38, 128, (130), 251–2
Sappho, 22, 26, 27, 33, 38, 128, 251–2
satire, *see* Horace, Juvenal
Saturn, 230
sauium, 252
scazon, 34, 36, 41, **253**
sculpture, generally: 161, 225; Greek and Roman, 45, 54, 75, 98, **147–8**, 199, 205, 206, 208, 211, 216, 228,

234-5, 240, 242-3, 246-7; medieval, 193-4; Renaissance, 65

Segesta, 53

senate, 184, 199, 231, 248

Severus, the arch of, 241

Shakespeare, personality, 55, 79, 242; verse, 162; *As You Like It*, 95; *Hamlet*, (130); *Julius Cæsar*, 231; *King John*, 127; *King Lear*, 127; *Merchant of Venice*, 89, (152); *Midsummer-Night's Dream*, 173; *Romeo and Juliet*, 28, 55; *Taming of the Shrew*, 55; *Twelfth Night*, (129); *Two Gentlemen of Verona*, 55

Shelley, 18, 75, 227-8

Sibyl: of Cumae, 73, 81, 122, 211, 214, 220; of Tibur, 122, 123, 125

Sicily, 12, 19, 53, 63, 75, 220

Silenus, 148

Sirens, 73

Sirmio (Sirmione), **40-6**, 254

Siron, 79

slaves and slavery, 23, 33, 93, 103-4, 114, **115-7**, 138, 142-3, 147, 157, 159, 187, 207, 215, 225; and love, 33, (86), 252

Social War, (115), (180), (187), (191)

sonnets, 20, 34, 54, 128, 137

Spain and the Spanish, 17, (33), 46, 69-70, 75, 137, 219, 225, 254

Spello (Hispellum), 86, 256

stadium of Domitian, (239)

stanza-form, 37, **90**, 128-9, 130, 165-6, 251-2

Sterne, Laurence, 162

Stoics and Stoicism, 77

style, 87, **161-4**, 166, 181

Subura, 103, 105, **219-221**, **223**

Sulmo (Sulmona), 178-80, 191-6, 261

Swift, Jonathan, 125, 255, 258

Swinburne, 114

Taormina, 53

Tarentum, 74, 141, 157

Tarpeian Rock and Park, 92, 230, **247**

temples and shrines, Greek and Roman, 40, 68, 96, 98-9, 112, 121, 122, 126, 144, 146, 159, 199, 207-8, 210, 212, 226, 228-9, 232, 238, 246-7

Tennyson, 14, 43-4, 114, 126, 163, 254, 258

Terence, 50, 225

Thackeray, 114

theatres, **53**, 96, 208-10

Theocritus, 63

Thomas Aquinas, St., 203, 211

Thomas, Dylan, 129, 131, 153

Thunderer: the emperor Domitian, (246); the god Jupiter, (230)

Tiber, father Tiber, 46, 97, 220, 226, 229-30

Tiberius, 43, (186), 236, 238

Tibullus: character, 11, 163-70, 173-6, 189, 195, 248; life, 164-7, 167-70, 173-6; poetry generally, 90, 163-74, 176, 185, 197, 252; elegies separately:
    1.1: **167-9**
    1.2: 169-70
    1.5: **168, 189**
    2.1: **170-4, 176**

Tibur (Tivoli), 15, 102, 105, 106, **121-6**, 137, 145, 155, 157, 214, 253, 254, 258

Titus, arch of, 241

Tivoli, *see* Tibur

tragedy, 47, 75, 89, (172), 201

Trajan, 224

translation, generally, 126, **162**; Greek to Latin, 26, 154; Latin to English, **12-15**, 33, 84, 87, 126, 130, 133-4; Latin to Italian, 194

triumph, 71, 125, **244-6**

Troy, 21, 24, 72, (74), 229

Tuscany, 83; *and see* Etruria

Umbria, **83-6**

Umbricius, 16, 202, 214-7, 218

U.S.A., 26, 57, 62, (69), 75, 233

Van Goyen, Jan J., 70

Varia (Vicovaro), 143, 145

Varius Rufus, L., (78), 118, 156

Vatican, 12, 234

Veii, 234

Venus, 28-9, 96, 103, 113, 154, (179), 182, 184, 193, 246, 252

Venusia, 115-6

Vergil (P. Vergilius Maro): character, 56-8, 61, **63**, **66-72**, **73-9**, 81-2, 102, 114, 118, 159, 191, 197, 242, 248; life, 12, **56-60**, **62-4**, **72**, **73-9**, 154, 155, 159, 225, 229, 248, 256, 264; poetry generally, (17), 102, 163, 179, 237, 242; and Dante, 46, 113; poetic works:
Aeneid, (56), (61), 72, **73-4**, (76), **77-9**, (81), (111), 112, 127, 190, (211), **229-31**, (240), (248)
Bucolics generally, (57), **58-64**, 72, 77, 127, (195), (197)

Vergil (*continued*)
  separate poems,
  Bucolics 1 : 56, (58), **61–2**, 64, 77
    3 : **58**
    9 : **62, 63**, 255
  Catalepton 13 : 252
  Georgics generally, 66, 69, 72, 76–7,
    127, 188–9, (197), 225
  Georgics 2 : **40, 66–9, 71–2, 97**
    4 : **76–7**
Verlaine, (129)
Vermeer, Jan, 30
Verona, 17, 19, 22, 26, 28, 40, 42, **52–5,**
  179, 249, **250**, 255
Vespasian, 146, 199, 210, 235, (258)
Vesta, 109, 122, 123, **243–4,** 248
Vesuvius, 76

Via Appia, 215, **217–8**, 219; Via
  Latina, 205–6, 215; Via S. Lucia in
  Selci, 223; Via di S. Vito, 223
Vicovaro (Varia), 145
Viminal Hill, 221
Virgiliana, La, 65–6
Virgilio, 64

Wilder, Thornton, 23
Wolf, Hugo, 132
word-order, 87, **130–3**
Wordsworth, (129), (131), 137

Yeats, 18–19

Zagarolo, 175, 260

OTHER NEW YORK REVIEW CLASSICS*

J.R. ACKERLEY Hindoo Holiday

J.R. ACKERLEY My Dog Tulip

J.R. ACKERLEY My Father and Myself

HENRY ADAMS The Jeffersonian Transformation

CÉLESTE ALBARET Monsieur Proust

DANTE ALIGHIERI The Inferno

DANTE ALIGHIERI The New Life

WILLIAM ATTAWAY Blood on the Forge

W.H. AUDEN (EDITOR) The Living Thoughts of Kierkegaard

W.H. AUDEN W.H. Auden's Book of Light Verse

ERICH AUERBACH Dante: Poet of the Secular World

DOROTHY BAKER Cassandra at the Wedding

J.A. BAKER The Peregrine

HONORÉ DE BALZAC The Unknown Masterpiece *and* Gambara

MAX BEERBOHM Seven Men

STEPHEN BENATAR Wish Her Safe at Home

ALEXANDER BERKMAN Prison Memoirs of an Anarchist

GEORGES BERNANOS Mouchette

ADOLFO BIOY CASARES Asleep in the Sun

ADOLFO BIOY CASARES The Invention of Morel

CAROLINE BLACKWOOD Corrigan

CAROLINE BLACKWOOD Great Granny Webster

NICOLAS BOUVIER The Way of the World

MALCOLM BRALY On the Yard

JOHN HORNE BURNS The Gallery

ROBERT BURTON The Anatomy of Melancholy

CAMARA LAYE The Radiance of the King

GIROLAMO CARDANO The Book of My Life

DON CARPENTER Hard Rain Falling

J.L. CARR A Month in the Country

BLAISE CENDRARS Moravagine

EILEEN CHANG Love in a Fallen City

UPAMANYU CHATTERJEE English, August: An Indian Story

ANTON CHEKHOV Peasants and Other Stories

RICHARD COBB Paris and Elsewhere

COLETTE The Pure and the Impure

JOHN COLLIER Fancies and Goodnights

CARLO COLLODI The Adventures of Pinocchio

IVY COMPTON-BURNETT A House and Its Head

IVY COMPTON-BURNETT Manservant and Maidservant

BARBARA COMYNS The Vet's Daughter

EVAN S. CONNELL The Diary of a Rapist

HAROLD CRUSE The Crisis of the Negro Intellectual

ASTOLPHE DE CUSTINE Letters from Russia

LORENZO DA PONTE Memoirs

ELIZABETH DAVID A Book of Mediterranean Food

L.J. DAVIS A Meaningful Life

VIVANT DENON No Tomorrow/Point de lendemain

TIBOR DÉRY Niki: The Story of a Dog

For a complete list of titles, visit www.nyrb.com or write to:
Catalog Requests, NYRB, 435 Hudson Street, New York, NY 10014

ARTHUR CONAN DOYLE The Exploits and Adventures of Brigadier Gerard
CHARLES DUFF A Handbook on Hanging
DAPHNE DU MAURIER Don't Look Now: Stories
ELAINE DUNDY The Dud Avocado
ELAINE DUNDY The Old Man and Me
EURIPIDES Grief Lessons: Four Plays; translated by Anne Carson
J.G. FARRELL Troubles
J.G. FARRELL The Siege of Krishnapur
J.G. FARRELL The Singapore Grip
ELIZA FAY Original Letters from India
KENNETH FEARING The Big Clock
FÉLIX FÉNÉON Novels in Three Lines
M.I. FINLEY The World of Odysseus
MASANOBU FUKUOKA The One-Straw Revolution
CARLO EMILIO GADDA That Awful Mess on the Via Merulana
MAVIS GALLANT The Cost of Living: Early and Uncollected Stories
MAVIS GALLANT Paris Stories
THÉOPHILE GAUTIER My Fantoms
JOHN GLASSCO Memoirs of Montparnasse
P.V. GLOB The Bog People: Iron-Age Man Preserved
EDMOND AND JULES DE GONCOURT Pages from the Goncourt Journals
EDWARD GOREY (EDITOR) The Haunted Looking Glass
A.C. GRAHAM Poems of the Late T'ang
VASILY GROSSMAN Everything Flows
VASILY GROSSMAN Life and Fate
PATRICK HAMILTON The Slaves of Solitude
PETER HANDKE Short Letter, Long Farewell
PETER HANDKE Slow Homecoming
ELIZABETH HARDWICK Seduction and Betrayal
ELIZABETH HARDWICK Sleepless Nights
L.P. HARTLEY Eustace and Hilda: A Trilogy
L.P. HARTLEY The Go-Between
NATHANIEL HAWTHORNE Twenty Days with Julian & Little Bunny by Papa
HUGO VON HOFMANNSTHAL The Lord Chandos Letter
RICHARD HOLMES Shelley: The Pursuit
ALISTAIR HORNE A Savage War of Peace: Algeria 1954–1962
WILLIAM DEAN HOWELLS Indian Summer
RICHARD HUGHES A High Wind in Jamaica
RICHARD HUGHES In Hazard
RICHARD HUGHES The Fox in the Attic (The Human Predicament, Vol. 1)
RICHARD HUGHES The Wooden Shepherdess (The Human Predicament, Vol. 2)
MAUDE HUTCHINS Victorine
HENRY JAMES The Ivory Tower
HENRY JAMES The New York Stories of Henry James
HENRY JAMES The Outcry
TOVE JANSSON The Summer Book
TOVE JANSSON The True Deceiver
RANDALL JARRELL (EDITOR) Randall Jarrell's Book of Stories
DAVID JONES In Parenthesis
FRIGYES KARINTHY A Journey Round My Skull
YASHAR KEMAL Memed, My Hawk
YASHAR KEMAL They Burn the Thistles

MURRAY KEMPTON Part of Our Time: Some Ruins and Monuments of the Thirties
ARUN KOLATKAR Jejuri
DEZSŐ KOSZTOLÁNYI Skylark
TÉTÉ-MICHEL KPOMASSIE An African in Greenland
GYULA KRÚDY Sunflower
SIGIZMUND KRZHIZHANOVSKY Memories of the Future
PATRICK LEIGH FERMOR Between the Woods and the Water
PATRICK LEIGH FERMOR Mani: Travels in the Southern Peloponnese
PATRICK LEIGH FERMOR Roumeli: Travels in Northern Greece
PATRICK LEIGH FERMOR A Time of Gifts
PATRICK LEIGH FERMOR A Time to Keep Silence
GEORG CHRISTOPH LICHTENBERG The Waste Books
JAKOV LIND Soul of Wood and Other Stories
ROSE MACAULAY The Towers of Trebizond
NORMAN MAILER Miami and the Siege of Chicago
JANET MALCOLM In the Freud Archives
OSIP MANDELSTAM The Selected Poems of Osip Mandelstam
OLIVIA MANNING Fortunes of War: The Balkan Trilogy
OLIVIA MANNING School for Love
GUY DE MAUPASSANT Afloat
GUY DE MAUPASSANT Alien Hearts
JAMES MCCOURT Mawrdew Czgowchwz
HENRI MICHAUX Miserable Miracle
JESSICA MITFORD Hons and Rebels
NANCY MITFORD Madame de Pompadour
HENRY DE MONTHERLANT Chaos and Night
ALBERTO MORAVIA Boredom
ALBERTO MORAVIA Contempt
ÁLVARO MUTIS The Adventures and Misadventures of Maqroll
L.H. MYERS The Root and the Flower
DARCY O'BRIEN A Way of Life, Like Any Other
IONA AND PETER OPIE The Lore and Language of Schoolchildren
RUSSELL PAGE The Education of a Gardener
BORIS PASTERNAK, MARINA TSVETAYEVA, AND RAINER MARIA RILKE Letters, Summer 1926
CESARE PAVESE The Moon and the Bonfires
CESARE PAVESE The Selected Works of Cesare Pavese
LUIGI PIRANDELLO The Late Mattia Pascal
ANDREY PLATONOV The Foundation Pit
ANDREY PLATONOV Soul and Other Stories
J.F. POWERS Morte d'Urban
J.F. POWERS The Stories of J.F. Powers
CHRISTOPHER PRIEST Inverted World
RAYMOND QUENEAU We Always Treat Women Too Well
RAYMOND QUENEAU Witch Grass
JEAN RENOIR Renoir, My Father
GREGOR VON REZZORI Memoirs of an Anti-Semite
GREGOR VON REZZORI The Snows of Yesteryear: Portraits for an Autobiography
TIM ROBINSON Stones of Aran: Labyrinth
TIM ROBINSON Stones of Aran: Pilgrimage
FR. ROLFE Hadrian the Seventh
TAYEB SALIH Season of Migration to the North
TAYEB SALIH The Wedding of Zein

GERSHOM SCHOLEM Walter Benjamin: The Story of a Friendship

DANIEL PAUL SCHREBER Memoirs of My Nervous Illness

JAMES SCHUYLER What's for Dinner?

LEONARDO SCIASCIA The Day of the Owl

LEONARDO SCIASCIA Equal Danger

LEONARDO SCIASCIA The Moro Affair

LEONARDO SCIASCIA To Each His Own

LEONARDO SCIASCIA The Wine-Dark Sea

PHILIPE-PAUL DE SÉGUR Defeat: Napoleon's Russian Campaign

VICTOR SERGE The Case of Comrade Tulayev

VICTOR SERGE Unforgiving Years

GEORGES SIMENON Dirty Snow

GEORGES SIMENON The Engagement

GEORGES SIMENON Monsieur Monde Vanishes

GEORGES SIMENON Red Lights

GEORGES SIMENON Tropic Moon

GEORGES SIMENON The Widow

CHARLES SIMIC Dime-Store Alchemy: The Art of Joseph Cornell

TESS SLESINGER The Unpossessed: A Novel of the Thirties

VLADIMIR SOROKIN The Queue

STENDHAL The Life of Henry Brulard

ADALBERT STIFTER Rock Crystal

THEODOR STORM The Rider on the White Horse

ITALO SVEVO As a Man Grows Older

A.J.A. SYMONS The Quest for Corvo

HENRY DAVID THOREAU The Journal: 1837–1861

TATYANA TOLSTAYA White Walls: Collected Stories

EDWARD JOHN TRELAWNY Records of Shelley, Byron, and the Author

LIONEL TRILLING The Liberal Imagination

LIONEL TRILLING The Middle of the Journey

IVAN TURGENEV Virgin Soil

MARK VAN DOREN Shakespeare

ELIZABETH VON ARNIM The Enchanted April

ROBERT WALSER Jakob von Gunten

ROBERT WALSER Selected Stories

REX WARNER Men and Gods

SYLVIA TOWNSEND WARNER Lolly Willowes

SYLVIA TOWNSEND WARNER Mr. Fortune's Maggot *and* The Salutation

SYLVIA TOWNSEND WARNER Summer Will Show

C.V. WEDGWOOD The Thirty Years War

SIMONE WEIL AND RACHEL BESPALOFF War and the Iliad

GLENWAY WESCOTT Apartment in Athens

GLENWAY WESCOTT The Pilgrim Hawk

REBECCA WEST The Fountain Overflows

EDITH WHARTON The New York Stories of Edith Wharton

T.H. WHITE The Goshawk

JOHN WILLIAMS Butcher's Crossing

JOHN WILLIAMS Stoner

EDMUND WILSON To the Finland Station

RUDOLF AND MARGARET WITTKOWER Born Under Saturn

FRANCIS WYNDHAM The Complete Fiction

STEFAN ZWEIG The Post-Office Girl